Nicholas C. Edsall
July 1962

BURKE, DISRAELI, AND CHURCHILL

The Politics of Perseverance

BURKE, DISRAELI, AND CHURCHILL

The Politics of Perseverance

✣

STEPHEN R. GRAUBARD

HARVARD UNIVERSITY PRESS
Cambridge, Massachusetts
1961

Distributed in Great Britain by Oxford University Press, London

*Publication of this book has been aided
by a grant from the Ford Foundation*

Library of Congress Catalog Card Number 61–6349
Printed in the United States of America

For
John Conway

PREFACE ·

These essays are based on materials available in any well-stocked library. If an excuse is required for yet another study of men who, individually, are scarcely neglected in our literature, it is that masters need occasionally to be "rescued" from their disciples. Several generations of Conservatives, old as well as "new," have succeeded so well in advertising their particular hero's virtue that the term "Burkean" (horrible invention) is a word of opprobrium among many who hear his praise but neglect to read his works. Disraeli, the nineteenth-century Tory Party leader, remains almost exclusively the property of those who resemble him only superficially, but who feel some necessity to give him his due. He did serve their cause, after all, strange man though he was. When others intrude to write about him, it is generally to prove him exotic and quaint. Winston Churchill is said to be known intimately, but of his mind, rather than his deeds, few have chosen to speak. His histories may, in fact, make us too uncomfortable, painfully aware of lost opportunities.

I am indebted to many friends and colleagues for reading and discussing these essays in various stages of their preparation. For any errors that remain, and for all interpretations, I am, of course, alone responsible. I would thank most particularly Walter Jackson Bate, Crane Brinton, John Bullitt, John Clive, John Conway, Klaus Epstein, Howard Mumford Jones, Walter Kaiser, Henry Kissinger, Kenneth Murdock, David Owen, Dorothy Thompson, and Eric Weil. For editorial assistance, I am grateful to Miss Ann Louise Coffin; for help in typing and proofreading, to Miss Virginia Shaw.

S.R.G.

Cambridge, Mass.
October 5, 1960

CONTENTS

INTRODUCTION

To PRONOUNCE the names Edmund Burke, Benjamin Disraeli, and Winston Churchill in any company even superficially acquainted with their works is to invite a stock response — British Conservatives. In this way, the twentieth century pays its unconscious tribute to the nineteenth, and to a political mentality capable of dubbing St. Thomas Aquinas "the first Whig," or exclaiming with Gilbert and Sullivan:

> That every boy and every gal,
> That's born into the world alive,
> Is either a little Liberal
> Or else a little Conservative.

While Victorian opinion has fared badly in the twentieth century, many of its political maxims survive. Thus, the Liberal-Conservative division, with its neat and simple formulation, offensive to no one, and hospitable to even the wildest political stray, gives order to a political scene which might otherwise appear cluttered and unkempt. By its standards, Burke, Disraeli, and Churchill belong to the same camp; if only an ideological line can be drawn between them, suggesting even a tenuous discipleship, the order will be perfect. Burke will emerge as the spokesman for eighteenth-century Conservatism, Disraeli as its nineteenth-century voice, and Churchill as its twentieth-century representative. If liberties need to be taken to confine the three within the same orthodoxy, this is a small price to pay for symmetry.

Unfortunately for those who crave systematic compartmentalization, the facts in this instance resist such impolite coaxing. While learned treatises may be written about the "British Conservative tradition," naming those who deserve a place within this political Pantheon, many of these works are only slightly concealed forms of special pleading. It is a strange irony that the twentieth century, otherwise so inhospitable to inherited forms and institutions, should show an almost excessive concern to establish the ancestral respectability of existing things. Ideas, even more than men, seem today to require their progenitors; a movement is thought to be lacking in substance if its genealogy cannot be traced. So, Conservatives, like Liberals, search for their forebears, seeking to justify themselves by claiming association with those whose greatness is no longer contested and whose contributions are no longer denied. A "Conservative tradition" that originates with Burke and leads to Churchill is an idea almost too congenial to be admitted. Its architectural perfection warns us to be wary, lest our zeal for pattern blind us to the possibilities of error.

That the careers and thought of Burke, Disraeli, and Churchill do show certain identities, no one would think to deny. These, however, will not be appreciated if too crude a measure is used to express them. It is not so much that the "Conservative" label is wrong when applied to these men, as that it is insufficient. It ignores large differences between them, and expresses their agreement too generally; perhaps, too emotionally. Also, it emphasizes unity while another measure, susceptible to greater nuance, might serve to suggest divergence. To dwell on their so-called "conservatism" may be to prejudge the issue, making the bond between them an ideological one, when it is in fact of quite another sort. Also, it withdraws attention from the men themselves — from their characters and personalities — making them "spokesmen," the very thing which they may never have been. Finally, and perhaps most importantly, the term implies a resistance to innovation except under quite special circumstances. It ignores the "creative" aspect of their careers, making them appear as the repairers of dikes when their ambition may have been of a higher order. The term "Conservative" carries no hint of that "critical" and "dissenting" spirit which was central to their being, and made them, out of habit or necessity, curiously insensitive to the opinion of their day. Burke, speaking to friends in 1778, remarked that he had "always been in the minority." Disraeli and Churchill, in their long political careers, would not have been thought arrogant if they had uttered the same boast.

To join Burke, Disraeli, and Churchill in a common study, therefore, is not to suggest intellectual or political agreement. As this book will show, there were many differences between them, some of exceedingly great importance. Nor should it be imagined that they are brought together because they made politics their profession and Parliament their home. Disraeli and Churchill enjoyed a political success substantially different from anything experienced by Burke; they made their way, however belatedly, to Number 10 Downing Street; Burke never even sat in a Cabinet. The fact that they were not adherents of the same political party ought not to be lost sight of. Burke lived and died a Whig; Disraeli gave his allegiance to the Tory Party; Churchill began as a Tory, belonged to the Liberal Party for over two decades, and returned, in middle age, to Toryism. Some would argue that he was never entirely faithful to any of the political parties that he served; no one would think to say that of Disraeli. As for their social origins and personalities, they could not have been more different. Burke, born in Ireland, in a century when there was no love lost between that kingdom and England, lived his adult life on a bare margin of financial security. Only his services to the Whig Party, and to his chief, Rockingham, provided him with the means to pursue an active

parliamentary career. Disraeli, born a Jew in a nation not given
to any special regard for members of that race, gave his services
to a party whose suspicions about him were only gradually and
partially allayed. Churchill, the son of Lord Randolph, and
member of the Marlborough family, boasted a heredity which
no Englishman could gainsay, and which no argument could
demolish. These political careers started with very different
prospects and proceeded to quite different conclusions. Within
the House of Commons, their reputations were as various as
their abilities. Burke, in an age proud of the eloquence of Pitt,
Fox, and Sheridan, never achieved great distinction as a parliamentary orator. Disraeli enjoyed a remarkable success almost
from the beginning; men listening to him and Gladstone in
later years wondered whether the House of Commons had ever
known more skilled debaters. Churchill was not listened to
sympathetically until 1940, and then, for long periods, was
heard with almost excessive respect. His early reputation was
somewhere between Burke's and Disraeli's, probably closer to
Burke's.

Why, then, given all these differences, should these men be
considered together? The reasons are many; some fairly obvious, others less so. To begin with, they are all literary men.
To say this is to comment on something other than their occu-
pations. It is to suggest something about their characters. Each
began life as a writer, and each continued in this career when
politics laid heavy claims on their time and energy, making
authorship a chore. They wrote for money in the beginning; for
other reasons at the end. The temptation to divide men into
those who pursue and prefer a contemplative life and others
who choose active careers needs always to be guarded against.
There is something of the contemplative in every active man, as
there is of the active even in those who choose to spend their
lives in the silence of their studies. This notwithstanding, the
intellectual preoccupations of the man who leaves no written
record is frequently difficult to discover. For the man in politics,
parliamentary speeches provide only partial information; such

speeches are most often *ad hoc* pieces, addressed to a specific point, and not calculated to survive by many days their delivery. Even with individuals who achieve the highest offices, information about their thought is frequently lacking. While diaries and correspondence will offer some data, complemented by the record of things done, these are poor substitutes for the carefully produced literary work which is at once a more permanent and personal document. We would know about Burke, Disraeli, and Churchill even if none of their tracts, novels, and histories had survived. We know more about them because they have. Their minds show a dimension which calls for explanation; their thoughts are scarcely less important than their deeds, since they contribute to clarifying those deeds.

In every generation, thousands of members enter and depart the House of Commons. The greatest number, satisfied to enjoy the privilege of belonging to London's "first club," know no greater fame than that which comes from entering a lobby to register a vote in response to a bell. These men, anonymous in their day, are forgotten the moment they leave Westminster, constituting only a statistic for the historian who thinks to consider them. Their plight is in part a function of the size of the House; in part, a comment on their abilities, but principally a statement about the character of every legislative assembly. Only a few names survive, and these for various reasons. In the British Parliament, until quite recently, politics was not a profession for the greatest number of those who attended. In the eighteenth century, and in the nineteenth to only a slightly lesser extent, a parliamentary seat existed as evidence of status; it was rarely conceived of as an avenue to status. Those who sat in the House of Lords arrived in obedience to a personal summons from their sovereign; these men enjoyed the right of attendance. Members of the House of Commons came as the result of some sort of election. With few exceptions they were men of great property, enjoying a large local influence, who were prepared to spend a part of each year away from their lands. Most of the principal offices of state circulated among

men of this description. It was not uncommon for certain of
them to hold their appointments reluctantly, half hoping that
an adverse vote might relieve them of their duties, retiring them
to their lands, the turf, and the pleasures of travel. In any case,
politics at Westminster figured as only one of their interests.

Beginning in the eighteenth century, another sort of person
began to make his appearance in Parliament. This was the "professional" who lacked rank and fortune, but expected intelligence and ambition to serve in their stead, bringing as their
prize political office. As parvenus, these men were in a delicate
position; in an assembly of wealthy and independent "amateurs,"
they needed to be wary lest they strike a discordant note. To
differ from the majority in opinion, manner, or speech was to
risk giving offense; they must appear like the others, even to
the extent of adopting their habits and values, crowning whatever success they might achieve with the symbols recognized
by an aristocratic society. Since these men entered Parliament
not to challenge the system, but to profit from it, such requirements were easily satisfied. Burke and Disraeli belonged to this
category of men. By the time that Churchill entered on the
scene, the House of Commons was populated principally by
"professionals," men prepared to spend the greater part of their
time in active political effort at Westminster. Churchill, though
born into the "governing class," acted as a "professional."
Nothing pleased him so much as politics; he showed not the
slightest anxiety to be off to some sylvan retreat with guns and
aristocratic friends.

Burke, Disraeli, and Churchill never thought to exchange
their existence for some other which might prove equally
agreeable; they had no wish to make politics a secondary matter
in their lives. This, despite the fact that each of them suffered
an extraordinary amount of personal abuse, which might have
led lesser men to crave a release from the battle. In parliamentary
government the politician needs to expect occasional rough
handling and frequent periods on the Opposition benches, but
the obloquy suffered by these three went far beyond what was

commonly meted out. For one reason or other, each experienced particularly painful exclusions; these left their wounds and made their political lives peculiarly tempestuous.

Unless the quality of dissent is recognized in these careers, its most distinctive element is missed. These were not men parroting the opinions of their day and pandering to a taste which others had created. In every age, great men will seem unique; it is rare, however, that an individual puts you in mind of no other. Something like this needs to be said of Burke, Disraeli, and Churchill. Dr. Johnson, on his sickbed, remarked of Burke: "That man calls forth all my powers. Were I to see Burke now it would kill me." The Irish Whig, with his impassioned prose, rapid talk, and uncontrollable anger scarcely resembled the others whose interest he served in so many ways. In Victorian England, it was impossible to think of Disraeli except as unique; that strange alien figure who stalked the lobbies and sat in inscrutable silence through long hours of debate fitted no category known to his times. Churchill, in this century, was sometimes compared to his friend and colleague, David Lloyd George, but as the 1930's proceeded, that comparison seemed increasingly inadequate. Between the brothers Chamberlain, between Arthur Balfour and Herbert Asquith, between Bonar Law and Stanley Baldwin there was distance, but nothing compared to that which separated Lord Randolph's son from all of them.

If the three were out of tune with their times, and if they showed no particular impatience with their situation in the minority, then the hostility directed toward them, even the discomfort which so many felt in their presence begins to explain itself. Burke, Disraeli, and Churchill required a particular sort of courage to withstand the shafts directed against them. If their confidence had not rested on certain firm convictions, their adversaries would certainly have carried the day. They aroused hostility because of their views, but also because of themselves. The two cannot be divorced, since each depends on the other. If they had been different, they would have thought differently, and had they done so, their careers would have taken quite other turns.

What, then, may one expect to learn from a comparative study of these three minds and of the careers which developed from them? First, and most importantly, that to treat men like fauna, labeling them with tags which express our perceptions and needs, and not theirs, is an error to be avoided. It distorts the men, and, also, their times. Nothing is gained by making one appear like the other, or by detaching each from his environment, leaving him to float in a theoretical ether which is entirely of our own invention. Burke and his contemporaries lived in a society fundamentally different from that into which Churchill was born. In the questions which Burke faced, and in the manner in which he proceeded to deal with them, he showed habits of mind which could not survive his century. Burke wrestled principally with what our century would call "political" issues. The problem, for most of his life, was to define the limits of royal authority, to suggest the pressures which political parties might legitimately exert in the political process, to offer principles for the governing of overseas colonies and dominions, and to consider the role of expediency and prudence in all of these matters. Only toward the end of his life did Burke need to study the question of revolution seriously. In approaching this problem, he used, necessarily, the insights he derived from a lifetime of political endeavor. Burke, early in his career and late, challenged orthodox and traditional opinions. His concern was not to find what ailed the world, so much as to express what conscience and reason suggested might be improved in it. This was a man capable of transforming the smallest grievance into a question of transcendental importance. His passion, which ought to have been his friend, proved to be his enemy. Men refused to believe in anger so long continued and so liberally expended.

Disraeli entered the House of Commons more than four decades after Burke's retirement. The wars of Napoleon had accelerated that rapid industrialization which, while enthroning iron and cotton, brought new misery to workers recently removed from their country toil. When Disraeli managed to divert his attention from himself, he considered ways of coping with these problems. To maintain certain institutions in the face of demands for political power and economic advantage from groups previously excluded from the political process was a challenge suited to his romantic intelligence. In his criticism of middle-class standards and values, Disraeli went against what others believed to be the ascendant opinion. More than that, he accepted and exploited the fact of class divisions, and constructed a theory which promised to resolve them. Disraeli's myth — which emphasized the union of the landed gentry and the common people, and which dwelled on the natural alliance between those who owned the land and those who tilled it — looked forward to a new society while protesting fidelity to the old. Workers, yeomen, landlords — the Tory Party, under Disraeli's leadership, pledged itself to each, refusing to admit that their interests might be competing. Living in a revolutionary age, when foreign crowns fell almost too easily, and Chartists threatened in angry demonstrations, Disraeli understood the necessity of offering a program which would at one stroke advance his own career and serve the cause of domestic peace. For England he proposed a remedy in the refurbished Tory Party, with its insistent appeal to "national" ideals and interests. For the rest of Europe, plagued even more seriously by political and economic discontent, Disraeli's rhetoric offered no solution.

While social and economic questions continued to preoccupy political Britain throughout the first half of the twentieth century, Churchill remained remarkably aloof from these concerns. In his Liberal years, he supported his Party in its reform efforts, but this never commanded more than a tithe of his energies. As Churchill's life proceeded, he became increasingly concerned to dwell on the conditions which would enable Great Britain to survive as a world power. This problem would have been meaningless in the eighteenth century and unthinkable in the nineteenth. Yet, the rapid change of the first decades of the twentieth century, in threatening and destroying so many established institutions, made it imperative that the nation establish a new image of itself. While many individuals recommended caution, and saw in social reform the answer to Britain's problems, Churchill believed such a mood to be ill-suited to the times. European civilization was threatened by forces more serious than any loosed by the French Revolution, and only a policy which recognized the nature of the emergency could be expected to cope with it. Churchill's interest was not in diplomacy, in the old sense, or even in war, as he had known it in his youth, but in each as revolution and technology had transformed them. To come to terms with the exploding "democracy" which made popular values and ideals a new element in the chemistry of politics, and which dismissed his own views as those of an aristocratic adventurer, was Churchill's principal task. While Great Britain argued about unemployment insurance, education and welfare, nationalization and public ownership, Churchill gave his attention to arms, diplomacy, national security, and imperial policy. In these areas, he imagined, lay the future safety of the realm. While certain men were prepared to go along with him on specific policies, few found it possible to follow him on many.

Unless the views of Burke, Disraeli, and Churchill are examined against the background of a rapidly changing political and social order, their meaning will be lost. Burke lived in a society which made politics the preserve of the aristocracy; political parties were loose combinations expressing family alliances as frequently as intellectual agreements. Burke tried to use the instrument of party to raise his friends to power; he expected to achieve his own elevation by the same device. It is a comment on his day that men thought him too partisan, rejecting him on these as well as on other grounds. Burke could not live down his Irish birth and his impecunious condition; both argued against his suitability for high office even when his friends came to power. With Disraeli, the situation was different. Disraeli understood the uses which might be made of party organization in the realization of his ambitions. In dedicating himself to the Tory Party, in becoming indispensable to its success, he created a niche for himself which a more aristocratic age would never have admitted. The partisan excess which would have been dismissed as "raving and ranting" in Burke, with Disraeli, was accepted, even admired. In Victoria's reign party government came to be the norm; Disraeli did a great deal to make it so. In the twentieth century the aristocratic hold on politics was further reduced. Churchill, though born in the Marlborough connection, could not expect that this alone would give him a claim to office. He needed to fight for the positions to which he aspired. While aristocratic birth gave some preference, it could also be a handicap, particularly to one who was not prepared to abide by the political conventions of his day. If Churchill had been a loyal party member, never leaving the Tory Party, and never questioning its leadership, his political exclusion from 1931 to 1939 would not have happened. Politics changed considerably after the eighteenth century; Burke was condemned for being too partisan; Churchill for being insufficiently loyal. The "party-less" man had become a true outsider in the twentieth century, and no amount of personal talent could compensate for an unwillingness to accept party control.

While these and other differences need always to be recalled, it is important to recognize the issues on which these men did agree. Thus, if one may generalize very broadly, it would not be inaccurate to say that each was a romantic who lived by a myth, sometimes recognized as such, more frequently incorporated into the basic structure of his thought. These were historically minded men who found in historic example the arguments they required. They romanticized the past, although in different ways, with different purposes, and with varied success. Burke used the past as a standard by which to judge the present; the lessons of 1688 had a permanent importance for him. Disraeli constructed an original interpretation of the past, which he used for the advantages which might accrue to himself and to the Tory Party. Churchill thought the past more glorious than the present, and, in a democratic age, advanced the dangerous notion that not only was the past better, but that greater fortitude, intelligence, and imagination had been required in earlier times. The idea that giants had ceased to roam the earth, and that smaller men had come to take their place, was not one particularly congenial to Churchill's society.

On specific issues, a minimum agreement existed, but again, with important differences in emphasis. Each, for example, expressed serious reservations about democracy and seemed to prefer aristocracy. And yet, to put the matter so baldly is to risk a serious misinterpretation of their individual positions. In Burke's day, the advantages of aristocratic government were scarcely debated; only at the end of his life, and then only in isolated quarters, did men seriously question the adequacy of existing aristocratic institutions. Burke's fears about the French Revolution derived in part from his anxiety lest the French example be used by its English disciples as a device for overthrowing aristocratic forms in Britain. By Disraeli's time, democracy's advance could no longer be ignored. Disraeli hoped that he might construct a Party which would maintain traditional institutions while effectively channeling popular demands into enterprises which carried no threat to the nation. "Tory democracy" was the answer of one who wished to maintain an association with the past while emphasizing an acceptance of the present. In giving way on "nonessentials," Disraeli hoped to secure harmony in the nation. Churchill knew that the problem of democracy versus aristocracy had already been settled, and that a reversal of the process was inconceivable. He accepted this situation and tried to accommodate himself to it. This, however, did not prevent him from extolling the aristocratic past, or making clear his reservations about the democratic present.

On other substantive issues there was less agreement. Burke spoke in a Whig idiom — criticizing the monarch, emphasizing the liberties of the subject, and hearkening back to the glories of 1688. Disraeli, in his romanticism, emphasized the role to which history had summoned the Tory Party. It was the agent which would restore the Queen to her rightful inheritance and the Church to its ancient dignity, while satisfying the people in their legitimate demands. For Churchill, these questions scarcely figured at all. In a style which owed a great deal to Gibbon and Macaulay, but which imitated neither, he warned Britain of its enemies, foreign and domestic. Churchill never doubted the seriousness of the plight in which twentieth-century Europe found itself, and never imagined that the past could be restored by diplomacy alone, however adroit, or by even the most ingenious military policy. He believed, however, that a lesser or greater catastrophe might be avoided by courage and intelligence; he set himself the task of creating a model for both.

The chasm which separates the views of Burke, Disraeli, and Churchill will be understood only if an effort is made to explain these differences in the context of what we know of their personalities and needs. It is not without significance that Burke wrote political tracts, that Disraeli chose the novel as his medium, and that Churchill preferred to write history and biography. While it is possible to imagine Burke writing history (he did so in the *Annual Register*, and made other more ambitious attempts on a larger scale), it is impossible to imagine him as a novelist. Churchill, as a youth, wrote a novel, but never thought to produce a second. Disraeli never tried his hand at history, but would almost certainly have been dissatisfied if he had. The choice of literary form, in each instance, was not an accident.

Burke, writing in an aristocratic age, intended that his works should be known by those who governed the country. The parliamentary arena was Burke's natural forum. He could imagine no other. Even when he wrote long and passionate tracts, sometimes in the form of letters, he composed them with a parliamentary audience in mind. The imagery and idiom testified to his interest in communicating with this particular group.

Addressed to such an audience, the works required style and dignity, both in thought and expression. They were necessarily impersonal, dwelling on public issues that merited the attention of political men.

When Disraeli wrote, he wrote for himself primarily. If this appears to be a contradiction, it may be explained by Disraeli's continuing preoccupation with himself and his progress in the world. In the tales which he invented, Disraeli sought to reassure himself about what the individual might achieve by his own effort and intelligence. Writing at a time when fiction formed a staple in the reading diet of many, Disraeli knew the advantages of writing for this public. The novel suited Disraeli's purpose; it broadcast his views, made his personality known, and gave free rein to his imagination. Disraeli believed in the hero in history and imagined that destiny had selected him for such a role. The novel, more than any other literary form, permitted him to explore the possibilities of individual action.

Churchill used his histories to report on himself, but this was incidental to a larger purpose. Living at the center of affairs at a time when criticism was common, Churchill knew better than others how much in fact there was to criticize. His originality lay in his reflections on the character of the epoch in which he lived; even when writing about another age, as he did in his *Marlborough*, comparisons with the present were always implicit. At the sunset of one epoch and at the start of another, he knew how to appreciate the first without becoming maudlin or slipping off into easy despair. Understanding that the critic who offers nothing but reproof is a poor friend of humankind, Churchill sought to avoid that snare. Pride in his family, in his country, and in his own achievements led him to write history and biography. Inevitably, these became essays also in autobiography — of thought no less than of action.

The extension of the suffrage and the growth in power and prestige of political parties — developments of the nineteenth and early twentieth century — touched in fundamental respects the independence and influence of every member of the House

of Commons. The political party, by sanctioning certain proposals and enlisting support for them, made the task of reform
infinitely easier. This service, however, had its price; the party, a
jealous mistress, insisted that its own interests be safeguarded.
This made independence a difficult and dangerous matter, not
recommended to those who valued safety. Popular pressure
also intervened to alter the political process. So long as members
debated among themselves, with only garbled reports reaching
the outside for the interested few, Westminster responded
slowly to changes in the popular mood. When, however, members spoke as often for the audience outside as for each other,
new arguments were heard. Just as party development worked
to reduce the individual member's freedom, so the democratizing
process tended in the same direction. A member came to have at
least two masters; the party whip, always present, and the anonymous public, frequently listening in.

These changes ought not to be ignored in a study of British
politics which starts with Burke and concludes with Churchill.
They ought not, however, to be made paramount. The careers
of Burke, Disraeli, and Churchill do reveal remarkable identities,
even if these express situational rather than intellectual or political affinities. In politics each found his work, and in parliamentary combat each sought to excel. Although they differed
about the past, and measured the present by standards which
derived as often from personal as from political necessities, they
agreed in repudiating any system of analysis which made politics
appear a science. Their perceptions were those of the artist; they
ignored the regularities which governed human affairs in favor
of the accidental and the mysterious. They were all contemplative men actively engaged, who used language as a weapon, and
sought inspiration in history. In and out of Parliament they
preached to a society which mocked them as often as it praised
them. Their ideas, rarely conventional, were frequently dismissed as myth and fantasy. Even their friends and supporters
sometimes felt uneasy about their words, sensing incongruities
in them. They were not "representative" men in any sense, and

appeared neither as the spokesmen of their day nor as the heralds of a new and better order which they saw immediately impending. Not one of them was content with his age, and, though rebellion never figured as their remedy, criticism remained a constant occupation. It is this which makes their lives interesting, and their minds as worthy of study as their deeds. Their careers cannot be easily and conveniently capsuled and made to appear like a hundred others. The differences between them, and between the political worlds which they inhabited need always to be recalled; only in this context is their accomplishment given substance and meaning. Because such lives provide a comment on the society which made them possible, the history of Great Britain since the middle of the eighteenth century may be given a new dimension in a study which dwells on their thought.

EDMUND BURKE

❧ *The Old Whig* ❧

Edmund Burke was born in 1729 in Dublin of a Protestant
father and a Catholic mother. Reared in his father's religion, he
escaped the legal disabilities which continued to afflict those
who remained loyal to the older faith. Burke belonged to that
tiny minority in Ireland — socially privileged — who could
buy, sell, and inherit land without hindrance, and serve the state,
if such was their pleasure, in both civil and military capacities.
None of these possibilities existed for those who refused to ab-
jure their Papist beliefs. Burke's education was a good one; as a
boy, he attended a small school outside Dublin maintained by
a Yorkshire Quaker; later, he went to Trinity College, Dublin.
The poverty and degradation of Ireland, so shocking even to
the casual visitor, did not entirely elude Burke, though he was
shielded from its immediate effects. The condition produced by
absentee landlords, excessive rents, primitive agricultural methods, and mass illiteracy made Ireland one of the most backward
of the dominions over which George II ruled. While Dublin,
with its graceful neoclassic architecture, provided a cover for
the misery elsewhere apparent, Burke saw enough to realize the
plight of the unhappy island.

In 1750, he left Dublin for London. Enrolled in the Middle Temple, he began that slow though not very arduous training which would permit him to follow his father in the legal profession. While Burke's talents were not unsuited to the law, he showed no great interest in its study. A literary career seemed infinitely more compelling, and after a short time he abandoned the pretense of taking his dinners in the Temple. Realizing the likely consequences of his rebellion, Burke was undeterred by the prospect of his father's denying him further support. The literary apprenticeship, with its demands, took precedence over every other consideration. While no record exists to suggest how Burke fared in the period 1750–1756, hardship and frustration appear to have been his lot. The silence of the record testifies to the bleakness of the time. As an unattached youth in London, without entree to society, literary or social, Burke came to rely heavily on other Irish residents of the city. He became especially close to a "kinsman," William Burke; this friendship remained always important to him. An illness brought him into touch with an Irish physician, Dr. Christopher Nugent, whose daughter he subsequently married. There is scarcely any mention of English friends; if they existed, they were of small consequence to him. How Burke spent these years it is impossible to say; his literary output was negligible, and no other interest seemed to engage him. It was not until 1756 that anything appeared which suggested actual literary employment.

A Vindication of Natural Society, published anonymously in 1756, revealed a curious image of the Irish youth who till that moment had made no impression on literary London. The work was more philosophical than literary, and attempted through the use of irony to ridicule arguments which asserted the superiority of natural over political society. This was an unorthodox position in the eighteenth century — a time when worship of *nature* and the *natural* seemed almost an article of religious faith for those who thought themselves enlightened. That Burke should have been led to attack this opinion suggests an independence of mind, but also, a seriousness of purpose. By using irony as his device, however, he failed in his object. The irony was either unrecognized or misunderstood, and, what Burke intended to mock, many of his readers imagined he sought to praise. Confronted with a total confusion about the meaning of the tract, he hastened to publish a second edition, in which he admitted his authorship, and added a preface to explain his meaning. The preface stated: "It is an observation which I think Isocrates makes in one of his orations against the sophists, that it is far more easy to maintain a wrong cause, and to support paradoxical opinions to the satisfaction of a common auditory, than to establish a doubtful truth by solid and conclusive arguments." Burke had intended to construct a fanciful thesis with sufficient reasonableness to recommend it to the unwary, but without any element of truth in it. Bolingbroke, the old Tory leader, who died in 1754, had frequently expatiated on the superiority of "natural religion" to "revealed religion." Burke thought Bolingbroke's arguments specious, and imagined that equally preposterous proofs might be adduced to prove the superiority of "natural society" to "political society." He expected that the grotesqueness of his argument would be seen, and that it would be ridiculed, as Bolingbroke's deserved to be. Through irony he intended to strike a blow against all who used easy rationalist explanations to explain complex and difficult phenomena.

The preface removed the ambiguities; the irony, previously obscured, emerged in all of its stridency. The proofs of the evil tendencies of the state, expressed mathematically in numbers killed in war, appeared exaggerated and crude, as Burke had intended they should. Blaming political society for the whole of the carnage that had taken place since antiquity, Burke contrasted this unhappy scene with the peaceful one offered by nature; he wrote: "How far mere nature would have carried us, we may judge by the example of those animals, who still follow her laws, and even of those to whom she had given dispositions more fierce, and arms more terrible than ever she intended we should use. It is an incontestable truth, that there is more havoc made in one year by men, of men, than has been made by all the lions, tigers, panthers, ounces, leopards, hyenas, rhinoceroses, elephants, bears, and wolves, upon their several species since the beginning of the world; though these agree ill enough with each other, and have a much greater proportion of rage and fury in their composition than we have. But with respect to you, ye legislators, ye civilizers of mankind! Ye Orpheuses, Moseses, Minoses, Solons, Theseuses, Lycurguses, Numas! with respect to you be it spoken, your regulations have done more mischief in cold blood, than all the rage of the fiercest animals in the greatest terrors, or furies, has ever done, or ever could do!''

Burke, in his ironical mood, equated political society with tyranny, inequality, and injustice. Only a reader who detected the irony could understand that his intention was to prove the opposite. Burke did not think of the state of nature as a time of bliss from which man had been rudely taken. On the contrary, the benefits of society were too apparent for Burke to deny them. Like Locke, in the previous century, he thought of the state as lawgiver and judge. Locke, in describing man's condition in nature, had dwelled on the disorder stemming from each individual's judging his own cause, with no authority existing to adjudicate between rival claims. He saw political society as a blessing, creating an order and harmony previously unknown. Burke viewed the matter in much the same way; man's nature made the state necessary. Political society served to defend legitimate interests; inequalities and injustices, where they existed, were not to be charged to the state. Those who read Burke's *Vindication* and failed to detect its ironical intent emerged with the impression that it was another argument in favor of the "natural" over the "artificial"; nothing was further from his mind.

Whether the fault lay with Burke, inexperienced in the use of a difficult literary device, or with his public, insufficiently attentive to the nuance contained in his prose, the tract, even with its preface, never gained a sympathetic reading. If Burke had hoped for some sort of recognition as a result of its publication, he must have been sorely disappointed. In 1757, however, with the publication of a treatise on aesthetics, Burke experienced his first literary triumph. *A Philosophical Inquiry into the Origin of Our Ideas of the Sublime and Beautiful* — an essay many years in preparation — refuted conventional eighteenth-century definitions of *nature*, which tended, too often, to repeat Shaftesbury, who saw nature as "all-loving, all-lovely, all-divine." Burke employed a different critical approach; distinguishing between the "beautiful," which pleased man by its order, proportion, limitation, and simplicity, and the "sublime," which moved the observer by its lack of proportion, he concluded that the first tended to make men happy, the second, afraid. The sublime, Burke wrote, caused man to feel "a sort of tranquillity tinged with terror." This was the higher enjoyment, since it made possible a feeling of exaltation. The sublime gave the individual a sense of power, independence, and aloneness. Courage, even more than happiness, was the gift bestowed by the sublime. The beautiful, Burke explained, served to unite men; the sublime to isolate them. The beautiful acted as a civilizing influence; the sublime afforded man a new understanding of himself.

With the appearance of this essay, Burke's life was totally transformed. Men who had never heard his name sought him out, and lifted him from his isolation. Within a year, he knew the greatest and most gifted members of the London literary and artistic world. Dr. Johnson, who was then at the height of his fame, came to know Burke through an introduction effected by Garrick. Sir Joshua Reynolds, famous for his painting but also for his generous hospitality, took Burke into his circle of intimate friends. Oliver Goldsmith praised the *Sublime and Beautiful* in an unsigned review in the *Monthly* in May 1757, and was soon acquainted with its author. Robert Dodsley, Burke's publisher, thought so highly of his young Irish protégé that he offered him the editorship of the *Annual Register,* which made its first appearance in 1759. After many lean years Burke seemed launched on the road to literary distinction.

While the attentions paid Burke were of course gratifying, he

from the king's service. British politics since the accession of George III in 1760 had run an erratic course. Unlike his Hanoverian predecessors, George III had no intention of seeing his powers reduced by Whig politicians who claimed a permanent right to govern in his name. The Whigs acted as if the services of their families to the royal family in a now somewhat remote past placed the king permanently in their debt. George III, displaying from the first days of his reign an independence inconceivable in the time of George I or George II, aspired to a more active role in the governing of his kingdom and in the choice of his ministers. Rumors of the creation of a "court party" and a "court interest" circulated almost immediately after his accession. The rumors gained support from various royal interventions. Taking advantage of divisions among his Whig ministers, George III contributed to the destruction of the great War Ministry in 1761. Pitt, and his brother-in-law Temple, perhaps the most prominent of the ministers who had managed the war since 1756, went into retirement. A royal favorite, wholly lacking in political importance — Lord Bute — took charge of the king's affairs. This experiment collapsed in 1763; the nation, and even more, the House of Commons, would not tolerate the Scot who took such pride in being the king's loyal and devoted servant. The king turned next to George Grenville; his government, while not subject to the same criticisms, proved no more durable. In 1765, against his will, but in despair of avoiding the inevitable any longer, the king commissioned Rockingham to form a ministry. It was at this moment that Burke appeared on the parliamentary stage.

The Rockingham ministry survived only till the first days of July 1766. Its greatest achievement — the repeal of the Stamp Act — sealed its fate. The king refused to abide any longer a ministry capable of such action. In dismissing Rockingham and in asking Pitt to serve in his place, George III showed his habitual fear of being controlled by party and politicians. The king hoped to use Pitt to free himself of the Whig dominance. Knowing Pitt's own reservations about party, and believing that an alliance with the "great commoner" would bring to an end the dictation suffered at Whig hands, the king planned with his prime minister a government which would be above party and which would stimulate all manner of men to serve in its ranks. This experiment in "nonparty" government never had a fair trial; it was doomed by the physical collapse of its chief member. Pitt, elevated to the House of Lords, conducted affairs for only a few months. Physical and mental ailments compelled him to retire to the country where no minister could possibly reach him. The Duke of Grafton became the acting head of government; aware of the weakness of his position, he negotiated with the Rockingham party in the hope of bringing the group back in a new ministry. It was apparent by the summer of 1767 that Rockingham had no intention of serving in any ministry in which he did not himself hold the principal place. Neither Grafton nor the king were prepared to pay this price for Rockingham's support. Political agitation increased, and Burke achieved his first prominence as a Whig politician.

His place as a Whig apologist had already been established in 1766 immediately after Rockingham's dismissal. Burke chose that moment to publish *A Short Account of a Late Short Administration.* This, a sharp political polemic, suggested party warfare during the time of Anne. Burke's aim was a simple one; he hoped to prove that the Rockingham administration, which had lasted only a year and twenty days, had not just been another ministry, indistinguishable from a dozen others. Burke wished to create an image which would make its achievements appear distinctive; the Rockingham period, he said, had seen the Americans becalmed, Englishmen confirmed in their liberties, trade and manufacture expanded, and the king's business handled efficiently. In short, the ministry had made a record which it wished to be remembered for. Burke constructed a myth in which the "services of a year" seemed so exceptional as to tell their own tale. The implication was clear; Britain would again enjoy such government when the king saw fit to recall Rockingham and his party to his service.

In 1766 Burke expected such a call to be imminent. By 1770, he had reason to wonder whether it would come at all. The king, by judicious interventions, achieved what few had imagined possible. Even the withdrawal of Chatham (Pitt), the sudden death of Charles Townshend, who was expected to succeed Grafton, and the gradual dissolution of the ministry through repeated crises and alarms were not sufficient to upset the prevailing order. It was with some sense of urgency that Burke decided to produce a manifesto which would establish authoritatively the identity and policy of the Rockingham party. He took upon himself the task of giving the party its platform; this he did in 1770 with the publication of a long tract entitled *Thoughts on the Cause of the Present Discontents.*

Burke was determined to convey to the public a sense of the gravity of affairs. Reviewing the events of the last years, he found that they augured ill for the future. Great Britain, he said, was in the midst of a crisis, the seriousness of which it failed to comprehend. While it was common for every age to imagine itself peculiarly ill-governed and ill-used, he had no doubt that the grievances of his own time were genuine. Disorder existed everywhere, and honest men agreed that remedies were needed. Burke admitted that the people were often wrong in their disputes with established authority, but he refused to accept the theory that they were always wrong. On the contrary, he argued that the persistence of a complaint suggested some defect in the constitution or in the governing authority. It took no great mind to see the tyranny of an earlier time; Burke had little respect for what he called "retrospective wisdom." The challenge was to detect tyranny in its new forms, and to act to prevent its continuance. He reminded his readers that there were "few statesmen so very clumsy and awkward in their business, as to fall into the identical snare which proved fatal to their predecessors." A new arbitrary tax, when it was introduced, would not "bear on its forehead the name of *Shipmoney.*"

Burke admitted that he saw no designs on Parliament itself,

but he asked whether the growth of the royal power did not constitute a real danger. The king, he argued, was seeking to accomplish through Influence what certain of his predecessors had attempted to do through Prerogative. Surrounded by a court faction, the king seemed determined to undermine the position of the Whig leaders. According to Burke, the "king's men" hoped to remove from places of influence all those who enjoyed a real popularity in the nation. The court party sought to create a situation where the people were left with no spokesmen in Parliament, and where all honor obviously reflected royal choice. Understanding the necessity of concealing its ambitions, the court party spread the rumor that it intended only to protect the constitution against a factious nobility and an irresponsible rabble determined on its destruction. "Would to God, it were true," Burke wrote, "that the fault of our peers were too much spirit! It is worthy of some observation," he said, "that these gentlemen, so jealous of aristocracy, make no complaints of the power of those peers (neither few nor inconsiderable) who are always in the train of a court, and whose whole weight must be considered as a portion of the settled influence of the crown." Burke charged the "king's friends" with violating the spirit even more than the letter of the constitution. The discretionary powers, which were properly the king's, were being used to please the prejudices and whims of courtiers. He did not question the king's possession of these discretionary powers, but he insisted that their use ought always to reflect a public interest. The king's choice of certain men over others touched the constitution in a fundamental way; "constitute government how you please," Burke wrote, "infinitely the greater part of it must depend upon the exercise of the powers which are left at large to the prudence and uprightness of ministers of state." Since power had to be distributed among men, and since no constitution could guarantee the proper use of that power, the only guarantee lay in the character of the men selected. "Men are in public life as in private," Burke wrote, "some good some evil. The elevation of the one, and the depression of the other . . . are the first objects of all good policy."

Parliament, Burke thought, existed as a check on the king. If the monarch decided unwisely in the selection of his ministers, support should be refused them. The king made a mistake when he chose as ministers men unknown to Parliament. Only those who were known and respected could be safely entrusted with the responsibilities of government. Burke, without naming Bute, obviously intended that his words should be understood as applying to such royal appointees. He accepted the fact that government was difficult, and that even the best encountered more criticism than it deserved while the worst never received the complaint that it merited. However, the question was never one of "absolute discontent" or "perfect satisfaction"; it was always a more relative matter. Government, he implied, should always seek to do those things which called forth the greatest support from the people.

Burke looked with a special fondness on the House of Commons, and sought to explain its many excellent qualities. He reminded his readers that the Commons was not originally intended to be a "part of the standing government of the country." It was devised as a control, deriving its power from the people, existing for a time, and losing its identity in the people again. The power of the House of Commons was meant to be transitory. While certain people argued as if only the House of Commons represented the people, this was an error; the king, the lords, the judges represented the people no less than did the Commons. They all represented the people because they all held a trust from the people. According to Burke, no power was ever given for the sole benefit of the person who exercised it. Government — an institution of divine origin — in its forms and in the persons who exercised authority in its name, originated with the people.

Referring to the Wilkes affair, and to the effort to keep a legally elected member from his seat in Parliament, Burke remarked that the House of Commons "was not instituted to be a control *upon* the people, as of late it has been taught, by a doctrine of the most pernicious tendency." On the contrary, "it was designed as a control *for* the people." Other institutions existed to check "popular excesses"; if they were not adequate to their task, they ought to be made so. The House of Commons existed to oversee executive and judicial bodies and listen to public complaint. Burke was offended by a House of Commons which asserted that everything was going well in the kingdom when in fact the nation was lost in despair. He could not abide a House of Commons which applauded ministers who were detestable to the country. When the public protested, Burke wrote, the Commons could not simply ignore its charges and proceed as if nothing required to be done. Parliament's nature was totally corrupted when it gave indiscriminate support to all ministers or when it sought to interfere with free elections. Parliament needed to rediscover its old purpose and act again as an effective control on government.

Writing about the Wilkes case, Burke made it appear that the "king's friends" were responsible for the whole affair. Their aim, he said, was to convince members of the House of Commons "that the favor of the people was not so sure a road as the favor of the court even to popular honors and popular trusts." He looked for a Parliament in which independent men were always inquiring into the operations of government; the "court party," he charged, sought only the presence of docile and consenting puppets. By prosecuting Wilkes, they hoped to teach the lesson that popularity, if not fatal, was at least dangerous. Before the Wilkes affair, men were right in believing that popularity served to gain the greatest gifts within the king's giving. The "king's friends" wished members to understand that the favor of the court was "the only sure way of obtaining and holding those honors which ought to be in the disposal of the people." He summed up his charge with the statement: "Resistance to power has shut the door of the house of commons to one man; obsequiousness and servility, to none."

The idea that Wilkes was punished for indecent publications, or for possessing impious materials, Burke thought preposterous. Only the fact that Wilkes had stood up against royal oppression led the ministry to decide on the measures which had kept him from his rightful place in Parliament. Burke worried lest the Wilkes case lead others to believe that political success came not from popularity with the people but from proving oneself agreeable to the court. If once men became convinced that such was the avenue to position and power, they would soon seek to qualify in those terms. Dissatisfaction with the existing state of affairs had led to various reform proposals, including some which would operate to shorten the lives of individual parliaments and prevent all or most "placemen" (royal office holders) from sitting in Parliament. These recommendations were generally pressed in the form of proposals for a triennial or a place act. Burke opposed both remedies, on the ground that they would not achieve the results contemplated. Frequent election, he explained, would only operate to the advantage of the Crown whose funds were far more ample than those available to private individuals. With such elections, even the seats of independent country gentlemen would be endangered; no one could afford repeated contests with the Treasury. Also, Burke worried lest the effect of frequent election on the populace be increased disorder. His opposition to a place act was equally firm. The barring of great and powerful interests from Parliament would prove harmful. Such interests, prevented from participating in an institution with which they wished to be associated, would probably retaliate by seeking to undermine or destroy that from which they were excluded. As for the Crown, he imagined that it would soon exercise its influence through the granting of contracts, bribes, and other forms of secret help, if it discovered that the granting of office disqualified a friend from sitting in Parliament. Such influence, because it was secret, had particularly dangerous possibilities.

The only remedy, Burke argued, lay in a proper appreciation by Parliament of its real function. As a controlling agency, its responsibility was to differ with every administration, and to refuse automatic support to any proposal emanating from the ministry. The member who supported every administration was a man who subverted government. Membership in Parliament acquired its dignity from the fact that it expressed independence. A member should expect his parliamentary actions to be scrutinized by his electors, and, if it became evident that he had sold his freedom, defeat in the next election might well prove the price exacted for his surrender. The "court party," Burke wrote, had sought to propagate the notion that all political connections were by definition factious. This, he vehemently denied. While men organized in political parties might prove narrow, bigoted, or selfish, he failed to see why this should invariably be true. In one of the most fortunate periods in English history, during the reign of Anne, a "Whig connection" governed. Those men, according to Burke, understood the value of party and never imagined that it interfered with their proper patriotic sentiments. Lord Sunderland, Lord Godolphin, Lord Somers, and Lord Marlborough — all "wise men" — knew that they would be criticized as an ambitious junto, but this did not deter them from their purpose. They remained faithful to a principle of party which saw them loyal to each other and also to the doctrines on which they agreed. Party served as an instrument which permitted individuals to join with others of like mind, to achieve more easily those things which were both good and necessary. Burke, who had never forgiven Chatham for upsetting the Rockingham ministry in 1766, attacked those who imagined they might proceed without any connection at all. Honest combination was a necessity; dishonest combination, based on private inclination and a desire to act contrary to the interests of the people, he found contemptible.

Convinced that a wicked combination in the form of a "court party" existed at that moment, Burke emphasized the hazards of the situation. Until independent men were introduced into the House of Commons, prepared to listen to the public and pay heed to the traditions of the body to which they had been elected, there was no hope of restoring Parliament as "an agency of control." When the king understood that such men were prepared to serve him, and that no others were better suited to his service, then the constitution would again be secure. Burke's *Thoughts on the Cause of the Present Discontents* was from first to last a party statement. It aimed at incorporating elements of a traditional Whig myth with policies suited to the interests of the Rockingham party. In his concern for the dignity of the House of Commons, in his interest that Parliament function as a "control," in his suspicions about royal intentions, and in his defense of "political connections," Burke expressed ideas which had been common in Whig circles before the Hanoverians entered England. His insistence that power be viewed as a "trust," and that the individual possessing power admit his responsibilities, reiterated a classic Whig dogma. Locke, a century earlier, had argued that government existed for the community, and that no government could ignore the people. Burke almost certainly exaggerated the menace represented by the "court party," but he did so with a clear conscience, convinced that in its essentials his argument was true. If the Crown succeeded in dominating Parliament, there would be no defense of the subject's liberties; Whigs before and after 1688 had often believed this.

The meaning of the tract was obvious; through Burke, the Rockingham party served notice on George III that it proposed to treat him as Shaftesbury and Sunderland had treated Charles II. His actions would be scrutinized, his ministers interrogated, and his policies questioned. The king's plan to put an end to party strife was declared impossible; to do that would be to put an end also to liberty. Burke created a platform for his party, sanctioned it by appealing to history, and, in effect, summoned others to join in the battle which was forming. He made it appear a struggle between traditionalists who insisted that the House of Commons retain its function as a "control" on government and others who cared only that Parliament authorize what the king and his ministers insisted on. The engagement, thus opened, would end only when the king submitted to the will of

Parliament as George I and George II had done. Ten years experience of George III had led the Rockingham party to this position.

The king understood the nature of the threat; aware of the risks, he prepared to meet his adversaries with the powerful support available to him. If he relied on his "friends," he depended also on that very ample patronage, always at his disposal, which made possible the winning of new friends. The opposition, in turn, depended on its support, and particularly on its talented spokesmen in Parliament. Burke and others would seek to reduce the latest of the king's "favorites," Lord North, to impotence. He would be hounded from office as Bute and Grafton had been before him. The political scene in 1770 seemed to promise quick results; the deepening crisis in the American colonies offered a real possibility. The Rockingham party, if it did not have a vested interest in disaster, knew at least the likely advantages that would flow from a major embarrassment of the ministry. In the House of Commons, Burke became the principal critic of the government. On the difficulties with the American colonies, he developed a policy different from that of Lord North. The implication was clear; when and if Rockingham was again summoned to serve the king, such a policy would be inaugurated.

In 1774, when the tension between the mother country and the colonies had reached an intensity which threatened disaster, Burke made a major pronouncement in the House of Commons. His speech, widely reported, argued for a return to the system of taxation which had existed before the controversy began. Because so much of the discussion had been on a theoretical plane, involving disputes about the limits of Parliament's powers over the colonies, the reality of the so-called distinction between internal and external taxation, and differences about the representativeness of the Parliament which sat at Westminster, Burke claimed that the real issues had been lost sight of. He expressed his fatigue with this endless discussion and theorizing; his wish was for peace, which he thought could be obtained if the mother country continued to regulate trade and if the colonies were permitted to tax themselves.

Burke, showing sympathy for the American complaints, reminded his fellow-members that a rich man like Hampden would never have been inconvenienced by being required to pay twenty shillings ship money. Hampden's opposition in the seventeenth century had been based on a principle; he believed that he would be forfeiting his freedom if he capitulated before an unjust tax. Burke claimed that the American colonies had accepted without complaint until 1764 the navigation acts which regulated their commerce. Accustomed to these regulations, they obeyed them without any thought that their freedom was reduced as a consequence. This was a form of commercial servitude, but the American colonists, free in every other respect, saw no reason to object. It was not perfect freedom, Burke said, but "comparing it with the ordinary circumstances of human nature, it was a happy and liberal condition." Only when Parliament attempted to introduce new principles of government did the colonies see fit to object. The decision to "raise a revenue" in America was a departure from all precedent; wisdom dictated the abandonment of these novel practices and the return to old usages. With some feeling, Burke exclaimed, "revert to your old principles — seek peace and ensue it — leave America, if she has taxable matter in her, to tax herself." He had no wish to go into the abstract rights and wrongs of the situation; "I am not here," he said, "going into the distinctions of rights nor attempting to mark their boundaries. I do not enter into these metaphysical distinctions; I hate the very sound of them. Leave the Americans as they anciently stood, and these distinctions, born of our unhappy contest, will die with it." For Burke, precedent constituted the "arguments of states and kingdoms"; abstract theories could be left to "the schools." If the Parliament at Westminster admitted that its authority extended only to the British Isles, that the colonial legislatures had come to exercise certain powers, and that these needed to be respected, subject always to a general superintending authority which remained in London, the troubles would end immediately. Parliament's meddling, Burke said, had led to a loss of peace, union, commerce, and revenue; the road back to reason lay through experience.

In March 1775, when relations with the colonies were fast deteriorating, he launched a new attack on ministerial policy. His hope was for reconciliation; his quest, he said, was for peace, not achieved through war, but looked for "in its natural course, and in its ordinary haunts." Burke claimed that peace could be obtained if "plain good intention" was shown. Peace implied a willingness to make concessions, and the mother country, as the superior power, should make the first gesture. She had no reason to fear that her initiative would be misinterpreted and taken as evidence of weakness. America was worth keeping, and it could never be kept by the use of force which was a "feeble instrument," unlikely to achieve any but unsatisfactory results. Force, Burke explained, gave only a temporary solution to a problem; a nation was not being governed when it had to be perpetually reconquered. Also, force, when it failed utterly, left no opening for compromise; an "impoverished and defeated violence," was a peculiarly barren thing. Even when force succeeded, it did so generally at the expense of the object recovered. Burke had no wish to see America and the mother country wasted in a needless but brutal quarrel. He reminded the House of Commons that the mother country had no experience in the use of force as a method for governing its colonies.

When Burke reflected on the character and temper of the American people, he discovered additional reasons for counseling immediate reconciliation. The colonists, English in origin, boasted a remarkable and intense devotion to freedom; they viewed freedom not abstractly but concretely; like their English ancestors, they feared especially a tyranny originating in unjust and arbitrary taxation. Most of the colonists were Protestants; they were drawn to dissent, and their competence in the law made them skilled adversaries in their encounters with government. Geography, which caused the colonies to be separated from the mother country by three thousand miles of water, served also to enforce a lenient rule on those who governed from London. Even if the mother country had wished things to be otherwise, circumstances intervened to thwart its ambition. The colonists, accustomed to freedom from the beginning, would never tolerate or accept voluntarily an infringement of that happy condition. The mother country, Burke thought, could respond in one of three ways: it could seek to alter the American spirit; it could call that spirit criminal and prosecute it; or it could admit its permanence and come to terms with it. He considered each of the possibilities and concluded that only the last gave any promise of a permanent solution. Believing that "the temper and character, which prevail in our colonies, are . . . unalterable by any human art," Burke warned the Commons that "an Englishman is the unfittest person on earth to argue another Englishman into slavery." It was impossible to ignore the colonists' complaint that they were being taxed by a legislature in which they were unrepresented. Pleading for a realistic assessment of the situation, he said: "The question with me is, not whether you have a right to render your people miserable; but whether it is not your interest to make them happy. It is not what a lawyer tells me, I *may* do; but what humanity, reason, and justice, tell me, I ought to do." The only statesmanlike act was one which effected a reunion of the colonies with the mother country. If the colonists were reassured about their liberties they would welcome a continuing association with Great Britain. Freedom, Burke insisted, was the only commodity of which Britain enjoyed a monopoly.

In this speech as in others, Burke argued as a man who knew which objectives were worthy and how they might be secured. Theoretical rights held no interest for him; they only served to confuse the issue. The union of the mother country and the colonies, with its economic and political advantages to both, constituted the most telling argument for a return to the situation as it had existed in 1763. Burke, in his matter-of-fact and empirical manner, showed the temper of his Whig predecessors.

Godolphin, in 1707, in effecting the union of Scotland and England, had employed a similar reasoning. In that negotiation, there had been a willingness to compromise by the stronger of the two parties, and also, a readiness to court risks stemming from the admission of Presbyterians into the Parliament at Westminster. The advantages and the necessity being clear, there only remained the problem of devising a formula suited to the situation. Had Burke enjoyed a ministerial office in 1775, he would have sought a solution of the American problem in these terms.

His concern with the American situation increased after the outbreak of hostilities. In letters to friends and colleagues he expressed the fear that the Tories might succeed in concealing their blunders. Burke wished the Whigs to maintain their opposition and to confound Tory propaganda which played on patriotic sentiment. While undertsanding the difficulty of the Whig position — in war, its opposition was frequently made to appear factious and treasonable — there seemed no escape from such hazards. Unless the ministry was constantly pressed, and its actions subjected to a minute and continuous scrutiny, the most terrible results could be expected. In any case, Burke had become so much a party man that he could not imagine abandoning an opportunity which might in the end cause the ministry to collapse.

In 1777, when Britain's troubles were serious but not yet grave, Burke addressed a letter on the war to the sheriffs of Bristol; he intended the letter also for his constituents in that city. Reviewing the events which had followed the outbreak of hostilities, he dwelled on the political consequences, which he thought particularly pernicious. The suspension of habeas corpus, he deemed an unwarranted and unnecessary interference with the liberties of the subject. This, Burke wrote, was a dangerous act, for, in the event that it established a precedent, it could do irreparable harm to the constitution. In time of war, laws were frequently corrupted; in civil war, the temptation to ignore principles of equity and justice was particularly strong. Burke expressed the shame he felt at Britain's posture — cringing and fearful before old enemies likely to take advantage of her misfortunes, but belligerent before those who had formerly accepted her tutelage. This was an intolerable situation. While German "boors and vassals" manned England's hired armies, the Americans looked to the old enemy, France, for support. Such was the condition to which Lord North had led a once united empire.

There was no point in the British continuing to pretend that they had been wronged, and that the colonists' grievances were entirely without foundation. Burke reminded his readers that no conqueror in history ever "professed to make a cruel, harsh and insolent use of his conquest." To approach the colonies, sword in hand, professing good will, but all the time demanding absolute surrender, made no sense at all. Nothing would be achieved by such a policy. Burke claimed that rebellions or revolts of a whole people were always provoked, and that they were resolved when the grievances which caused them were removed. The government needed wisdom and honesty, and not additional arms.

Burke admitted that, when he first took his seat in the House of Commons, he believed, as did others, that Parliament enjoyed an unlimited legislative authority over the colonies. While he wished to maintain this right in its original form, not only for the advantage of the mother country, but "principally for the sake of those, on whose account all just authority exists," the "people to be governed," he soon realized that it was not expedient for the whole of the authority to be used. Just as in England Parliament enjoyed complete legislative authority, but accepted the fact that it ought not to attempt to do certain things lest it offend the opinions and feelings of the people, so in the colonies prudence dictated that some part of the admitted powers not be used. Parliament, by neglecting to use a power, did not invalidate it. To use a power simply to prove that it existed was to engage in a dangerous and foolish act, which, in the end, would probably not achieve its purpose.

Remarking on differences between nations, Burke suggested

[38]

that government always had to conform to the character and circumstances of the people involved. "I was never wild enough to conceive," he wrote, "that one method would serve for the whole; that the natives of Hindostan and those of Virginia could be ordered in the same manner." Given the character of the American people, none except a free government would satisfy them. If asked what such a government would be, his answer was: ". . . it is what the people think so; . . . they, and not I, are the natural, lawful, and competent judges of this matter." Freedom was always "a blessing and a benefit," taking different forms in different times and places. Absolute freedom existed nowhere, and could never exist. Liberty had to be limited in certain ways; the aim of the wise governor was to discover with what little restraint the community might subsist. "Liberty," Burke wrote, "is a good to be improved, and not an evil to be lessened."

Burke accepted the fact that his age was not all that certain men wished it to be. However, the only check to further decline was a correct judgment about what was good in the age, and an attempt to exploit that. He was unhappy about the spirit which placed such a heavy reliance on the idea of domination. The virtues of freedom needed to be recognized; freedom, even in its excess, he wrote, was preferable to servitude with its vices. "We are taught," he said, "to believe that a desire of domineering over our countrymen is love to our country; that those who hate civil war abet rebellion, and that the amiable and conciliatory virtues of lenity, moderation, and tenderness to the privileges of those who depend on this kingdom, are a sort of treason to the state." Burke hoped to teach the opposite lesson, not only for the good of America, but also for the benefit of England and its people. The war had already damaged the country severely. Its continuance could only compound the evil. An immediate and honorable peace was the only reasonable course.

The American war, by the political crisis that it created in Great Britain, established the basis of Burke's fame in Parliament. In the complex machinations that followed on the king's resolve to maintain Lord North at the head of his affairs, party lines grew increasingly taut. The American-French alliance of 1778 and the Spanish entry into the war in 1779 dealt heavy blows to a ministry already severely handicapped by inefficiency and growing despair. In these circumstances, the sustained criticism of the Opposition, which knew how to exploit every opportunity, added a burden of almost insuperable weight to those which already existed. North, on several occasions, sought relief from the onerous charge which the king had laid on him, but George III had no intention of seeing his trusted friend leave his service. As the king explained to a meeting of ministers in June 1779, the great mistake of his life had been to appoint Rockingham in 1765 and to agree to the repeal of the Stamp Act. That mistake, he had no intention of repeating; Rockingham and his Whig friends, by embarrassing his ministers, only made them more dear to their sovereign.

The year 1779 was, in certain respects, the most critical of the war for Great Britain. The existence of a French fleet in the Channel, the marked unreadiness of the British fleet to risk an engagement, and the growth of revolutionary sentiment in Ireland created dangers without precedent since the time of Elizabeth. On the naval front, the king did what he could to instill some sense of danger among those commissioned to guard Britain's coasts. The ministry was prepared to make concessions in Ireland, hoping thereby to reduce tension and convert criticism into gratitude. As early as 1778, Burke and his party argued for a modification of trading regulations so as to give the Irish a more equitable share in the profits of that trade. Burke claimed that the world was large enough for England and Ireland to flourish together. The granting of new mercantile privileges to Ireland, he said, could only serve to increase the well-being of both kingdoms. According to Burke, this had happened earlier in the century when Scotland acquired comparable privileges. However, even if Ireland proved to be the sole beneficiary, England would profit from having a happy and prosperous people within its Empire. In the fashion of Adam Smith, he dwelled on the advantages that would follow from a wide distribution of wealth. By these arguments, Burke hoped to persuade his Bristol constituents that their own interests would be served by certain propositions introduced by Lord North to relieve Ireland of various restrictions on its trade. The growth, however, of a large English mercantile opposition to these proposals finally dissuaded North from seeking to incorporate them in legislation, and the bills passed in 1778 went only a short distance toward satisfying Irish hopes.

The Rockingham Whigs refused to accept this as a final settlement of the problem. In May 1779, when the news from Ireland was grave, Rockingham, in the House of Lords, moved for an inquiry into ways of improving trade between the two countries. He reminded the Lords that "the American war commenced in addresses and petitions; that when those were turned a deaf ear to, they were followed with non-importation agreements." Ireland, he said, "was precisely in that situation which, if not speedily remedied, would, in the opinion of many, justify resistance." The implication was clear: if an Irish rebellion occurred, it could expect support from the Rockingham Whigs at Westminster. Lord North was in an impossible position; while he himself favored further Irish trade reforms, the commercial opposition of the previous year was fresh in his memory. He took the position in the House of Commons that Ireland had already gained immensely from the new legislation, and that no further changes could be made without endangering English commercial interests.

The Rockingham Whigs would not leave off their attack. Charles James Fox, who had visited Ireland in 1777, led the campaign to force the ministry into further reforms. Irish opinion was mobilized; petitions poured into Westminster. The Speaker of the Irish House of Commons, in a private note to Lord North, said: "It is my duty, though it is not in my department, to inform your Lordship of the desperate state to which this kingdom is reduced. If it is attacked in its present state, it will certainly be lost, perhaps without a blow." While the possibility of a French invasion threatened, the Irish Parliament showed an increasing opposition to policy as it emanated from Westminster. Henry Grattan, in moving an Amendment to the Speech from the Throne, asked for a "free export trade for Ireland," and "called upon the mob to do themselves justice." The Amendment, carried through without a division, read: "That it is not by temporary Expedients but by a Free Trade alone that this Nation is now to be saved from impending Ruin." The Volunteers, raised to resist a French invasion, showed on November 4, the anniversary of William III's birthday, that they were prepared to challenge British authority if it did not quickly reform itself. On November 15, rioting broke out in Dublin. Almost immediately a rumor circulated that a shipment of Irish wool was preparing to challenge the British navy; an Irish version of the Boston Tea Party was planned. The ministry, recognizing the hazards of further delay, made a total capitulation. On December 13, Lord North introduced a bill which made large concessions, and which went beyond what the Irish, in their most optimistic moments, had been led to expect. Because Burke knew that North had been forced into this situation, he saw no need to congratulate him for what he had accomplished. Burke's silence was misinterpreted in Ireland, and, in 1780, he thought it necessary to explain his position in a letter to a member of the Irish House of Commons.

In the Irish crisis, as in the American, the Rockingham party used every available weapon to bludgeon the ministry. The object was always to harass and embarrass, under cover of a more neutral motive — that of informing and instructing. In the precision of the Opposition's recommendations, and in the idealism which permeated its imagery, the hand of Burke was always visible. Burke hoped to establish an irrefutable case against the ministry, while providing his House of Commons colleagues with some sense of the gravity of the times through which they were living. He spoke, primarily, for political purposes, but always, with some attention to the larger implications of his words. An image of the Whig Party was being created; Burke intended that it should have substance and historical dimension.

If Burke's party interest led him to concentrate on questions having immediate political relevance, his strength derived from his capacity to convert these parochial incidents into larger and more compelling issues. For him, the distinction between the moral and the political was slight; when considering the American or the Irish situation, he thought as a politician, but also as a moralist. Ireland's economic discontent provided the Rockingham party with an issue useful in its campaign against North, but Burke saw the matter in another dimension also; the moral aspect of an unjust treatment of a dependent kingdom could not fail to absorb his attention. In the penal laws, which subjected the Roman Catholic majority in Ireland to heavy and humiliating disabilities, he found an example of injustice which moved him deeply. Burke knew that many of the private disabilities were in varying degrees ignored, and existed only on the statute books, but the fact that they existed as law, and that the public disabilities were enforced, seemed to him a perversion of reason and justice. Soon after joining the Rockingham party, Burke began to write a tract on "the laws against Popery in Ireland." While his many political obligations prevented his completing this work, enough was written to suggest his contempt for the principles on which this whole body of legislation claimed to be based.

Burke believed that the various laws had only one purpose — to ruin those who persisted in their Catholic faith. Tampering with the rights of inheritance, for example, was calculated to reduce Catholics, of whatever wealth or situation, to penury and obscurity. Laws encouraging children to enter a Court of Equity to plead against their Catholic parents, thereby uncovering the size of their parents' estate and forcing a division in their own favor, tended to reduce the influence of Catholic parents. The granting of special rights over her children to a Catholic woman who renounced her Catholicism was another device for curtailing the authority of the Catholic father. The laws against property-holding and office-holding were bad enough, Burke wrote, but those involving education were even more pernicious. Existing law made it extremely dangerous for a Catholic education to be offered to a Catholic child inside or outside the kingdom. Such laws, Burke said, were "unjust, impolitic, and inefficacious." Their effect on the prosperity, morality, and safety of the Irish nation had been disastrous. In one way or another, two out of every three citizens of the Irish state suffered some major loss through legislation introduced under quite different circumstances in the previous century. Burke wished to see this whole code scrapped; he called for laws which would not injure even a single Irish national. He admitted that there were difficulties in a wholesale abandonment of legislation, but he saw no alternative to attempting this delicate but necessary operation. The penal laws were a "misapplication and abuse of our reason."

Burke believed that a legislator's chief concern ought to be the happiness of the people. A law against the majority of the people was a law against the people itself. Law, he wrote, depended for its validity on the consent of the people. The exclusion of great numbers of men from the common advantages of society could never be legislated. Even if the people, in their foolishness, consented to such injustice, their decision would not serve to make such a practice law. Consent, Burke explained, was only one prerequisite for law. An act became a law if it did not run counter to the principles of a superior law which no community — not even the whole race of men — could alter. This superior law was "the will of Him who gave us our nature, and, in giving, impressed an invariable law upon it." "It would be hard," Burke said, "to point out any error more truly subversive of all the order and beauty, of all the peace and happiness of human society, than the position, that any body of men have a right to make what laws they please; or that laws can derive any authority from their institution merely, and independent of the quality of the subject matter. No arguments of policy, reason of state, or preservation of the constitution, can be pleaded in favor of such a practice." Burke thought there were only two proper foundations of law — equity and utility. Human laws were "only declaratory," having a power to change the mode and application of law, but powerless to alter the principles of original justice. The intolerance condemned in the unjust acts of Louis XIV could not be condoned when England caused an even larger number to suffer in Ireland.

Burke argued, as Locke had, that man's enjoyment of his natural rights defined the ultimate purpose of civil society. Government justified itself to the extent that this objective remained a principal concern. No man, Burke wrote, suffered evil voluntarily or happily; to subject individuals who adhered to particular religious principles to harsh penalties because their conscience forbade them to do otherwise was to make a travesty of justice. Religious persecution was an evil to be avoided. The coercive powers of the state ought to be limited to such acts as guaranteed its existence. Those who supported the penal legislation wished to make it appear that religious toleration would in some way endanger the state. Burke believed this to be a false issue. The repeal of the penal laws could only operate to increase the happiness and well-being of the Irish nation, and, in the long run, to cause trade and industry to prosper also. The only real danger to a state, Burke said, was to "render its subjects justly discontented"; the repeal of the penal laws could not but have the opposite effect.

Burke's Irish birth made him particularly susceptible to the problems of that unhappy island, but his interest in religious toleration was more than personal or political. He regarded religious toleration as a problem involving questions of justice, and hoped to make others see the matter in a similar light. In 1773, in a speech on a bill for the relief of Protestant dissenters, Burke said that he "would have toleration a part of establishment, as a principle favorable to Christianity, and as a part of

Christianity." A penal law which was not put into effect was both dangerous and absurd. If the evil which it sought to restrain was a real one, then to ignore the law was to permit the evil to continue. If the evil was not real, then legislation ought not to exist which threatened those who fell under its terms. An individual should be restrained in his religious freedom, Burke believed, only when he dissented not for reasons of conscience, but in order to raise faction in the state. Freedom for those who believed in Christianity, whatever its form, served to strengthen Christianity. The real enemy was not the dissenting Christian, but the unbeliever. It was he who sought to undermine all truth and loosen the bonds of civil society. The unbeliever could never be tolerated since his ideas represented a threat to political order. Burke, in going this far in his defense of religious toleration, spoke not as a politician, but as a man concerned with justice and with the security of the state. The defense of civil society needed to be the state's concern, but the persecution of those who in no way threatened the state revealed a temper which Burke deplored.

Burke's capacity to insinuate moral principles into politics showed itself again in 1780 with the introduction of his *Plan for Economical Reform*. In plotting the destruction of certain traditional and ancient offices in the King's Household, Burke claimed to be motivated by one interest only. His aim, he told the House of Commons, was "the reduction of that corrupt influence, which is itself the perennial spring of all prodigality, and of all disorder; which loads us, more than millions of debts; which takes away vigor from our arms, wisdom from our councils, and every shadow of authority and credit from the most venerable parts of our constitution." The king, he said, was the head of "a prodigal court" which depended on an "ill-ordered revenue"; this same situation, in the time of Louis XIV, had sapped the foundations of France. Men were by nature acquisitive, but Burke asked whether society profited when these instincts were satisfied with gifts from a court. He pre-

[46]

ferred to believe that men should seek their fortunes in other ways. Minor jurisdictions, which added nothing to justice but were expensive, he proposed to abolish. The Crown should be compelled to sell much of its landed property; such property, Burke argued, was more suited to private than to public ownership. Within the King's Household, he urged the destruction of various offices; such reforms, he estimated, would reduce the pension list by some 40,000 pounds annually. Those offices in which a real public service was performed, Burke proposed to treat differently. For such offices, the holder needed to be amply paid, so that the sacrifice of his private convenience received a just reward. Also, in order to maintain the practice of having the greatest nobles of the realm in close communication with the monarch, Burke recommended no changes in the offices of honor surrounding the king's person. He expected to achieve two objectives with these reforms: the reduction of the Crown's influence through the abolition of certain temptations to corruption; the demonstration of Parliament's concern for the opinions and well-being of the people outside. Burke continued to think of Parliament chiefly as an agency of control, and it was in these terms that he made his proposals.

Burke's plan failed to commend itself to the House of Commons, and on April 4, 1780, he wrote to one of his Bristol constituents: "I must fairly own that I feel myself totally defeated. . . . By refusing to destroy the subordinate treasuries, or to enter the household, the House has, in my opinion, rejected the whole plan." If the Rockingham campaign was defeated on this front, it refused to capitulate on others. Petitions, in response to incendiary speeches from the chief Whigs, came in increasing number to Parliament. On April 6, John Dunning spoke on the forty or so petitions which had descended on the House in recent months. Not since Charles I, Dunning said, had the House been asked by so many to redress grievances. The moment for a decisive act seemed at hand; Dunning moved a resolution for which there was no precedent; it read: "That it is the opinion of this committee [of the House of Commons] that the influence of the crown has increased, is increasing, and ought to be diminished." A second resolution read: "That it is competent to this House, to examine into, and to correct, abuses in the expenditure of the civil list revenues, as well as in every other branch of the public revenue, whenever it shall appear expedient to the wisdom of this House to do so." In these motions, introduced by Dunning, the whole thrust of Burke's argument since 1770 seemed to be contained. The issues, anticipated by Burke in 1770 in his *Thoughts on the Present Discontents*, seemed to have been confirmed by the events of the intervening decade. Dunning's motions expressed a fear of the royal power, and of the uses to which it had been put. The motions asserted Parliament's right to "control," about which Burke had always been insistent. In 1780, the House felt a sufficient disillusionment with the ministry to vote for the Dunning resolutions. Had the Opposition, at that moment, known how to exploit its victory, it might have succeeded in bringing the North ministry down. However, in the absence of a firm resolve, it procrastinated, and satisfied itself with yet another Dunning motion, brought forward on April 24. This motion read: "That an humble Address be presented to his Majesty, praying that he will be graciously pleased not to dissolve the parliament, or prorogue the present session, until proper measures have been taken to diminish the influence, and correct the other abuses, complained of by the petitions of the people." The ministry was prepared for the assault; it had spent the weeks collecting its forces. Dunning, in speaking on the motion, commented on the crowded condition of the House, and noted the presence of many military and naval officers summoned home by the ministry to do their duty by the king. Dunning begged these men to show zeal for their country also. When the votes were counted, the Opposition's defeat was recognized. Fox, angry at the result, called the vote "shameful, base, unmanly, treacherous." His words carried little conviction; in a fair contest between the ministry and its Whig opponents, the ministry had carried the day. The king, acting almost immediately, dissolved Parliament, and called a General Election.

This General Election posed serious problems for Burke. He had been sitting since 1774 as member for Bristol, and would have liked to continue to represent that powerful and populous borough. The sentiment for his reelection, however, seemed doubtful. In 1774, he had been chosen as one who could argue effectively the city's needs against an American policy which threatened its trade. Since that day, the city had become less obsessed with this issue, and more disturbed by its member's independence. Burke showed a peculiar disregard for his constituents' wishes; or at least such was the common opinion. He had revealed this independence even at the moment of his election; when Henry Cruger, the other elected member, thanked the citizens, he remarked on the "legality and propriety of the people's instructing their representatives in Parliament," and had spoken of himself as the "servant of my constituents, not their master, subservient to their will, not superior to it." Burke, under no obligation to comment on these remarks, decided to make them the principal point of departure in his own speech of thanks. While admitting that "it ought to be the happiness and glory of a representative to live in the strictest union, the closest correspondence, and the most unreserved communication with his constituents," serving them in every possible way, Burke rejected the notion that a member of Parliament ought to sacrifice his opinion and judgment to that of his electors. Burke told the crowd: "Your representative owes you, not his industry only, but his judgment; and he betrays, instead of serving you, if he sacrifices it to your opinion." Burke had no objection to receiving the views of his constituents, but he refused to be bound by their instructions or mandates. Parliament, he explained, was "not a *congress* of ambassadors from different and hostile interests" but a deliberative assembly of a single nation, whose members sat not for a local place, but for the whole people. Burke wished to be a representative, not a delegate; for his judgment, a gift of Providence, he demanded respect. While he undertook to be a faithful friend and devoted servant to those who had elected him, he would not be their flatterer.

There is nothing to indicate that Bristol appreciated this "declaration of independence" even in 1774. As Burke's term proceeded, and as he embarked on ventures which seemed to have no relation to Bristol's interests, the initial enthusiasm for him waned. Burke understood in 1780 that he could not hope to win the seat again unless he cleared himself of the charge of "neglecting" his electors. In coming before them in 1780, he dwelled on the theme that the existence of a court, prepared to support and reward competent men, tended to deprive the people of the services of such individuals. Court service offered emoluments which popular service could never rival. When an individual chose to serve the people, Burke said, it was important that he be given freedom to think on large matters, and to act on questions of national importance. If the electorate denied its representatives that freedom, service of the Crown would become the only school for statesmen. Were this to happen, then "the monopoly of mental power" would be added to the others already available to the Crown. The people would be left impotent, since they would lack the only strength which might weigh in a contest with the court; represented by men of narrowness and ignorance, they could never hope to have their interests sustained.

Aware of the charges that had been made against him, Burke proceeded to refute them. The notion that he had neglected his constituents' interests he dismissed summarily. He admitted only that in his desire to serve his constituents, there had been no time left to court them. He had heard criticisms of his Irish trade and religious policy, but he found no justice or wisdom in the voices raised against him. On Irish trade, Burke insisted that his actions reflected what he thought were the best interests of the nation. Given the conditions arising from the American war, it was mandatory for British statesmen to work for a strengthening of imperial ties. The ministry, slow, unimaginative, and halfhearted, had done nothing to improve the situation.

[50]

Only when rebellion threatened in Ireland did the ministry bestir itself. Burke admitted that in pressing for Irish trade reform he had ignored his constituents' instructions; his obedience, he said, had been to higher instructions. Understanding the danger in which the nation found itself, he could act no differently. His decision could not be guided by the "little, silly canvas prattle of obeying instructions, and having no opinions but yours." Such "idle, senseless tales, which amuse the vacant ears of unthinking men" would never have saved the nation from the menace that hovered over it. "What obligation lay on me to be popular?" Burke asked. "I was bound to serve both kingdoms." Bristol, in choosing him in 1774, he said, showed confidence in his judgment; he refused to believe that his constituents wished him to approach a problem only as it appeared at that moment and not as it would appear in the perspective of history.

Burke saw no reason to apologize for his views on Irish Catholicism. He asked whether anyone in his audience believed the penal laws were based on "common justice, common sense, or common honesty." Bad law, he insisted, was the worst of all tyrannies. Existing legislation, which put the Catholic at the mercy of an informer — the most unreliable of men — caused intolerable suffering. Burke was proud that he had joined with others in seeking to put an end to so iniquitous a system. The Catholic population of Ireland, at a time when the mother country was sorely tried by a colonial rebellion, had come forward to reiterate its loyalty. At such a moment, the spurning of a conciliatory gesture would have been an act of folly. Burke recalled the happiness he felt in thinking that at least one good thing had come out of the war with America, and that in at least one corner of the Empire there was a possibility of peace.

Certain men, Burke said, argued that Parliament had acted too hastily and had not shown a sufficient interest in deliberating. Burke believed the contrary to be true; Parliament had been too slow. "They took four-score years," he said, "to deliberate on the repeal of an act which ought not to have survived a second session." Burke refused to accept the theory that any system of government required the permanent subjection of a part of the people for its security. He was offended by the habit of "proscribing the citizens by denominations and general descriptions"; that, he said, represented the "miserable invention of an ungenerous ambition, which would fain hold the sacred trust of power, without any of the virtues or any of the energies, that give a title to it." Crimes were the acts of individuals and not of denominations. The arbitrary classification of men under general descriptions, and the punishment meted out to them as a consequence of such classification, saved the state the trouble of proving its case. That method, Burke said, was "an act of unnatural rebellion against the legal dominion of reason and justice"; he refused to admit its legality.

Burke knew that the Gordon riots, which had wrought such terrible damage in London, reflected the determined opposition of a minority to the actions taken by Parliament to relieve the Catholics. The riots made him all the more confident about the rightness of Parliament's action. "We knew beforehand, or we were poorly instructed," he said, "that tolerance is odious to the intolerant; freedom to oppressors; property to robbers, and all kinds and degrees of prosperity to the envious." Burke wished to please the people in their legitimate desires, but refused to "act the tyrant for their amusement." The interests of justice limited his desire to please. In considering the charges leveled against him, Burke noted that no one claimed he had sacrificed his constituents' interests in favor of his own ambition, fortune, or party, but only that he had pushed the principles of benevolence and justice too far. He found these accusations comforting.

His defense concluded, Burke proceeded to canvass the city to determine whether he stood any chance of retaining his seat. The results were disappointing; recognizing that defeat was virtually certain he asked his name to be withdrawn from the ballot. In taking leave of his constituents, he expressed the wish that his successor might resemble him in all things, "except in my abilities to serve, and my fortunes to please you." His difficulties, caused by personal as well as political factors, concealed a fundamental incompatibility. Bristol did not wish to be represented by so independent a member. In defending himself, Burke had spoken of his emotions at the time when the war with America was going badly; he said: "I am a royalist, I blushed for the degradation of the crown. I am a whig, I blushed for the dishonor of parliament. I am a true Englishman, I felt to the quick for the disgrace of England. I am a man, I felt for the melancholy reverse of human affairs, in the fall of the first power in the world." Burke, as a Whig, caring deeply for the honor of Parliament, could not please a constituency expecting a different sort of service. Bristol's notion of itself, he could never share; his feeling for Parliament, his electors understood only dimly. In these circumstances, a break was inevitable.

Burke had no difficulty in finding another seat, but the results of the election were disappointing to the Rockingham interest. The ministry's shortcomings did not result in any substantial change in the composition of the House of Commons. This was an additional factor contributing to increased agitation for the reform of Parliament. Many Whigs, including Charles James Fox, emerged as proponents of an expanded franchise and a redistribution of seats. In this agitation, Burke remained aloof at first; when he finally expressed himself, he stood not with his friends, but against them. Parliamentary reform was the one issue on which he refused to share the opinions of his Whig associates. In 1782, speaking on a motion for a committee to investigate the representation in the House of Commons, Burke, sounding both alarmed and angry, said: "Our political architects have taken a survey of the fabric of the British constitution. It is singular that they report nothing against the crown, nothing against the lords; but in the house of commons everything is unsound; it is ruinous in every part. It is infested by the dry rot, and ready to tumble about our ears without their immediate help." The critics were many, and, while their remedies differed, they seemed all to agree that immediate reform was necessary. Burke held dark suspicions about the motives of many of those who called for change. He found particularly offensive the school which argued that each individual had the right to govern himself, and that, if this proved impossible, he ought to be represented by an individual chosen by himself. By this standard, Burke insisted, the existing House of Commons failed as a "representative" assembly and should be regarded as a usurpation on the natural rights of the British nation. Burke asked why these critics called only for a reform of the House of Commons. Why did they not insist also that the people choose the king, the judges, generals, bishops, and priests? The logic of their definitions of natural rights ought not to have stopped at the doors of the House of Commons.

Burke believed that rights existed independently of election. By prescription, by the fact that something existed from time out of mind, an institution also acquired legitimacy. Prescription, he said, was the "most solid of all titles, not only to property, but, which is to secure that property, to government." According to Burke, "it is a presumption in favor of any settled scheme of government against any untried project, that a nation has long existed and flourished under it." He went further to argue that "it is a better presumption even of the *choice* of a nation, far better than any sudden and temporary arrangement by actual election." The nation was not "an idea only of local extent and individual momentary aggregation," but "an idea of continuity, which extends in time as well as in numbers and space."

That Burke should have chosen the issue of parliamentary representation as the one on which to make his most sweeping defense of the *status quo* was not without significance. While genuinely impressed by the fact that he could find no evidence to suggest that constituencies with large electorates enjoyed advantages denied to others, his failure to discover widespread popular sentiment for reform also impressed him. Suspicious about the motives of those who agitated for reform, he wondered whether their object might not be the upsetting of the British constitution, first by discrediting the existing House of Commons, and then by exploiting the doubts raised as a consequence. Burke thought it an evil day when men were "no longer quarrelling about the character or about the conduct of men, or the tenor of measures," but instead, had "grown out of humor with the English constitution itself." In an impassioned peroration, he exclaimed: "It is for fear of losing the inestimable treasure we have, that I do not venture to game it out of my hands for the vain hope of improving it. I look with filial reverence on the constitution of my country, and never will cut it in pieces and put it into the kettle of any magician, in order to boil it, with the puddle of their compounds into youth and vigor. On the contrary, I will drive away such pretenders; I will nurse its venerable age, and with lenient arts extend a parent's breath."

Even after the Election of 1780, in which the king had used his influence recklessly to secure the election of men friendly to his interest, Burke refused to join those who said that the representation should be changed. Horace Walpole, writing after the election, said: "There are several new Members, but no novelty in style or totality of votes . . . the court may have what number it chooses to buy." Burke refused to despair; for him, the problem remained much as it had been since 1770. The king would go on trying to use his influence to gain support; the Whigs would have to resist him. Burke, returned to the House of Commons in 1780 as a member for the "pocket-borough" of Malton, a seat in Rockingham's control, felt no misgivings about the system which permitted him to continue to serve. He persisted in voicing traditional Whig arguments against a king determined to maintain Lord North at the head of his affairs. The continuing decline in the ministry's popularity gave Burke some reason for confidence.

[55]

Given the strength of the ministry's support in the House of Commons, only a catastrophe of the first order could have upset it. In November 1781 such a catastrophe occurred. The surrender of Cornwallis with the whole of his army at Yorktown meant, for all practical purposes, the end of the American war. News of the debacle reached London two days before a scheduled meeting of Parliament. Burke and Fox, when they spoke in the Commons, attacked North with such violence and effectiveness that it appeared the ministry could not survive further abuse. The Christmas recess intervened to prolong its life a little longer, but in March 1782, its demise finally occurred. With great reluctance the king accepted the resignation of the man who had served him faithfully, though often unwillingly, for a dozen years. The king, understanding that an election would only result in the coming together of an even more rebellious Parliament, tried to prevail on Shelburne, Chatham's old friend and disciple, to form a new ministry. This proved to be impossible, and after prolonged negotiations, in which the king went so far as to contemplate abdicating, he accepted the inevitable and commissioned Rockingham to form a new ministry. Thus, after sixteen years, the Rockingham Whigs were at last restored to a position of governing responsibility.

The new ministry, with Rockingham at its head as First Lord of the Treasury, included Charles James Fox as Secretary of State for the Foreign Department and Shelburne as Secretary for the Home and Colonial Departments. Lord John Cavendish held the office of Chancellor of the Exchequer, and Burke came in as Paymaster of the Forces. This office, which gave a salary of four thousand pounds per annum, did not bring Burke into the Cabinet. No appointment symbolized more perfectly the character of British politics in the eighteenth century. Given Burke's contributions to his party, and given his role in formulating its policy and pressing for its adoption, a more considerable office was certainly expected. It is doubtful whether Rockingham seriously considered his trusted lieutenant for a more conspicuous place. It was not, as some suggested, the fact that Burke had demonstrated too great a "violence and in- temperance in debate" that kept him from a seat in the Cabinet; Fox was guilty of the same fault many times over. Burke re- ceived no greater office because Rockingham could not con- ceive of him as anything but an "agent," gifted and industrious, a boon to the party, but still its servant and not a "principal" within its ranks. Burke had come into Rockingham's service without funds, influence, or position; everything that he owned, including his estate, Gregories, at Beaconsfield, he owed to Rockingham's patronage. Fox's position was entirely different; as the son of Lord Holland, he joined automatically the ranks of those who had a right to govern. No one ever thought to compare his abilities with those of Burke, and judge between them. Such a calculation would have been meaningless. When Rockingham chose his ministers, he chose with reference to other criteria. While competence and service counted for some- thing, birth and influence weighed more heavily. The Duke of Grafton seemed entitled to be Lord Privy Seal; his position in British society, and his influence in Parliament gave him an almost prescriptive right to be consulted in government. Burke, the "professional" in politics, had no comparable right. Under the prevailing forms, he was entitled to nothing, and had to be grateful for what he received.

Whatever disappointment Burke may have felt about his position in the Rockingham ministry was nothing compared to the larger unhappiness which he felt over the sequence of trage- dies that befell the ill-fated ministry. The trouble started even before the ministry was formed. George III, refusing to treat with Rockingham personally, conducted all negotiations through an intermediary, Shelburne. The ministry had existed only a few weeks when it became obvious that major differences divided the Cabinet, and that a growing antipathy of Fox for Shelburne threatened a break-up of the government. Shelburne, a gifted and able statesman, was one of the most distrusted men of his day. Politicians who shared no other opinion seemed to agree that he was a devious schemer, whose purposes could never be known and whose word could never be trusted. Fox's differences with Shelburne became so serious that, in a talk with the Duke of Grafton, Fox implied that Shelburne was "as fully devoted to the views of the Court as Lord North had ever been." Given such an opinion, it was inconceivable that the two could long continue to sit in the same Cabinet. The crisis, which would certainly have come in any case, was hastened by Rockingham's death in July 1782. Shelburne believed that he was entitled to succeed Rockingham, and the king's preference for him over Fox, whom he feared and detested, assured him of the first place. Fox, followed by almost all of the Rockingham Whigs, went into opposition.

In the months that followed, Burke took the lead in attacking Shelburne. His old invective against North seemed mild beside that which now overwhelmed Shelburne. At times, it seemed scarcely possible that such language could be used about an individual who had, so recently, served in a ministry under Rockingham. While there were few who actively sympathized with Shelburne, there were many who believed that Burke was going too far in his attacks. If his words had led only to Shelburne's downfall, they might have been forgiven. But, in the spring of 1783, there occurred a "revolution" in political alignments which made Burke's words seem all the more incomprehensible. North and Fox, inveterate enemies, suddenly indicated that they and their supporters intended to act together against Shelburne. No action could have thrown greater discredit on the theory of politics which Burke had propagated, in season and out, for almost two decades. His fine words about "party" and "Whig principles," about "influence" and "corruption" seemed suddenly hollow. How could a union of such different elements be justified? How could any party which claimed to be faithful to its past so ignore a decade of its own propaganda? Fox might say that "the American war was the cause of the enmity between the noble lord and myself," and that the end of the war meant the end of the enmity, but Burke could not justify his own position so easily. For too many years, he had attempted to give Great Britain a particular image of its political struggle; he could not suddenly and conveniently obliterate the record. While he and Fox might delude themselves into believing that they were only working to end the system of weak, divided, and dependent ministries which had so favored George III's purposes, the plea of "comprehensive ministry" did not sound well in the mouth of Burke. He had been too critical of Chatham in an earlier period to be able to use such an argument himself.

With Fox and North united in their opposition to Shelburne, the ministry's days were numbered. A resolution censuring Shelburne's American peace terms was introduced and it passed by a vote of 207 to 190 on February 22, 1783. Two days later, Shelburne submitted his resignation to the king. For the next several months, George III tried desperately to keep the Whigs out of office. He offered the chief post to Pitt, who was then only twenty-four, and, when it was refused, he asked others to take it. He begged North to come in, on the condition that Fox be kept out. Not one of these attempts succeeded. Fox insisted that the king appoint his friend and colleague the Duke of Portland to be head of the Treasury, and that he and North be joint Secretaries of State. Finally, on April 2, 1783, the king capitulated. He accepted Portland and told him to proceed to form a ministry along any lines that he thought advisable. The result was a ministry headed by Portland, in which Fox and North were his principal colleagues, and in which Burke, still without a seat in the Cabinet, returned to his post as Paymaster of the Forces.

The Coalition ministry did not survive the year. Its only major piece of legislation, a planned reform of the East India Company, passed the House of Commons but failed to secure the approval of the Lords. Burke played a major role both in the framing of the bill and in defending it in the Commons. Arguing for its passage, he claimed that considerations of humanity, justice, and policy required a reform of the government of India. The natural rights of men, he said, were sacred, and no charter could run against them. The great charters only confirmed man's natural rights and made them more secure; Magna Charta, he called "a charter to restrain power, and to destroy monopoly." The charter of the East India Company, as it existed, expressed a contrary principle; it established commercial monopoly and created political power. Neither could be listed among the rights of men. Political power, which necessarily limited man's enjoyment of his natural liberties, could be justified only by the advantages which it bestowed. Political power represented a trust, and was revocable when the trust was broken. Parliament, he said, had created the power vested in the East India Company, and the Company was answerable to Parliament for its use. The Company, Burke claimed, had abused its power; it was only right therefore that consideration should be given to the revocation of the original grant.

The Company's rule had been unsatisfactory, its governors had shown an avarice which neglected nothing in its hope for gain, and there had been too little attention given to the necessity of creating an adequate system of public works to benefit the Indian population. According to Burke, the Company's servants had been guilty of terrible chicanery. They seemed to know only two ways of dealing with native princes; they either controlled them by making them financially dependent, or ruined them by making them puppets, easily recognizable as such. The Company's financial impositions, which were irregular and excessive, Burke deplored. There was no hope of the Company's reforming itself. For all of these reasons, he proposed to alter the charter to recommit the government of India to a body of seven Commissioners, nominated in the Act, whose successors would be chosen by the Crown. These men were to hold office for at least four years, and to govern with the aid of nine Assistant Commissioners. The Commissioners would sit in England. Whatever the merits of the bill, its defeat in the Lords meant that no such changes would be made. Within twenty-four hours of the bill's defeat, the king asked for the ministry's resignation. With obvious pleasure, he commissioned Pitt to form a new government.

So ended another brief interlude in office for Burke. In the General Election that followed a few months later, the supporters of Fox and North suffered terrible defeats. Some hundred and sixty members, most of them from the Opposition, failed to keep their seats. Pitt returned to a House in which his friends boasted an overwhelming majority. Burke felt deeply the humiliation of his party's situation. While he might go on criticizing the king for improper and illegal interventions, and dwell on the royal pressure that induced the Lords to reject the East India Bill, these and similar complaints fell on deaf ears. Fox's mistake in allying himself with North could not be undone. The nation, in an unmistakable fashion, had shown its displeasure with a party which took so lightly its traditional claims. Words alone would never suffice to undo the harm caused by an error of such magnitude.

Burke sensed the difficulty of his position. Pitt was not Lord North, and the arguments used against an inefficient and ineffective administration would not serve a second time. The king at last had gained a minister in whom he could place his confidence, and who might be expected to govern intelligently and energetically. For those who continued to follow Fox, the prospect was bleak. The House of Commons, with its many new members, showed little patience with the Whigs who during the years of the American war had commanded its attention. Burke, for many of the members, became the "dinner bell"; his rising was the signal for a mass departure. Burke felt these insults keenly, but, given the situation of his party, could do nothing about them. Increasingly interested in Indian affairs, his speeches during the period 1784–1789 reflected this concern. While he could not hope seriously to embarrass the ministry with his criticism, the issues were such as called forth that idealistic and moral impulse which always lay near the surface of his mind.

In 1785, speaking on certain debts owed by the Nabob of Arcot to Europeans, Burke gave full expression to the misgivings he felt about British rule in India. He reminded Parliament of the obligations imposed by empire, and asked whether Great Britain's record in India would bear investigation. Burke's description of the Nabob of Arcot's plight showed what he thought the situation to be. Private adventurers loaned the prince money which they did not possess, but for which they charged exorbitant rates of interest. Burke estimated that on a debt of 880,000 pounds, the Nabob of Arcot probably never received as much as 100,000 pounds in real money. Burke explained how debt was piled on debt, with money lenders promising to make payments which in fact were never made. These methods, Burke said, made princes the debtors of inconspicuous and penurious adventurers, who then emerged as great and powerful men, laying claim to vast fortunes. Burke summarized the procedure as follows: "The nabob falls into an arrear to the company. The presidency presses for payment. The nabob's answer is, I have no money. Good. But there are soucars who will supply you on the mortgage of your territories. Then steps forward some Paul Benfield, and from his grateful compassion to the nabob, and his filial regard to the company, he unlocks the treasures of his virtuous industry; and for a consideration of twenty-four or thirty-six percent on a mortgage of the territorial revenue, becomes security to the company for the nabob's arrears." Burke could not understand why the mortgage was not made directly to the company. If the company thought such a policy too indulgent, it might charge 8 per cent interest. When, however, it pretended to be disinterested and permitted the nabob to become the debtor of an adventurer who was in fact a usurer, it failed in its duty. Adventurers and usurers, Burke said, had come to control the whole of the Carnatic, a territory as large as England. Such corruption and oppression could not continue, and he offered to stand with any man who brought before Parliament a plan to relieve "our distressed fellow-citizens in India."

Edmund Burke: The Old Whig

In the political situation then existing, Burke could do nothing better than maintain his interest in Indian affairs. In the spring of 1786, he and his friends set in motion a process which was destined to go on, with interruptions, till 1795. The Whigs decided to charge Warren Hastings, the late Governor-General of the East India Company, with high crimes and misdemeanors. The charge, as framed by Burke, was introduced into the House of Commons in the spring of 1786. When Pitt supported the motion that Hastings be tried for at least some of the crimes with which he was charged, Burke and his friends became confident that the House would eventually approve the move to impeach Hastings. This was accomplished by a vote of the House in April 1787. In February 1788, in Westminster Hall, before the House of Lords as judges, Burke introduced the charges drawn up by the managers of the indictment. The trial was, in its first days, the major concern of everyone in the capital. Its progress, however, proved unbelievably slow, and, as other, more crucial events engaged the attention of political London, interest declined rapidly. Burke, however, remained faithful to his declared intention, announced in Westminster Hall, that he would not rest till the Lords had found Hastings guilty.

Burke, in his opening speech, told the Lords that they were being asked to decide "whether the crimes of individuals are to be turned into public guilt and national ignominy; or whether this nation will convert the very offences, which have thrown a transient shade upon its government, into something, that will reflect a permanent lustre upon the honor, justice, and humanity of this kingdom." He claimed that the interests of the English Constitution were involved in the trial. The existence of the practice of impeachment, he said, guaranteed statesmen, accused of wrongdoing by statesmen, that they would be tried by statesmen, in accordance with principles of state morality. Hastings' crimes did not result from "lapses, defects, errors," but were in every instance the result of forethought and criminal intent. "We charge him with nothing,"

[63]

Burke said, "that he did not commit upon deliberation; that he did not commit against advice, supplication, and remonstrance; that he did not commit against the direct command of lawful authority; that he did not commit after reproof and reprimand, the reproof and reprimand of those, who are authorized by the laws to reprove and reprimand him." Burke called Hastings "the chief of the tribe, the head of the whole body of eastern offenders; a captain-general of iniquity, under whom all the fraud, all the peculation, all the tyranny, in India, are embodied, disciplined, arrayed, and paid."

Burke begged the judges to be impartial, so that Asia would not think that a European enjoyed rights denied to others. "God forbid," he said, "it should be bruited from Pekin to Paris, that the laws of England are for the rich and the powerful; but to the poor, the miserable, and the defenceless, they offer no resource at all." Given the dignity of his audience, these were extreme words. Burke thought them justified because, for him, the trial was not of a man, Hastings, but of a principle, of a trust broken, of justice set aside, and of ideas of equity and utility ignored. The House of Commons had taken the unusual step of citing an individual before the House of Lords for impeachment. Parliament's honor was involved, and Burke never placed a small price on that. Also, he knew that Hastings and his friends would go to almost any length to secure an acquittal. Burke was determined they should not succeed. He imagined that a favorable judgment would mean the vindication of certain principles of justice, would constitute a partial recompense to a people sorely tried, and would gain new honors for the ever-vigilant House of Commons, the guardian of the people's interest. With Hastings, as with George III, Burke tended to argue as a Whig very conscious of a historical tradition.

Had Burke died before July 1789, he would have been remembered in these terms. While his last years would have been seen as politically barren, the situation of his party would have figured largely in any explanation of his personal misfortune. Even his excessive language, used in the course of the Regency Bill debates, might have been excused as the inevitable consequence of a too great Whig partisanship. Because Burke lived on into the period after the French Revolution, and because these happenings stimulated him to an activity even greater than was his habit, the tale of his life cannot conclude on a purely domestic note. He became the spokesman for, and the creator of a wholly new opinion on the meaning of the French Revolution. His tract, *Reflections on the Revolution in France*, which appeared late in 1790, signalled the end of one stage of the British debate on the French Revolution and the start of another. Until that moment, most men had considered the events of 1789 as cause for feeling either satisfaction or jubilation. Those sympathetic to Enlightenment ideas, who felt keenly the injustices perpetrated by the old-regime institutions, imagined they were witnessing the start of a long-heralded and long-delayed new age. Less doctrinaire men believed only that the Revolution guaranteed a long period of French weakness, and that this was in Britain's interest. Until Burke's tract appeared, no one imagined that the Revolution represented a major new threat to British security.

Burke expressed these thoughts first in a speech on the Army Estimates, delivered in the House of Commons in February 1790. While the speech caused some excitement, garbled versions and a studied moderation in tone guaranteed that it would interest only a limited audience. Burke took a singular position; he spoke of the government of Louis XIV as having been "nothing better than a painted and gilded tyranny." France, the model for Europe, had been followed in its absolutist ways by other states; James II had tried to govern by the same principles. According to Burke, only the opposition of "the good patriots of that day" had prevented James from doing so. Having testified to his continuing belief in Whig explanations, Burke turned to consider the Revolution that had overtaken France. This Revolution, he said, introduced a new evil into

Europe. England, geographically France's neighbor, could not expect to be untouched by the "distemper" raging across the Channel. Should England elect to imitate the French example, the result would be confiscation and plunder in the name of democracy, and the replacement of religion by atheistic belief. Burke claimed never to have opposed reformation; his whole political life was devoted to that end. However, the French were acting not as reformers but as destroyers, intent only on obliterating that which had come down from the past. Those Englishmen who thought to compare the French Revolution with the Revolution of 1688 in England were making a fundamental error. Neither in objectives nor in methods, Burke said, did the two events resemble each other.

Those who heard Burke and pondered his words must have recognized the intensity of his feeling when he announced that he "would abandon his best friends and join with his worst enemies" if he found his friends on the side of the revolutionaries. These remarks ought to have prepared them for the blast which appeared later that year as *Reflections on the Revolution in France*. Burke's message was simple: the Revolution created a crisis not only for France, but for Europe, and, in the end, for all mankind. As a Whig member of Parliament, concerned with the defense of the British constitution, Burke felt it necessary to warn his readers against those at home who had already begun to broadcast French revolutionary principles. He directed his anger against these apostles of a new and foreign creed. The sermon preached by Dr. Richard Price at the Old Jewry became the chief object of his attack. In that sermon, Burke discovered all the false notions about the nature of the French Revolution which others, in their ignorance, had also accepted. The idea that the French in 1789 were simply following the English example of 1688 offended him. As Locke had once used Filmer to discredit an absolutist theory of government, so now, Burke used Price to discredit a theory about the democratic and revolutionary implications of the events of 1688.

Burke, the loyal Whig, refused to accept a theory which suggested that the men of 1688 had aimed at establishing a right "to choose our own governors," "to cashier them for misconduct," and "to frame a government for ourselves." Price had enumerated these as the revolutionary principles of 1688; Burke set out to prove the grotesqueness of his claim.

Employing the Declaration of Right of 1688 as the basis of his argument, Burke showed the discrepancy between these principles and those advanced by Price. The Revolutionary Settlement had not touched the hereditary principle, Burke explained; it had only qualified it by joining to it the requirement of Protestant belief. A denial of the hereditary principle would have brought into question the legality of the title of every sovereign of England. Even James, a bad king, had enjoyed a good title; he was not a usurper. Burke saw in the principle of hereditary royal succession a guarantee of the liberties of the English people. No government would long survive, Burke said, if it could be overthrown by "any thing so loose and indefinite as an opinion of *misconduct*."

Burke repudiated also the idea that the king existed as the servant of the people. Although the king's concern had to be the well-being of the people, he was not under their rule. In England, the subject owed obedience to the king, and not the other way around. It was not the duty of the subject to judge the king. As for the right of "cashiering" him, it did not exist. Price had spoken of the right of "framing a government for ourselves"; Burke reminded his readers that the Revolution of 1688 had as its purpose not the creation of a new government but the preservation of an old one, under which Englishmen had enjoyed law and liberty. The Englishman, from the time of Magna Charta, had viewed his liberties as inherited; he wished to preserve and guard them and did not imagine that he needed to win them. The idea of inheritance was pleasing to the English people; it gave promise of protecting what was already enjoyed without denying the possibility of future change. In an heredi-

[67]

tary monarchy, a hereditary peerage, and a House of Commons enjoying inherited rights, Burke saw the chief guarantee of stability and freedom.

Against those who might seek to use the French experience as a guide for Britain, Burke set his aim. The two revolutions were entirely unrelated; all that had happened in France since July 1789 proved this. When Burke turned to consider those "melancholy events," he expressed himself in conventional Whig terms. His comparisons, implicitly and explicitly, were always with 1688. The French had rebelled against a "mild and lawful monarch," whose hand held out only "graces, favors, and immunities." It was unnecessary for him to mention James II; his meaning was clear. The English, in 1688, goaded into action by royal tyranny, looked to their natural leaders for direction. Without naming Marlborough, Somers, Godolphin, or any of the others, Burke made his point. The Third Estate, in France, was not composed of the most considerable men in the kingdom, called by a lifetime of service and education to lead the people to a necessary and proper action. In a passage which was to become celebrated, Burke showed his contempt for the new governors of France. They were not the great and gifted people which an old and creative civilization had served to produce; they were mostly lawyers recently come from the provinces who had spent their lives worrying about the small matters which provided them with their meager incomes. Such men could not be depended on to give leadership to a kingdom. Men of this sort had played no role in the events of 1688; this was implicit in the whole of Burke's argument.

Burke's commitment to the principles of an aristocratic political order was so absolute and so unthinking as to admit no other possibility. Burke knew that in an aristocratic society the man of property accepted the obligation of governing the state. In such a society there could be no conflict between private and public interest; the two were inextricably joined. When he looked at France, and saw men without property or experience seeking to govern the country, he could think only one thing. These men wished to govern because they saw in government a means of improving their own private situation. Their aim was not the public good but their private advantage. Burke scrutinized these new governors and declared them small men, interested in improving their personal standing and profiting from the disequilibrium which they had helped to create. An assembly dominated by such men had nothing in common with what the English proudly called their House of Commons.

In the common sin of envy, Burke discovered the explanation for much that the French revolutionaries had done. He was not impressed by the fact that the French assembly claimed to represent the whole people; as he explained, "a government of five hundred country attorneys and obscure curates is not good for twenty-four millions of men, though it were chosen by eight and forty millions; nor is it the better for being guided by a dozen of persons of quality, who have betrayed their trust in order to obtain that power." Ambition and envy did not produce men capable of the difficult and complicated tasks of government. The incident of election did not convert small men into great men.

Burke's preoccupation with Price's sermon was such that he returned repeatedly to consider the words uttered in the Old Jewry. Feigning surprise at a doctrine which suggested that England was not a free country, and that she would become one when she followed France in her new ways, Burke asked Price what he meant for the English to imitate. Was freedom to be won through the annihilation of monarchy and all other ancient institutions; would it be secured when church lands were sold "to Jews and jobbers"; or was it necessary to imitate France in other of her monstrous military and administrative devices? Showing contempt for the new "democratists" who spoke as Price did, Burke suggested that they spoke approvingly of the masses when they were on their guard, but that they showed little love "for the humbler part of the community" when they were less cautious in their reflections. Having defended the system of representation which prevailed in England throughout his life, Burke was little disposed to find fault with it at that moment. He defied the enemies of that system to prove that it was not "adequate to all the purposes for which a representation of the people can be desired or devised."

Burke argued that he had no wish to deny the *real* rights of men; he took issue only with those who sought to enumerate pretended rights. Writing very much in the tradition of Locke, Burke said that civil society was the "offspring of convention" and that one of its fundamental rules was "that no man should be judge in his own cause." Obviously, to believe this was to surrender a liberty and accept an obligation, but, "the restraints on men, as well as their liberties, are to be reckoned among their rights." Liberties and restraints would vary with time and place, and it was foolish, Burke said, to imagine that they were immutable.

The construction of a commonwealth was an immensely complex thing. It could not be achieved by the simple adoption of a priori principles. Experience had to be referred to, because experience contained one of the elements necessary for an understanding of the problem. Simple governments, Burke said, were always defective. Theorists who spoke of rights spoke only in extremes; in good government, where the citizens' advantage was considered, right was often a combination of goods, or of good and evil, and sometimes, even of evils. Burke could not sympathize with those who talked continually of resistance and revolution; such men made "the extreme medicine of the constitution its daily bread." Worse, they made "the habit of society dangerously valetudinary," insisting as they did on "swallowing down repeated provocatives of catharides" to demonstrate their love of liberty. He claimed that most republicans he had known had ended their lives as thoroughgoing courtiers, and he had little use for such men who thought the alternatives to be war and revolution or nothing. These men, true adventurers, cared only for those things which advanced their own crazy schemes, and, by implication, their own petty careers.

Returning always to his indictment of Price, Burke accused him of wanting no "cheap and bloodless reformation"; that would never satisfy a palate such as his. Price wished for a "magnificent stage effect" with a good display of plot, massacre, and assassination. His words, "their king led in triumph, and an arbitrary monarch surrendering himself to his subjects" offended Burke deeply. He could find no excuse for such jubilation. Providing his readers with an account of the capture of the monarch, Burke sought to communicate something of his own disgust and shame. Could anyone who admired justice and courage feel differently? He recalled seeing Marie Antoinette many years previously at Versailles when she was still *dauphine,* and he mourned that no one had risen to prevent the indignities to which she had since been exposed. The day of chivalry had passed, and with it one of the glories of European civilization. Burke believed that Europe owed to the chivalrous spirit much that was best in its way of life. That spirit had made for equality without destroying rank; it had tamed power and given a sanction to law. But all this was now changed, for "a king is but a man, a queen is but a woman; a woman is but an animal; and an animal not of the highest order. . . . Regicide, and parricide, and sacrilege, are but fictions of superstition, corrupting jurisprudence by destroying its simplicity. The murder of a king, or a queen, or a bishop, or a father, are only common homicide; and if the people are by any chance, or in any way gainers by it, a sort of homicide much the most pardonable, and into which we ought not to make too severe a scrutiny."

If this view prevailed, Burke wrote, laws would be obeyed only because the penalty attending disobedience was feared, or because obedience gave some private advantage. Men would no longer feel love or loyalty for their governors, but only terror. A new ethic would dominate in a society in which the people were always ready to rebel. They would be eternally jealous of those to whom they had temporarily given power. In such a society, kings would be tyrants, since only tyranny would offer a safeguard against the constant threat of revolution.

[71]

Burke argued that European civilization had depended on two principles, which he called the spirit of a gentleman and the spirit of religion. The nobility and the clergy had kept learning alive even in the most difficult times; theirs was a complex union, but it worked. He felt no confidence in the new order which seemed to be establishing itself in France. He found "coarseness and vulgarity" and a "poverty of conception" in all that the Revolution taught; their "liberty was not liberal," their science, "presumptuous ignorance," and their humanity "savage and brutal."

Burke was not awed by the noise which issued from France, nor was he apologetic about the silence in which the English people seemed to slumber. As he explained: "We are not the converts of Rousseau; we are not the disciples of Voltaire; Helvetius has made no progress amongst us. Atheists are not our preachers; madmen are not our lawgivers. We know that *we* have made no discoveries; and we think that no discoveries are to be made, in morality; nor many in the great principles of government, nor in the ideas of liberty, which were understood long before we were born, altogether as well as they will be after the grave has heaped its mould upon our presumption, and the silent tomb shall have imposed its law on our pert loquacity. . . . We fear God; we look up with awe to kings; with affection to parliaments; with duty to magistrates; with reverence to priests; and with respect to nobility. Why? Because when such ideas are brought before our minds, it is *natural* to be so affected; because all other feelings are false and spurious, and tend to corrupt our minds, to vitiate our primary morals, to render us unfit for rational liberty. . . . We are afraid to put men to live and trade each on his own private stock of reason; because we suspect that this stock in each man is small, and the individuals would do better to avail themselves of the general bank and capital of nations and of ages."

Burke's love for that which he called "prejudice" was based not on a fear of change but on a respect for that which experience had shown to be operable. He did not ask that reason leave untouched what history had served to produce; he only asked that it approach such things with reverence and with a concern to improve rather than dismantle. Because the French, in their Revolution, had been animated by a different spirit, and hoped for different things, he refused to see anything to praise in their effort.

The seventeenth-century Whig had never thought to destroy the traditional institutions of England. In his respect for the religious establishment, he recognized, Burke said, "that religion is the basis of civil society, and the source of all good and of all comfort." Burke reminded his readers that Englishmen were Protestants not out of indifference but out of zeal. They had no desire to change their belief for a supposedly better one which bore the name of atheism. He spoke of the ways in which a religious establishment served to mitigate power; it taught those in authority that they held power as a trust and that their ultimate responsibility was to God. A power which was said to come from the people was not similarly controlled. The people, confident of their own virtue and goodness, never stopped to consider whether they might be misusing authority. Arbitrary power was dangerous in any hands, but most of all, Burke suggested, when exercised by the people.

Society was a contract, but not one to be renegotiated at any moment. In this contract, which extended into many domains, and which linked dead men with those yet to be born, some place had to be given to God. It was God who had willed the state; his intention was that men should draw advantage from it. For this reason a church establishment was not simply a convenience for the state; it was a necessity. Church and State were not separable entities. Dwelling on the services which the Church performed in England, Burke suggested that the confiscation of Church property in France had rendered impossible such services by the French Church. The impoverishment and humiliation of a whole class of men, he could only view as the work

[73]

of a tyrant. Returning to his old theme, Burke saw this as the work of small and envious men who lusted after that to which they had no right.

While prepared to admit that the French state had its imperfections, these, he argued, provided no excuse for what the revolutionaries had done. Persecution and confiscation were not to be justified by the argument of imperfection. History taught that "pride, ambition, avarice, revenge, lust, sedition; hypocrisy, ungoverned zeal, and all the train of disorderly appetites" produced misery. These vices, Burke said, were responsible for France's troubles. "Religion, morals, laws, prerogatives, privileges, liberties, rights of men" were only the pretexts. The ordinary actors in great public events were "kings, priests, magistrates, senates, parliaments, national assemblies, judges, and captains." It was possible to change the names of these authorities, but in essence, they remained. So long as communities existed, power would also exist.

France's troubles did not originate with rapacious clerics; those who had punished the Church did so for reasons of plunder. The new religious establishment would never attract honorable men to its service, and, in the end, the lowest sorts of people would come to control the Church. When this happened, and when the bankruptcy of the Church was recognized by all, the philosopher would enter upon the scene, and suggest that it be done away with entirely. Atheism would be finally triumphant.

Burke, offended by persecutions and confiscations, refused to believe that such actions were ever defensible. He heard men say that their origin was not wanton rapacity, but that they were great measures of national policy. He refused to admit this. As he explained, justice was the great standing policy of civil society, and no departure from it under any circumstance could be countenanced. The men who decreed the destruction of office and property were not lawgivers; they had no understanding of the dignity of their office. Had they possessed understanding, they would have felt love and respect for their fellow men, and fear of their own ambition. Such men hated vice too much and loved men too little; this being the case, they were incapable of serving others, however much they protested the contrary. They lacked patience, love, and a proper doubt about their own wisdom. They were adventurers, susceptible to all the vices of that condition.

Reflections on the Revolution in France indicated as much as any of Burke's previous writings a continuing loyalty to traditional Whig principles. The tract, in its purpose and argument, expressed attitudes and a point of view which repeated what he had been saying for over two decades. Burke claimed that he had chosen no new path; there was nothing in the work to suggest that he had. In 1791, he published a *Letter to a Member of the National Assembly in Answer to Some Objections to his Book on French Affairs*. In this, he wrote: "I published my thoughts on that constitution, that my countrymen might be enabled to estimate the wisdom of the plans which were held out to their imitation." Burke's chief purpose had been to instruct Englishmen who might be led astray by Price and others into believing that 1789 and 1688 were in some way related, that in fact they were not. He was prepared to go to almost any lengths to prove this. The reputation of 1688 was a matter of no small moment to him; Burke, as a conscientious Whig, was not prepared to see that reputation sullied. The Revolution of 1688 had aimed at conserving traditional forms, and Burke refused to admit any other interpretation. The French Revolution, he insisted, was the work of ambitious and self-seeking men who wished only to improve their own situations. In the end, Frenchmen acted as they did out of envy and lust. The French revolutionaries claimed to be fighting injustice and corruption; Burke's argument was that they were the embodiment of both. The English Revolution was made against a monarch who had trespassed on the liberties of his subjects; the French Revolution was made by a rabble which created a folk tale to conceal its activity. If the tyrant in 1688 was James II, only in French revolutionary mythology did Louis XVI occupy the same place.

Whigs were in the habit of searching for would-be tyrants; Burke discovered the tyrant in France in precisely those people who were profiting from the change. Individual tyranny assumed one form, collective tyranny, another. If there was one thing that Burke never doubted, it was his capacity to recognize the face of tyranny.

In all his later works, in which he became even more violent in his argument, Burke returned to these same few simple themes. In his 1791 *Letter to a Member of the National Assembly*, he dwelled again on the sordid qualifications of those who wished to lead France. Plans produced by such men could only be wicked. This was a new tyranny, and Burke, as a Whig, felt compelled to bring it down. The French revolutionaries menaced all Europe; they were "a college of armed fanatics." They sought to propagate principles of "assassination, robbery, rebellion, fraud, faction, oppression, and impiety." Rousseau was their hero, and it was fitting that he occupy that place. He loved mankind, but had no love for individual men; his life was a monument to vanity. Burke argued that the chief purpose of the French tyranny was the destruction of those gentlemen who had previously governed France. To accomplish this, the revolutionaries were destroying the institutions and relations which made great men powerful and secure. The new revolutionary principles taught the servant to betray his master, and left the father unsafe in his own home. The French revolutionaries had succeeded, Burke said, not by using the powers and policies of statesmen or military commanders, but by being incendiaries, assassins, housebreakers, robbers, spreaders of false news, forgers of false orders, and so on.

Burke's tenacity was never more severely tested than in the years after 1790. Only an extraordinary self-confidence and a calculated indifference to criticism provided protection against the obloquy which descended upon him. That he never wavered in his opinions and never ceased to argue for them testified to the assurance with which he felt them. Others might call him mad, mistaken, perverse, inconsistent, ignorant, or ill-informed; Burke believed them all to be unjust. He treated his critics with varying degrees of scorn and anger, judging the times to be too serious for a more sympathetic estimate of their failings. England and Europe, besieged by Jacobinism, required for its defense the services of men who understood the times in which they were living. Burke could not believe that his critics possessed that understanding. They were seeking to make his fears appear unwarranted, his recommendations unnecessary, and his diagnosis inaccurate. Burke was determined to prove the insufficiency of all such sanguine opinion; they, not he, had fallen into error.

It is not without significance that, in his quarrel with Fox and other of his former colleagues, Burke chose to emphasize the extent to which his opinions accorded with Whig principles and traditions. In 1791, *Appeal From the New to the Old Whigs* sought to prove both his orthodoxy and his consistency. Burke had no desire to divorce himself from the tradition which he had defended from his earliest days in Parliament. To lose friends was a sad thing, but to be accused of betraying principles was a matter at once more grave and more urgent. Burke sought to defend himself against that charge. Basing his argument on testimony which had been given in a famous trial some eighty years previously, he invoked the historical record in his defense. In 1710, the Whig Ministry had caused an Anglican divine, Dr. Sacheverell, to be impeached for sermons which he had preached and published; these, the Whigs argued, had called into question the legitimacy of the rebellion of 1688 and the settlement which had followed. Burke suggested that in the record of this trial the most faithful rendering of Whig doctrine was to be discovered. That doctrine, he insisted, bore no resemblance to anything that the Jacobins and their English friends were arguing for at that moment.

Burke placed a high value on his reputation for consistency; he refused to permit his enemies to rob him of it. Reviewing his own career, he found in it no evidence of the inconsistency with which he was charged. Fox and others had attributed to him words which he had never spoken and sentiments which he had never felt. He remained what he had always been — a loyal Whig. Burke recollected that he had joined the Whig connection at a time "when he was in the prime and vigor of his life." He knew quite well how Whig principles differed from those held by Tories, and he had not made his decision without a full understanding of its meaning. He had joined with those who were able to feel an absolute identification with the men who had forced James II from his throne, in order that the liberties of Englishmen might be secured. Burke recalled that Sacheverell, who had brought the legitimacy of that resistance into question, had been impeached by a Whig ministry and a Whig House of Commons, and had been tried by a House of Lords in which Whigs predominated. The whole proceeding was undertaken so that the "true grounds and principles" of the Revolution might be known. Burke claimed to be supporting these same principles against men who wished to assert that others more faithfully expressed Whig intentions. These "new Whigs," as he styled them, insisted that sovereignty originated in the people, and that no government was legitimate except one which expressed the will of the people. In examining the Sacheverell trial record, he found no evidence of such a Whig principle. Instead, he discovered explicit references to the fact that resistance ought to be the "last remedy" of a people, and that only the destruction by the king in 1688 of the "original contract" with his people had led to rebellion. To preserve their liberties, after the "greatest deliberation and judgment," the people had acted. Only dire necessity justified resistance.

Among those who had managed the impeachment for the Whigs was the young Robert Walpole. Burke, in his essay, went to great lengths in his praise of this "honorable and sound" man. Walpole, he said, did not govern, as his enemies claimed, by corrupt means. He was not the man who "first reduced corruption to a system." Burke saw the great Whig prime minister as a wise and prudent man who loved peace and whose policies gave prosperity to the kingdom. Walpole and the other Whig managers knew that Sacheverell had tried to insinuate that the

Revolution of 1688 had brought about a profound change in the constitution. They claimed precisely the opposite — that it had restored the ancient constitution. Burke suggested that his own views were exactly those of his Whig predecesors. The English Jacobins had propounded a new doctrine, which they claimed to be ancient, and which made the popular will the legitimating factor in all government. Burke found no justification for such a doctrine in English history. Also, because he understood that men enjoyed hearing about their rights and were less disposed to admit their duties, he thought it necessary that they be reminded of these. The true statesman knew that duty did not express will and was not the result of option; it derived from the moral law which bound men independently of their volition. Burke recognized an entity called the PEOPLE when he saw "great multitudes act together, under that discipline of nature." He wanted no new Whig principles which betrayed their origin in a French Jacobin model.

By late 1791 the issue between Burke and his critics was fully joined. If Burke showed himself intemperate in his remarks, the opposition revealed no greater reserve in its own. The gravity of the question seemed to justify every excess in word and act. In December 1791, Burke issued another blast, which could only be thought provocative by those who disagreed with him. In *Thoughts on French Affairs,* he seemed to argue that Britain could meet its obligations and serve its interests only by going to war with Jacobin France. Burke saw the French Revolution as something more than a political incident; it was "a revolution of doctrine and theoretic dogma." To find a parallel for it, one would have to return to the Protestant Reformation. Only such events produced reactions against which the frontiers of geography and history provided no defense. These were international incidents from the moment of their happening. They set loose new ideas in the world which challenged traditional national loyalties. In the ancient world, Burke said, Sparta and Athens competed in the same way — each conspired to destroy the other. Each sought to increase its influence by converting the citizens of the other to its views. The French were seeking after a comparable influence at that moment. Appealing to the discontented of every sort, they were establishing factions which would in the end disrupt all existing governments. Men who hated the clergy and envied the nobility welcomed the opportunity to conceal their ambitions and make their avarice and lust appear as something else. Burke argued that the danger in England from these elements was large, and that it needed to be guarded against.

He remarked on the injustices and inefficiencies of the French regime, but gave no support to the notion that it would collapse as a consequence. On the contrary, he believed that a counter-revolution would not develop unless considerable external effort was made to bring it about. If the regime survived, its power would grow, and with the growth of power would come an intensified interest in upsetting established governments. Burke's meaning was clear. Europe could not survive unless it defeated the power which intended its own destruction. He was urging Europe to meet the French threat with war. A year later, some three months before the execution of Louis XVI, he was even more explicit about England's responsibility. A continental alliance needed to be formed, with England taking the principal role in its formation and operation. The enemy was French power and influence, and there could be no compromise with it.

In 1793, Burke's ambitions were partially realized. Europe went to war with revolutionary France. Believing that the conflict would "decide the fate of Europe forever," he directed his attention to ways of guaranteeing an Allied victory. Burke's criticism of those responsible for the destinies of the Coalition was intense and perpetual. He deplored the English ministry's failure to make greater use of French *émigrés;* it was almost as if England felt uncomfortable working in alliance with these elements. Burke thought the *émigré* group the only legitimate expression of that France which the Coalition was pledged to restore. Moral France, he said, was separated from geographic France, and, if ever monarchy and property were reestablished in France, it would be through the agency of those who had suffered in the defense of both. He saw the conflict as a "religious war," whose end would be the reestablishment of France's traditional religion. Burke knew that several of England's allies were hoping to profit from France's defeat and were beginning to consider ways of reducing the influence of that once great power. He had no use for any of their proposals. He believed that the liberties of Europe would be preserved only if France remained as a great power. The war was against Jacobinism and not against France.

Burke's criticisms and admonitions were a constant feature of the first years of the war. When, in 1796, it appeared that England might make peace with France, he made one final effort to dissuade his countrymen from even contemplating that possibility. He addressed and published three letters written to a member of Parliament entitled *The Proposals for Peace with the Regicide Directory of France*. Burke argued that England, a great power, could never enjoy security or respect if it compromised with evil. The war, he said, was with "an armed doctrine" which had not yet been defeated. Unless England was prepared to act greatly, and, as a consequence, suffer, she would court a disaster worse than any she imagined. Burke recognized that the English were divided, but he refused to be alarmed by this. The great majority, he insisted, were loyal, and it was to such men that he looked for support. He wrote: ". . . the desire of peace is essentially the weak side of that kind of men. All men that are ruined, are ruined on the side of their natural propensities. There they are unguarded. Above all, good men do not suspect that their destruction is attempted through their virtues. This their enemies are perfectly aware of: and accordingly, they, the most turbulent of mankind, who never made a scruple to shake the tranquility of their country to its centre, raise a continual cry for peace with France. Peace with regicide, and war with the rest of the world, is their motto."

The large group of loyal subjects to whom Burke appealed needed to recall the example of William III in the difficult years following his accession to power. Ruling a frightened people, and obstructed by an unmanageable Parliament, William persevered in his aims. At that moment, Burke said, the British nation showed its greatness. It knew that peace might "be made as unadvisedly as war" and that nothing was "so rash as fear." If the war against Louis XIV was just, then that being fought against Jacobin France was infinitely more so. It was, in Burke's words, a "war just, necessary, manly, pious." France, the home of regicide, Jacobinism, and atheism, threatened all of Europe. Its example could not be disregarded; its influence could not be escaped from. To be at peace with such a body of men was impossible.

Burke died in July 1797, and was thereby spared one final disappointment — the collapse of the First Coalition against France. The years 1790–1797 were tragic ones for Burke. Suffering alienation from political and personal friends, losing his only son and heir, seeing the Europe which he so much admired decline into chaos, he could not but feel the transient quality of all existence. That he was able to support these blows suggests the confidence he felt in the principles and policies which he enunciated. Burke would not listen to those who argued that he had abandoned the Whig tradition. His confidence derived in part from the fact that he believed himself the most faithful adherent of the Whig cause. Burke's constant preoccupation with the traditions of his own country, and with history, provided him with whatever strength he possessed. While he knew the Greek and Roman classics, understood natural law as well as contract theories, and appeared to be acquainted with works of Christian piety and theology, his ultimate understanding came from another sort of experience. Burke's chief indebtedness was to history. It was at this source that he acquired his principal insights, and it was in the service of this cause that he produced his most impassioned prose.

The events of 1688 ought not to have influenced Burke as much as they did. Only his romantic imagination transformed essentially parochial incidents into large and compelling principles. Because he believed in an aristocratic order, saw tyranny as the consequence of vain and perverse ambition, and respected the past for its wisdom and freedom, he found in 1688 the ideas for which he was searching. If the men of 1688 had failed to express verbally what their actions implied, Burke was prepared to perform that service for them.

Burke was the first man in England to sound the alarm against the French Revolution. He paid a heavy price for his insistent agitation. Old friends abandoned him, and he found no new ones. The Tory ministry, which went to war with France in 1793 and which owed a great debt to the man who more than any other awoke England to its danger, never accepted Burke as one of its own, but continued to regard him with the suspicion which it felt a Whig deserved. In April 1795, Burke wrote a poignant note to a friend, one of the Bristol sheriffs to whom he had addressed his American letter. The "old Whig" Burke claimed to have no influence with the ministry. "So good an old friend as you are to myself, & were to those much dearer to me than I am to myself, may well command my best services. But poor are those best from a person incapable of all exertion and possessed of no influence. I am touched to the heart to find, that so much to you depends upon what can be done by me. May the providence of the Almighty protect you! I have wrote this day, as strongly as I could, to Mr. Windham, with whom alone of the Ministry, I have the least communication; & him I have not seen this month or more for anything I can recollect. He has much weight with Lord Spenser, & if I can serve you at all, it is in this way." The letter was signed "Your affectionate melancholy friend, Edm. Burke."

In the end, Burke was alone. Old friends were gone; new ones did not exist. He had lost his party but held to his principles. Such a resolution of the problem gave small comfort to a man who for over three decades had prided himself on his Whig associations. If Burke had been less devoted to his party, he would have suffered less at its hands. But, if he had been less devoted, the excitement which he felt from the time that he first entered the House of Commons would never have been his. His great parliamentary achievement derived from the fact that he believed as a Whig and fought as one. The tragic end was of a piece with the triumphant beginning

The tragic dimension of Burke's life cannot be ignored. Apart from personal misfortunes, which were only incidentally created by politics, he suffered a career of peculiar and extensive calamity. If political power be the reward of victory in parliamentary combat, those who served under Rockingham's banner knew only the frustrations of almost continuous defeat. Rockingham's social position guarded him against the insult of loss, and Fox's bonhomie gave him a special sort of protection, but Burke had no comparable defense. Politics was his profession, and his whole life seemed bound by its rules. That he never attained a Cabinet position reflected mainly on the accident of aristocratic preference, but that his party was in opposition almost continuously after 1765 reflected in part on his own political miscalculation. Burke, and the Whigs generally, underestimated the royal power. When they found themselves barred from office, they thought only to force their way in. They believed that their myth would be sufficient to win for them the prizes which the first Hanoverians had been only too ready to offer them. They accepted too easily the fact of George III's dislike for them, and acted toward him as Tories had acted toward his predecessors. Wrapped in their cloak of "English liberties," they sought to represent themselves as the guardians of a Revolution which the whole nation acclaimed. They ignored the fact that George III himself was the beneficiary of that Revolution, and that he had no intention of disassociating himself from it. He would never act as a foreign-born prince had been compelled to, but he had no illusions about the extent of his power. George III wished to be a king in the way that William III had been; the Whigs would only accept him as another George I.

In the struggle that followed, the nation rallied around the king more than around his critics. Even the follies of the Ameri-

can war did not lose for the Crown the loyalty of most of its
subjects. National pride helped defeat the Whigs in their insistent attacks. The Whigs appeared too self-righteous, too disinterested, and too dogmatic. Burke, for all of his brilliance, contributed to establishing this caricature in the public mind. The
Rockingham Whigs wished to profit from being the party of
reform, but their reforms almost invariably included provisions
calculated to protect their own interests. When, for example,
they thought to reform the East India Company, it was characteristic that they should wish to nominate the first Commissioners
themselves. In another, even more celebrated instance, the Whigs
used Wilkes to establish a principle about parliamentary independence, but their treatment of the man suggested that their
motives were less pure than their words. Party, as the Rockingham Whigs defined it, made a virtue of what earlier generations
regarded as a vice. It thought to legitimate almost any act by the
mere fact of its approval. This innovation, the eighteenth century preferred not to accept.

Burke, by living on into the French Revolutionary era, gained
a momentary release from the cul-de-sac into which politics had
forced him. The prescience which he showed in his *Reflections*,
was admitted by almost everyone after 1793. The man who had
cried "wolf" frequently in earlier times, seemed in this instance
to be a worthy Cassandra. While the prophetic power was un-
deniable, there were some who wondered, however, whether
Burke understood rightly the events that he described. The explanations he gave for the French Revolution were perhaps too
simple; they were limited by a perception which refused to
leave the familiar ground of 1688. Burke, unable or unwilling
to study the psychology which had led hundreds of thousands
to riot against traditional institutions, looked too much to the
leadership of the rebellion. Seeing the origin of this unworthy
ambition in the common sins of unbelieving men, he made this
the motive cause. In doing so, he neglected to understand the phe-
nomenon whose future development he so accurately predicted.
The French Revolution unhinged Burke; many of his last writ-

ings show an excitement which cannot be thought normal, even in the extraordinary circumstances which attended their composition. He died a tired, broken, and disappointed man; his legacy was a political literature almost without parallel in the English language.

To seek consistency in that large and amorphous body of writing is perhaps to indulge in a vain and unnecessary inquiry. Yet, given Burke's own respect for continuity, there is some reason to ask whether his words reflect a constant intellectual position. On the most general plane, there is evidence to suggest that they do. Even before he joined the Rockingham party, he wrote critically of those of his contemporaries who generalized too much, and who, in their search for uniformities, distorted both man and nature. Burke did not share his century's hope of discovering new and fundamental attributes which would finally explain all physical phenomena. Perhaps his Christian belief limited a curiosity which might otherwise have breached the fragile frontiers of inherited opinion. Whatever the explanation is, Burke was satisfied to work within boundaries already established, and to seek solutions to specific and frequently modest grievances.

His greatest prose, perhaps, emerged out of the American crisis. This war suited Burke's talents as no other event did. The problem was finite, its solution depended on a sensible moderation and expediency; it appealed to his sense of justice, and it pointed to a reform requiring restoration rather than innovation. In his American writings, Burke showed consistent good sense. The same cannot be said for his reactions to other major political incidents. In these, the temptation to score a political victory, to scold under the pretense of instruction, and to construct impressive though insubstantial bogies, interfered with the main thrust of his argument. The failing, in part produced by political necessity, made him a more considerable political adversary, but a less important political thinker. Burke, however, even in those moments when he ranted and raved, thereby fulfilling suspicions which his enemies were always prepared to broadcast about the state of his mind, showed talents which made him something other than a political pamphleteer. He wrote for the moment, but also, even when he least intended it, for posterity. His mind rebelled against the restraints which a purely parochial political advantage recommended. His gifts — literary no less than intellectual — would not be denied. Disagreement with Burke's point of view was always possible, but it was more difficult to dispute the skill he showed in the use of his chosen instrument—words.

BENJAMIN DISRAELI

❧ *The Romantic Egotist* ❧

The life of Benjamin Disraeli, reproduced as fiction, would disconcert the modern reader; it would require him to believe in the improbable, to accept the role of accident in history, and to admit that the individual, even against the greatest odds, creates his own destiny. Only a romantic would find the tale credible; only a romantic would wish to spin it. Disraeli wrote such stories, believed them, and, in his own life, left the materials for another. Nothing about his life was conventional. Masking his personality with a face purposefully vacant, Disraeli pursued political power relentlessly, but knew better than to become the captive of his profession. An admirer of fashionable society, and an active participant in its rituals, he gave himself to neither, and managed to maintain a private existence from which both were excluded. Capable of deep, lasting, and generous friendship, Disraeli also knew the art of flattery; the first he reserved for men and women, some famous, some obscure, who struck his fancy; the second he showered particularly on one woman, the Queen, who had more need of him than he of her. Gregarious, Disraeli impressed his contemporaries as being reserved and aloof. He began his adult life as an author of novels, and, in 1880, when every political honor had been gained, and when death was known to be imminent, he found time for one last novel. Proud of his race, which was not English, given to writing about subjects having little to do with England, in manner, speech, and dress an alien, Disraeli wished to lead the party which he believed represented the virtue and genius of England. Enigmatic in the smallest things, Disraeli wrote constantly of himself, but managed to leave his message obscure and mysterious. What could such a man have meant when he confided to his diary: "My mind is a continental mind. It is a revolutionary mind." Why should a political Conservative seek so to describe himself?

The question admits of no easy answer; the words may have been rhetorical, intended only as a *jeu d'esprit*. If so, they defined Disraeli's mind better than he knew. They expressed, metaphorically, a reality which transcended politics but embraced character and personality. Disraeli's whole life was characterized by a preoccupation with himself; from early adolescence, he concentrated on the problem of making his way in the world. Had his quest been for local fame or modest fortune, it would have been quickly realized; his talents were more than sufficient for such success. His ambition, however, led him away from easy conquest; he dreamed of making a great place for himself in the political world. Disraeli aspired to the highest office; he wished to do things which would cause him to be remembered, not for a generation, and not as a name, but as a romantic hero who had overcome every obstacle in the pursuit of his destiny. Believing in heroic achievement, he wished to make himself the principal character in a heroic tale.

In his youth, as an aspiring novelist, he treated only one theme, that of individual heroism; the dimensions and the possibilities of success preoccupied him. In order to believe in himself, Disraeli needed to believe in the possibility of the individual conquering circumstance. Life had to be a revolutionary experience in which great men emerged out of the shadows of obscurity, driven by will, to do great deeds. Ambition and intelligence had to weigh more heavily than position or wealth; the first two, he possessed, the third he lacked, the fourth he could only hope to win or marry. Disraeli understood that ambition alone would never suffice to gain the greatest prizes; a man who aspired to greatness needed to consider how he might engage the services of others to join him in his odyssey. The capacity to prophesy the future, not in detail, but in general terms, and to plan for the future, Disraeli imagined, was one of the sure marks of genius. The "revolutionary mind" excelled in this, as it did in the habit of exploiting situations, not by accepting them, but by using them for its own purposes.

Benjamin Disraeli was born in London in 1804, the second child of Isaac D'Israeli, an amiable literary scholar who was never happier than when he sat at home among his books. The boy gained an early appreciation of that vast body of literature which every wealthy Englishman owned, but which few had the time or inclination to study. Isaac D'Israeli enjoyed a leisured life, the gift of an ample though not immense inheritance. He lived quietly, surrounded by his family and preoccupied with his work. Occasionally, other scholars came to talk of books and to enjoy their host's learning; Benjamin, even as a boy, seemed at home in this company. It was not a worldly group, and not overly concerned with politics. The D'Israeli family was close-knit; in early nineteenth-century England, Jews did not move easily in English society. It was an accident that caused the D'Israeli children to leave the religion of their fathers and enter the Church of England. Isaac D'Israeli had no great interest in religion, but was prepared to remain a nominal member of the Synagogue if no demands were made of him. When, however, his congregation insisted that he serve a term as Warden, he refused. Relations grew so tense that the only solution seemed to be an open break. In the end, Isaac D'Israeli asked that his name be removed from the Synagogue's rolls. On the urging of a friend, he then permitted his children to be baptized into the Anglican communion. Chance had intervened to lead young Benjamin out of the faith which might otherwise have barred him from a political career. At the time, neither he nor his father imagined that the baptism had any such significance.

Public events scarcely intruded in the lives of members of the D'Israeli household. Isaac D'Israeli's personal fortune was sufficient to maintain the family in easy comfort, but its size did not give promise of supporting another generation in that happy condition. The problem of placing Benjamin and his younger brothers in profitable employ must have been a subject of serious discussion within the family circle. The decision, in Benjamin's case, was taken soon after his seventeenth birthday; articled to a firm of solicitors, the family expected that the profession would provide him with a proper income. Only a few years' experience suggested the error of that decision; the law did not suit the talents of the eldest of Isaac D'Israeli's sons. Lacking any very precise notion of what he wished to do, Benjamin drifted into a career of pamphleteering and journalism. These pursuits provided little income and less pleasure. The only achievement of these years was a personal exploit, which ended in failure, but which provided an early hint of the extraordinary ambition animating the youth. Benjamin Disraeli, at twenty-one, conceived the grandiose scheme of establishing a new Tory daily newspaper. Convincing John Murray, the publisher and a friend of his father's, that the plan would succeed if Sir Walter Scott's son-in-law, J. G. Lockhart, consented to serve as editor, Disraeli, with Murray's blessing, traveled to Scotland to persuade Lockhart to support the venture. Meeting both Scott and Lockhart, Disraeli succeeded, after lengthy conversations, in satisfying Lockhart that the proposal made sense. Arrangements went forward for publishing the daily, now christened, somewhat grandiloquently, *The Representative*. The paper emerged, survived six months, caused Murray a loss of twenty-six thousand pounds, and made the old publisher wonder how he had ever agreed to such a folly. Recriminations followed, and Benjamin's parents, stung by criticisms leveled at their son, jumped to his support. It was scarcely needed; the failure was soon forgotten and did nothing to harm the reputation of the clever youth capable of conceiving such a remarkable venture.

If the experience provided no new employ for Disraeli, it gave him the idea for his first novel. How Disraeli came to consider writing as a career there is no way of knowing. However, given his acquaintance with books, the education he received in his father's house, his facile pen, and his ready wit, the decision is not surprising. In any case, no other professional path seemed open to him. Relying on his imagination to fill the spaces left vacant by a limited personal experience, in 1826 Disraeli published anonymously his first novel, *Vivian Grey*. The book made something of a stir, particularly before its author was definitely known. It was the work which later in life, Disraeli most regretted having written. Had he been able to withdraw it from circulation by preventing its republication, he would almost certainly have done so. It was only the piracy of foreign presses, particularly American and German, that persuaded him, years later, to permit the book to be reissued. To protect his readers he added a cautionary introduction; in middle age he wrote: "Books written by boys which pretend to give a picture of manners, and to deal in knowledge of human nature, must necessarily be founded on affectation. They can be, at the best, but the results of an imagination, acting upon knowledge not acquired by experience." Disraeli's mid-Victorian sense of propriety led him to regard his youthful indiscretion too solemnly; the book scarcely warranted so severe a condemnation. *Vivian Grey* was not a very good novel; like most of Disraeli's early efforts, it suffered from serious structural defects, only slightly mitigated by passages of considerable charm and wit. The lauding of youth, ambition, power, and will — constant themes in Disraeli's writing — appears at this early date, and gives the work its distinctive quality. The improbability of the tale only expressed the author's romantic preference, which no demand for rationality could ever extinguish. The hero, Vivian, is depicted as "a cunning reader of human hearts," who knows how to move others by the power of his oratory. Many of the novel's incidents were autobiographical; Vivian's ruminations about careers open to him suggests a problem which cannot have been too far from Disraeli's own mind at that moment. Whether he felt an equal bravado is doubtful, for Vivian is made to say: "The Bar: pooh! law and bad jokes till we are forty; and then, with the most brilliant success, the prospect of gout and a coronet. Besides, to succeed as an advocate, I must be a great lawyer; and, to be a great lawyer, I must give up my chance of being a great man. The Services in war time are fit only for desperadoes (and that truly am I); but, in peace, are fit only for fools. The Church is more rational. Let me see: I should certainly like to act Wolsey; but the thousand and one chances against me! And truly I feel my destiny should not be on a chance. Were I the son of a millionaire, or a noble, I might have all. Curse on my lot! that the want of a few rascal counters, and the possession of a little rascal blood, should mar my fortunes."

Disraeli, when he wrote *Vivian Grey*, knew as little about politics as he did about society. This did not deter him. His hero was a twenty-year-old boy whose ambition was to gain political power. Accepting certain limitations imposed by Vivian's age, Disraeli constructed a plot which depended on the boy's securing the support of others in an ingenious enterprise. Settling on the Marquess of Carabas, a disaffected ex-minister, Vivian succeeds in persuading him that he is not alone in having been ill-used by the ministry. If he and other such men will join forces, Vivian argues, and form a new political party, its force will sweep everything before it. The creation of the "Carabas Party" becomes the principal order of business. Youth must always encourage age, and Vivian achieves this with his rapid, witty, and confident talk, which, if not profound, is at least cheering; "that everything is possible" seems to be the chief of his several well-worn maxims. The notion of a boy of twenty conceiving so grandiose a scheme seemed entirely reasonable to Disraeli. Had he not himself conceived a similar plan with Murray and Lockhart? Using that experience to good effect, Disraeli involved his hero in a journey to Wales in search of Frederick Cleveland, erstwhile enemy of the Marquess of Carabas. Cleveland is needed to lead the party in the House of Commons, since all the other principals sit in the Lords. Vivian Grey, a perceptive youth, understands how he must treat Cleveland, on whom he forces himself. If Cleveland, knowing what his alliance with the Carabas party can mean, prefers "to pass the hours of his life in mediating the quarrels of a country village," there is no point in pursuing the matter. Touching Cleveland's vanity, and, also, his love of power, Vivian secures his prey. To that moment, his success has been complete. When, in the parts that follow, fortune turns, it is not the fault of Vivian Grey, but only that circumstance, beyond his control, conspires to defeat him. Chance, in the person of a jealous woman, wrecks Vivian's scheme. Disraeli did not know how to conclude his tale, and continued it beyond the point where it might reasonably have stopped.

What did Disraeli mean to suggest by the story? Why did he write it? An entry written in his diary while he was still young is illuminating. "My works are the embodification of my feelings. In *Vivian Grey* I have portrayed my active and real ambition. In *Alroy* my ideal ambition. The *Psychological Romance* [Contarini Fleming] is a development of my poetic character. The trilogy is the secret history of my feelings. I shall write no more about myself." How can *Vivian Grey* be said to express Disraeli's "real ambition"? In several senses. First, it accepts a world in which youth, fired by will, attempts great things and almost succeeds. Vivian's defeat is not preordained; had Mrs. Felix Lorraine not existed, it might not have occurred. Disraeli asserted the reality of the romantic hero and his accomplishment; he intended Vivian's project to be an almost impossible one, thereby testing the reader's readiness to believe in the improbable. Once it is admitted that great men exist, that they are not satisfied with what others find sufficient, and that their will transforms reality into what they wish it to be, then the first step has been taken toward the acceptance of a romantic philosophy analagous to the one in which Disraeli placed his faith. In extolling wit, ambition, and presence of mind, Disraeli praised those qualities on which he himself depended. Though prevented by circumstances from being involved in affairs, even as a youth, he yearned for the day when he would put his pen aside in favor of worldly pursuits. Vivian Grey accomplished the sort of things that excited Disraeli; it is in this sense that he spoke for his creator's "real ambition."

Disraeli suffered a period of intense emotional distress in the months following on the publication of *Vivian Grey*. The nature of his ailment is obscure; in part, because of the reticence of the nineteenth century on such matters, but also because its character was not understood. A two-month holiday on the Continent with friends did something to restore his spirit, but even the pleasures of travel in Paris, Geneva, Milan, Verona, Venice, and Florence provided only partial relief. In the years that followed, he kept much to himself, suffering the effects of a despondency which reduced his energies and stifled his ambition. It appeared, for a time, that he would have to be content to write as a hack, titillating the fancy of a predominantly female audience. *The Young Duke*, published in 1831, but written in 1830, showed evidences of pandering to a public taste created by publishers who knew their readers. Disraeli, at that moment, was in danger of becoming a "popular" writer, who used his pen only to entertain. *The Young Duke* emerged at a time when the author was traveling in the Middle East. Together with William Meredith, his sister's fiancé, Disraeli began in the spring of 1830 a trip which took him from London to Gibraltar, and then to Spain, Malta, Albania, Greece, Turkey, Cyprus, Syria, and Egypt. In Cairo, Meredith contracted smallpox, and after a brief struggle, died. Overwhelmed by grief for himself, but even more for his sister, Disraeli hastened back to England. The voyage, with its tragic end, had at least one good effect. His health was restored; the idea of using his experience only to amuse his readers no longer threatened. Disraeli possessed the materials to spin an infinite number of yarns, but that was no longer his interest. Preoccupied even more than before with a single theme — how to live a great life — he settled down to reflect and write on this matter. His travels in the Holy Land had made him all the more conscious of his race. How might he communicate his thoughts? What new sources of energy did they provide him? Disraeli chose the novel as his vehicle; it suited his subject, and he felt experienced in the problems it posed. *Alroy*, published in 1833, gave the first hint of what had transpired during Disraeli's years of illness and travel.

In *Alroy*, the novel in which he claimed to express his "ideal ambition," Disraeli employed an old Hebrew legend to sing another hymn to youth and heroic achievement. His hero, Alroy, a twelfth-century Jew, descended from David and known to his people as the Prince of the Captivity, is resentful of the Islamic power which holds the Jewish nation in thrall. The novel opens with a meeting between the youth and his uncle, a cautious and practical man who has summoned Alroy to explain why he must not continue to resist paying tribute to his Moslem masters. The dialogue is revealing of the character of each; the uncle's point of view is rendered in the simple expression, "the age of power is passed; it is by prudence now that we must flourish." Why, asks the uncle, has Alroy refused to show obedience? "Obedience," the youth answers, is a "word of doubtful import; for to obey, when duty is disgrace, is not a virtue." The conversation is a painful one; the uncle's wish is for repose and well-being; Alroy thirsts only for glory. The older man tries to reason with the boy; he urges him to walk in the bazaar of Bagdad, and see if the name of his uncle is not more powerful there than even that of the Caliph. Can such a reputation be, as Alroy suggests, the property of a slave? Alroy's answer is a simple one; "Uncle, you toil for others." "So do we all, so does the bee," the older man replies, "yet he is free and happy." "At least he has a sting," Alroy answers. "Which he can use but once," the uncle counters, "and when he stings," but he is interrupted by the youth who says: "He dies,

[97]

and like a hero. Such a death is sweeter than his honey." The older man sees the dreams of youth in all this talk and seeks to disparage it, but without success.

Disraeli, by opening his novel with this exchange, intended to show that his hero had come to feel, think, and act as a rebel even before circumstance forced him into that role. An accident that follows almost immediately on this conversation compels Alroy to flee the city. The flight is a difficult one, but Alroy is not a common mortal, and manages easily to survive it. During his flight, he encounters a mystic philosopher, a Cabalist, Jabaster, who has read in the stars of the approach of the son of David. While in the Cabalist's cave, Alroy has a vision in which the Lord appears and instructs him to go forward to raise the children of Israel from their bondage. Armed with a talisman and a ring, the gifts of Jabaster, he sets out for Jerusalem. Captured by bandits, he manages to effect his escape, only to be scorched by the sun, and eventually downed by wind and sand. He is found, unconscious, by a caravan making its way to Bagdad from Mecca. Bled, he is abandoned when his Jewish race is suspected. Only the accident of his being picked up by another member of the caravan who carries him to Bagdad saves him.

There, a seeming misadventure is suddenly converted into a stroke of good fortune. An Arab, gazing on the valuable ring which the weakened Alroy is wearing, swears that it is his and that the youth has stolen it. A great commotion in the bazaar follows, and Alroy, trying to withstand the mob, takes hold of the robes of a passerby, Honain, physician to the Caliph. Honain soon realizes that the ring is Alroy's; he orders the Arab punished for being a "liar, thief, and slanderer," and commands Alroy to follow him to his palace. Once in the palace, Alroy learns that Honain is in fact the brother of Jabaster, and also the original owner of the ring. Alroy, incapable of understanding how the brother of Jabaster can be a Moslem, is assured by Honain that in time this will be explained.

Honain claims to be "a man who knows men" and therefore

understands truth. Alroy tries to meet his skeptical arguments with an explanation of what it is to be a slave. Honain, after listening to his young companion, says: "I pray your pardon, sir; I thought you were Jabaster's pupil, a dreaming student. I see you have a deep ambition." To this Alroy responds: "I am a prince; and I fain would be a prince without my fetters." Honain's reply is not unlike the one which Alroy's uncle made when he first became aware of his nephew's rebelliousness. He tells Alroy of his own efforts, as a youth, to free the children of Israel. Those efforts came to nothing. Alroy is asked to profit from the lesson and abandon dreams which can only bring suffering and disappointment. Honain's offer is a generous one; he says: "Turn your late adventure to good account. No one can recognize you here. I will introduce you amongst the highest as my child by some fair Greek. The world is before you. You may fight, you may love, you may revel. War, and women, and luxury are all at your command. With your person and talents you may be grand vizir. Clear your head of nonsense. In the present disordered state of the empire, you may even carve yourself out a kingdom, infinitely more delightful than the barren land of milk and honey. I have seen it, child; a rocky wilderness, where I would not let my courser graze." The offer, needless to say, is refused. Honain says: "You are resolved, then, on destruction." "On glory, eternal glory," Alroy responds. "Is it possible to succeed?" Honain asks. "Is it possible to fail?" Alroy answers.

The sight of the Princess Schirene, the favorite daughter of the Caliph, does not deflect Alroy from his mission, but makes him feel a passion which is new and disturbing. Out of this encounter, engineered by Honain, will eventually come the destruction of all of Alroy's dreams. Alroy sees Jerusalem, organizes a Hebrew army, defeats the Moslems at Hamadan, and arrives at Bagdad as conqueror. His intention is to take Schirene for his wife. Jabaster, now the high priest of Israel, begs that he not commit this offense against the Lord who has brought him victory, but Alroy refuses to hear him out. His ambition is to become the conqueror of the world; to achieve that, he refuses to be bound by parochial prejudices. Jabaster continues to argue in the traditions of his race; he says: "Sire, bear with me. If I speak in heat, I speak in zeal. You ask me what I wish, my answer is, a national existence, which we have not. You ask me what I wish; my answer is, the Temple, all we have forfeited, all we have yearned after, all for which we have fought, our beauteous country, our holy creed, our simple manners, and our ancient customs." To all this Alroy replies: "Manners change with time and circumstances; customs may be observed everywhere. The ephod on thy breast proves our faith; and, for a country, is the Tigris less than Siloah, or the Euphrates inferior to the Jordan?" The King refuses to be guided by the Priest and the marriage between the Hebrew prince and the daughter of the Caliph is consummated in a week of great celebrations.

The story of Alroy's downfall follows hard on the one which has told of his success. Disaffection within, issuing quickly into rebellion, soon reduces to nothing the power which Alroy wields. Forced to flee, he is taken prisoner, and the Moslem power is entirely restored. All that remains for Disraeli to tell is the story of Alroy's trial and execution. Alroy, in a final meeting with his sister, moans that he has betrayed his country. "Oh, no, no, no!" she answers. "You have shown what we can do and shall do. Your memory alone is inspiration. A great career, although baulked of its end, is still a landmark of human energy. Failure when sublime, is not without its purpose. Great deeds are great legacies, and work with wondrous usury. By what Man has done, we learn what Man can do; and gauge the power and prospects of our race."

To compare this saga with that of *Vivian Grey* would be to treat unjustly a work which Disraeli intended to be grave and, in a certain sense, tragic. Yet the two works bear remarkable similarities. Disraeli, in the first edition of the novel, called it *The Wondrous Tale of Alroy*. As with *Vivian Grey*, he set out to tell a story which would test his readers. His hero, a youth possessed by an idea, violated every law of probability in the pursuit of his goal. Alroy's uncle and, later, Honain represented the voices of reason; they knew that Alroy could not succeed in his ambition. Theirs was a counsel of moderation because moderation represented reason. Alroy, secure in his faith, proceeded to achieve what they declared to be impossible. The tale was "wondrous" because it was improbable; to Disraeli, great accomplishment always belonged to the realm of the improbable.

Alroy's failure in the end did not alter the moral of the tale. Disraeli was intentionally ambiguous about the sequence of events which brought about Alroy's downfall. In one sense, the meeting with Schirene may be given as the cause of the tragedy. However, when one reflects on the magnitude of Alroy's ambition after his initial victories, it is obvious that the marriage with a Moslem princess was only one factor in a complex change. A man who could conquer, against such odds for Israel, might not remain satisfied with Israel's original aspirations. Disraeli avoided any suggestion that passion or disobedience of the law or injustice made Alroy's fall inevitable. He knew that each contributed to creating a political and military situation which Alroy could not master; beyond this, he refused to go. In a very real sense, Disraeli was uninterested in the decline of his hero. What made the tale "wondrous" was that he should have risen.

When Disraeli wrote that *Vivian Grey* expressed his "real ambition" and *Alroy* his "ideal ambition," he gave no hint of how he wished his words to be interpreted; several meanings are possible. One which commends itself by its plausibility is that Disraeli intended in both works to assert the reality of the heroic in human experience. His estimate of the two achievements did not depend upon their difficulty but upon their dignity. Vivian Grey, callow, ambitious, young, and shrewd, could conceive no greater project than his own elevation. Disraeli, while not alienated by such ambition, realized that there were others of greater merit. The verbal and mental gymnastics of his hero amused him, but he could not ignore their insufficiency; they were not calculated to produce great results. Alroy's quest was a far nobler one. Reared in an ancient and proud tradition, assured of comfort if only he would remain quiet, he thought such an offer a mockery of his belief. The faithful son of Israel could not accept the position of bondsman to the son of Ishmael. He had to rebel. That Disraeli should have believed that such a quest for glory expressed his "ideal ambition" cannot be surprising. He knew that no such opportunity for "great action" could be guaranteed to any man. He would himself probably spend his days in more prosaic endeavor. Like Vivian Grey he would attempt the difficult in politics, confident that the difficult might be achieved by a man possessed of courage and intellect. This was his "real ambition."

Alroy, partly because of its medieval Middle Eastern setting, expressed Disraeli's aspirations in a highly romantic idiom. Travel in the Orient only increased Disraeli's appreciation of the bizarre and the unusual, of the colorful and the exotic. To the extent that it led him to the unfamiliar, it contributed to diverting his attention from a total absorption in himself. This, as much as anything else, may have been the cure for the strange maladies which troubled him during these years. Travel, however, could never entirely resolve problems whose source lay in a deep malaise, too mysterious even to guess about. In *Contarini Fleming*, the most autobiographical of his novels, Disraeli hinted at some of the dilemmas which preoccupied him. It was the publication of this work in May 1832 that signaled the end of his morbid preoccupations with himself. While the novel may be studied as an extended dialogue, in which the hero is torn between two conflicting ways of living — the contemplative and the active — its publication coincided with an important decision on Disraeli's part; Contarini Fleming's doubts were no longer his own. He, Disraeli, had decided to opt for a life in the political world.

In *Contarini Fleming* even more than in his other novels,

Disraeli seemed to speak as much to himself as to his readers. The advice which a stranger offers his hero: "BE PATIENT: CHERISH HOPE. READ MORE: PONDER LESS. NATURE IS MORE POWERFUL THAN EDUCATION: TIME WILL DEVELOP EVERY THING. TRUST NOT OVERMUCH IN THE BLESSED MAGDALEN: LEARN TO PROTECT YOURSELF" sounds too authoritative to be intended only for a young boy. Certain of these injunctions Disraeli must have fashioned for his own use. The advice offered by Contarini's father is of the same character; while some of it is just inconsequential enough to suggest playfulness on Disraeli's part, there is enough to indicate seriousness. Thus, Contarini is told, "always know eminent men, and always be the master of the subject of the day." The father recommends a strict regimen; "Rise early and regularly and read for three hours. Read the Memoirs of the Cardinal de Retz, the life of Richelieu, everything about Napoleon: read works of that kind. . . . Read no history, nothing but biography, for that is life without theory. Then fence. Talk an hour with your French master, but do not throw the burden of the conversation upon him. Give him an account of something. Describe to him the events of yesterday, or give him a detailed account of the constitution. You will then have sufficiently rested yourself for your dancing. After that ride and amuse yourself as much as you can. Amusement to an observing mind is study." Disraeli, while pretending to write instructions for a youth still in his teens, was propounding principles for his own edification.

Was Disraeli not speaking to himself when he constructed a scene between father and son in which Contarini is told that he will be able "to influence men" only if he learns to control his imagination? Imagination, the older man explains, is Contarini's mortal enemy. Men possessed of great imagination, it appears, are usually failures in life. The poet may enjoy posthumous fame but this is no reward for the suffering he experiences in life. Even if Contarini could be a Homer, his father says, it would be better if he chose to be a man of action. In the end, the world sympathizes only with those capable of great deeds. Contarini is reminded that the "high poetic talent is the rarest in creation." It is probable that Contarini's imagination, like that of most others, is not "a creative faculty originating in a peculiar organisation, but simply the consequence of a nervous susceptibility that is common to all."

Contarini seeks, for a time, to heed his father's advice. Success comes, but Contarini finds it stale; he remains unhappy, sensing the meaninglessness of his existence. In desperation he turns to write a novel which he completes in seven days. He knows that the book is a crude performance, but he offers it to a bookseller for publication. Exalted by this experience, he takes a bold position at an important diplomatic meeting, and manages to win his point. His father, filled with pride, predicts that he will be Prime Minister one day, perhaps, something even greater.

At this moment of universal acclaim, Contarini's book appears. Although it is anonymous, the identity of its author is guessed. Contarini is made aware of its danger by the young lady who, unwittingly, inspired him to write it. She questions its judgment; it will make you many enemies, she warns. Contarini cannot understand why a book which speaks the truth should create difficulties for him. He is reminded that it is filled with ridicule, and that those injured by it are not likely to forgive him. Contarini's answer "There is nothing but truth in it" receives the reply, "You are not in a position, Contarini, to speak truth."

The prediction of trouble is proved correct. As soon as Contarini's authorship is guessed, a storm of criticism descends. Hurt and humiliated but refusing to be cowed, Contarini decides to quit his country and go abroad to write. He vows that the world will yet come to recognize his genius. Making his way rapidly to Venice, the city of which he has dreamed since his childhood, Contarini finds there the glory for which his romantic imagination has prepared him. A chance encounter with a young lady of great beauty, whom he discovers to be his cousin and the last of the Contarinis, leads to an explosion of his romantic sentiments. Alcesté says Venice is lighthearted and resigned; she begs Contarini not to bind his "lot to the fallen and the irredeemable." "In the north," she says, "you are a man; your career may be active, intelligent, and useful; but the life of a Venetian is a dream, and you must pass your days like a ghost gliding about a city fading in vision." To this Contarini replies: "It is this very character that interests me. I have no sympathy with reality. What vanity in all the empty bustle of common life!" Contarini marries his cousin, and on her death in childbirth, is inconsolable.

Except for convention, which dictated the length of a novel, it is difficult to know why Disraeli continued his story beyond this point. As with *Vivian Grey*, the plot is soon abandoned in favor of a fairly commonplace travelogue. In Rome, amidst the ruins which surround him, Contarini asks: "And where is Rome? All nations rose and flourished only to swell her splendour, and now I stand amid her ruins. In such a scene what are our private griefs and petty sorrows? And what is man?" Contarini is roused from his thoughts by the sudden appearance of Winter, the painter whom he had first encountered as a boy, who urges him to "act, act, act; act without ceasing, and you will no longer talk of the vanity of life." "But how am I to act?" Contarini asks. "Create. Man is made to create, from the poet to the potter," Winter replies. It is difficult to know from the final passages of the novel whether Contarini has understood or accepted Winter's advice. Coming into a large inheritance after his father's death, he determines to build a great villa, rivaling Hadrian's, in the vicinity of Naples. He intends to spend his life "in the study and the creation of the beautiful." This is Contarini's hope, but as he admits, he doubts that in the end it will prove to be his career.

Contarini Fleming, perhaps more than any other of his novels, expressed the dilemmas which made Disraeli's early adulthood troubled and painful. Conscious of his poetic temperament, but almost certainly aware that he lacked great poetic gifts, he argued with himself about the place that a man of his talent might occupy in the world. The feeling of intense isolation, which Disraeli ascribed to Contarini, he certainly felt himself. His illnesses, psychological as well as physical, suggest a constant tension which may have arisen in part out of a sense of frustration about how he was to spend his life. His ambition was great, but the field on which that ambition might play was obscure. The excitement which Contarini felt at being descended from the greatest house of Venice, Disraeli must have felt at the thought that he came from a race which was civilized and creative when Europe was a forest inhabited by painted savages. Like Contarini, he knew that the flat-nosed Franks (Europeans), who were masters of the world, would "toil, and study, and invent theories to account for their own incompetence," but would never guess that their inferiority was more fundamental, being racial. Disraeli, an alien in England, had to find his place in it. The difficulty of doing so was increased by the fact that he could not conceal the superiority he felt to those around him.

Disraeli, like Contarini, must have been offered a great deal of practical advice by his father, who, although not a man of affairs himself, appreciated the advantages of being one. Given Disraeli's known admiration for his father, there is reason to believe that he must have made strenuous efforts to heed that advice. To bridle his imagination, and realize his genius in some practical pursuit, must have appeared a reasonable answer to his problems. When he reflected on the virtues of his race, and considered how often they were linked to a life of action, his admiration for that solution must have grown. And yet, always, other possibilities recommended themselves. How could he be certain that the poetic instinct in him was not being denied? Was it right that he should abandon the contest so easily? Disraeli, agitated by his own indecision, and pulled toward the active life by its splendor and amplitude, finally chose the road recommended by his own character, Winter. His would be a life of constant worldly toil, in which the injunction "act, act,

act" always sounded. He would end his days not in "the study and the creation of the beautiful," but in the more frenzied pursuits of the politician.

It is impossible to know when, precisely, Disraeli made this decision. By the middle of 1832, when he contested a seat in Parliament for the first time, and lost, there was no longer any question about the nature of his ambition. Disraeli wanted to be in politics. In the years that followed, he made strenuous efforts to gain a footing on the political ladder, but circumstance seemed always to thwart him, making it appear, for a time, that he was destined to remain a novelist, admired only by those who knew how to appreciate his wit. While pursuing a political career unsucessfully, he managed to gain and hold a position in London society. What makes this achievement remarkable is that it occurred, and also that it did not immediately carry an equal advantage in the political world. Disraeli, as a youth, knew the society of his father's friends — publishers, scholars, solicitors — members of that large middle class whose existence the aristocracy scarcely acknowledged. After 1832, he moved away from this middle-class society into another whose tastes were of a quite different order. How did he manage to penetrate this world of titled people living in large and well-appointed houses who seemed committed to an existence of perpetual display? Disraeli owed his success, in part, to his talent and fame as an author, but the greatest debt was to a small circle of friends with whom he became early acquainted. Through them, he came into touch with men and women who would never have thought to enter his father's house.

The story of Disraeli's success in society is not without relevance to his political career. It suggests unusual ingenuity, a capacity to explore avenues not generally recognized as open, and an understanding of the advantages of patience. In 1829, Disraeli began a correspondence with Edward Bulwer (later Bulwer-Lytton; still later, the first Lord Lytton); Bulwer, Disraeli's contemporary, enjoyed a wide connection in London.

His reputation as an author, and his social position, only temporarily jeopardized by a quarrel with his mother which caused his income to be reduced, made Bulwer a central figure in London literary society. By 1832, Bulwer was introducing his friend to the men and women whose company he enjoyed. Bulwer's "set" in London was a very special one. It centered on Lady Blessington, who, in her great house at Seamore Place, received some of the most prominent literary and political figures of her day. Men thronged the Blessington mansion, leaving their wives behind to repeat tales about past indiscretions committed by this Irish lady, and, even more shocking, of continuing irregularities, involving certainly her son-in-law and "lover," the Count d'Orsay. Lady Blessington, one of the great beauties of her day, ignored the scandalous talk, and fought to maintain her position as one of London's great hostesses. Disraeli, like Bulwer, fitted easily into the circle. The charm of the conversation, the beauty of the house, the elegance of the company — all forming a pattern intended by the aesthetically fastidious woman who conceived it — made an impression on the young novelist for whom all this was strikingly new. Disraeli soon established a close acquaintance with Count d'Orsay, a "dandy" whose exploits provided fuel for London gossip. One introduction led to another, and, while some doors never opened to the "dandified Jew" who now became a conspicuous figure in society, a sufficient number admitted him to make his "progress" seem a remarkable one. With women especially — frequently older than himself — Disraeli had uncommonly good luck. In letters to his sister, he listed his invitations as a general might have cited his victories, taking great care to indicate always the rank and office of each of the persons captured.

During this period Disraeli cut a figure in society as a "dandy." Baudelaire, perhaps more than any other critic, understood the social implications of "dandyism." He knew that it was not simply "an exaggerated love of fine clothes and material comfort." Rather, he saw it as "primarily a desire to be individually original, but always within the limits of polite social convention." Dandyism appeared, Baudelaire said, "at times of transition, when democracy is only half powerful or when aristocracy is already tottering but has not yet fallen." It was the "last gesture of the heroic in an age of decadence." It was "a setting sun, magnificent but without warmth and full of melancholy." The society in which Disraeli moved welcomed him as a "dandy."

It was quite another thing in the political world. The impeccably garbed Disraeli, with his foreign face, his studied manner, and his romantic visions, spoke in an idiom which may have had its charm in drawing rooms, but which seemed peculiarly out of place on the hustings. In 1832, before the passage of the Reform Bill, Disraeli made his first unsuccessful attempt at securing a seat in Parliament. Later that year, he ran again for High Wycombe, claiming independence of all parties. In this election he was roundly beaten. The best evidence of the confusion which electors felt about this strange candidate is that he thought it necessary to explain himself in a short tract, which bore, appropriately enough, the title *What Is He?* Disraeli urged Tories and Radicals to unite in a new National Party which would pledge itself to the defeat of the Whigs. If Disraeli's tract served to make a confused policy seem somewhat less obscure, it did nothing to advance his cause; Tories had no great interest in his ideas, and Radicals remained suspicious and aloof. If Disraeli was to fulfill the ambition expressed to an incredulous Lord Melbourne in 1834, which was nothing less than to be Prime Minister, it was absolutely essential that he find a seat in Parliament. This was easier said than done.

In 1835, he contested High Wycombe for a third time, and failed again. By this date, Disraeli was beginning to move very purposefully in a Tory direction. Romantic notions about the establishment of a National Party were quietly laid aside. After his defeat, he wrote the Duke of Wellington, the Tory leader, and had the satisfaction of receiving a letter in return expressing regret at the results. Disraeli redoubled his attacks on the Whig Party. It was a class party, he wrote, oligarchic in its aims and composition, and interested only in establishing a despotism in Britain. Disraeli's criticisms of Melbourne became fierce, and, at times, tasteless; he called him a political profligate, a notorious place hunter, a despised and distrusted "political hack," incapable of managing public affairs. Melbourne, Disraeli wrote, was the Prime Minister of O'Connell, the Irish leader, and not of the king whom he pretended to serve. The Whig policy was "ever to smuggle in laws for the increase and consolidation of the power of their party under the specious guise of advancing the cause of popular amelioration." As for Toryism, Disraeli now saw it as "the national spirit exhibiting itself in the maintenance of the national institutions, and in support of the national character which these institutions have formed." The Tories would have been remiss to ignore entirely a pamphleteer of such ability. When Disraeli began to show an interest in joining the Carlton Club, there was no move to deny him admission. In his fourth attempt to secure a seat in the House of Commons, he ran as a Tory candidate. He failed to win at Taunton, but had the satisfaction of knowing that he had tied his fortunes to a thriving political party which was showing increasing interest in his polemical powers. In 1835, he published a long tract, the *Vindication of the English Constitution,* which summed up his political philosophy and established a new basis for Tory propaganda in its slashing criticism of Whig policy.

Disraeli opened the *Vindication* very much in the manner of Burke, with an attack on those who sought to discover universal political principles, applicable everywhere at every moment. Disraeli accused the Utilitarians, whom he found guilty of these easy generalizations, of gross ignorance. He warned new countries that any attempt to imitate in their constitutions the methods of already established states was doomed to failure. The English Constitution, he argued, was unique to England, expressed its particular history, and could not be exported. Dwelling on a favorite theme, he said the

House of Commons was no more the House of the People than was the House of Lords. "The Commons of England," he wrote, "as well as the Peers of England, are neither more nor less than a privileged class, privileged in both instances for the common good, unequal doubtless in number, yet both, in comparison with the whole nation, forming in a numerical estimation only an insignificant fraction of the mass." Disraeli wished to prove that an assembly could be representative without being elective. Members of the House of Commons, he insisted, "never were the representatives of the people. They always were, and they are still, the representatives of the Commons, an estate of the realm privileged as the other estates, not meeting personally for the sake of convenience, but by its representatives, and constituting, even with its late considerable accession of members, only a small section of the nation." To this point Disraeli had argued very much in the tradition of Burke. It was impossible, however, for a Tory politician to continue along lines made famous by the great Whig of the eighteenth century, and Disraeli had no intention of simply repeating Burke.

Reviewing the events of the seventeenth century, Disraeli dwelled on the attack launched against the Church of England during Charles I's reign. After the king's execution, Disraeli wrote, government "by the People" meant that there were "Courts more infamous than the Star Chamber in every county of England," and that "nearly one-half of the goods and chattels of the nation" passed from their rightful owners to others who had no just claim to them. Disraeli thought those events a dishonor to the nation which suffered them. After the Revolution of 1688 and the accession of the Hanoverians, a second tragedy occurred. The Whig oligarchs, Disraeli explained, seeking to impose their will on the nation, reduced the monarch to the position of a Venetian Doge. They exercised the real power, while the king existed only as a figurehead. This situation lasted for almost half a century. Only with the accession of George III, who "put himself at the head of the nation," was the Whig plan defeated. Under Pitt, the representative of the Tory or national party, England became, Disraeli wrote, "the metropolis of a mighty Empire, its Sovereign at the same time the most powerful and its people the most free, and second to no existing nation in arts or arms, in internal prosperity, or exterior splendour." Disraeli entertained no doubts about the integral connection between the Tory revival and England's prosperity. Under the Whigs, with their slogans about "Civil and Religious Freedom," England lived under a Doge without Bishops. The Whigs sought only the establishment of their own oligarchic power; they never represented the nation; only the votes of Irish and Scottish minorities maintained them in power. In Bolingbroke, the Tory who suffered persecution at Whig hands, Disraeli discovered the spokesman for national principles. The plea that Bolingbroke made at the height of Whig power, Disraeli repeated: let the Tory Party become the national party and its power would be invincible. "The Whigs," Disraeli wrote, "invoke 'the People'; let us appeal to the nation."

If the Tory Party had been searching for a political doctrine it could not have done better than adopt the one outlined by Disraeli — a political myth which defined British politics as a struggle between two groups, one representing a small propertied class, the other the nation; the first intent only on aggrandizement and destruction, the other anxious to conserve whatever the genius of the nation had painfully created, showed originality. To dismiss the Whig accomplishment as that of an oligarchy, and to make the reign of George III appear as the "golden period" in the eighteenth century suggested ingenious invention. The distinction between class and nation, the first basing itself on a selfish interest, only scarcely veiled, and the second on a democratic instinct which went beyond the counting of heads, revealed the art of a great polemicist. Had the Tory Party required a new idea, it could not have found a more useful one than that constructed by Disraeli. In fact, however, it seemed only mildly interested in Disraeli's invention. No one thought it imperative that such a brilliant polemicist be brought into Parliament immediately to strengthen the Tory contingent.

This was an unhappy time for Disraeli. The succession of electoral defeats had prevented him from taking even the first step up the political ladder. His financial situation grew increasingly precarious; although he continued to earn something as a novelist, this was scarcely sufficient for his needs. After 1832, he moved in fashionable London society, and these pleasures involved him in an expense which he had no means of paying. By 1837, he might well have begun to wonder whether he would achieve any of the distinctions that he had so confidently predicted for himself. His greatest asset remained his wit and intelligence; his greatest boon his friends. It was through a friend, Wyndham Lewis, that he finally had his chance. Lewis, a member of Parliament for Maidstone, persuaded the Tory leaders of that constituency that Disraeli would make an admirable candidate for the second seat. In the 1837 General Election, Disraeli ran and won; five years and five elections after his initial try, he at last attained his goal: he was a member of the parliamentary club.

His first years in the House of Commons were in no way spectacular. While he reveled in his new situation and supported his party loyally, there was not much that even the most gifted backbencher could do. Disraeli developed a parliamentary manner, gained proficiency as a speaker, and bided his time. He had reason to hope that his services to the Party would be recognized when Peel and the Tories were again in a position to form a government. The sudden death of Wyndham Lewis had no effect on Disraeli's political fortunes, but proved to be the most important event in his personal life. Solicitous for the widow of his late colleague and benefactor, Disraeli began to see a great deal of her, and finally asked for her hand in marriage. Her consent gave him the companionship of a woman who never for a moment doubted that he would attain the objects on which he had set his heart. Free of all financial worry, he could now give the whole of his attention to politics.

In 1841, Disraeli's hopes soared; the Whig ministry, defeated on a vote of confidence by a single vote, called a General Election. The results showed that the Tories had made impressive gains and that they would almost certainly form the next government. Disraeli, returned as member for Shrewsbury, expected that Peel, when called upon to form a ministry, would acknowledge his contribution by making a suitable offer. In this he was disappointed; as Peel proceeded to select his ministers, it became apparent that he had no intention of choosing Disraeli for even a minor post. Disraeli was mortified; swallowing his pride he wrote to Peel, asking that he be spared an intolerable humiliation. Reminding Peel of his services to the Tory Party, he told of the "storm of political hate and malice" to which he had been exposed. Disraeli said that he was supported in "these trials by the conviction that the day would come when the foremost man of this country would publicly testify that he had some respect for my ability and my character." Peel was moved neither by the argument nor by the flattery. A letter from Mrs. Disraeli, written without her husband's knowledge, begging Peel not to crush the political career of a man who had served so faithfully, received no greater consideration. The Tory government was formed, but Disraeli had no place in it.

Disraeli took pains to conceal whatever bitterness or humiliation he felt. He spoke in Parliament, continued as active as ever in London society, and by his general comportment seemed to suggest that he did not intend to regard the setback as a final defeat. His decision to spend the winter of 1842–43 abroad in Paris with his wife, showed that there was little for him to do at home. Disraeli, realizing that a major obstacle had been placed in the way of his advance, began to lay his plans. If Peel would not have him, then Peel would himself have to go. This idea, in some inchoate form, must have occurred to Disraeli during the months that he spent in France. He began, in Paris, to meet with a number of young Tories who for one reason or other were also disenchanted with Peel. The group, composed principally of young and well-born men, recently down from Cambridge, looked upon Disraeli as their chief; out of their conversations the idea of Young England developed. The doctrine of Young England was vague and romantic; it began as a protest against Peel's habit of deciding issues without reference to anything except personal or electoral advantage. The Tory Party, these men imagined, was losing its distinctive character; it was becoming too much like the other. Peel seemed to accept the notion that there would be times when the Tories governed, and times when they would form the opposition. His program lacked an obvious and consistent Tory bias. Young England took upon itself the task of bringing the party back to a greater consciousness of its historic traditions. During the summer of 1843, members of the group — and Disraeli especially — spoke critically of the Government in Parliament. Peel accepted the situation, bided his time, but at the beginning of the next session neglected to send a personal summons to Disraeli to attend at Westminster. In effect, Peel had ceased to consider him as a voting Tory. When Disraeli protested his political exclusion, the Prime Minister explained that he had not sent a summons because he was uncertain whether it would be welcome. Peel suggested that Disraeli's conduct at the end of the previous session had indicated such fundamental disagreement with the ministry that reliance on his support seemed impossible. Reassured by Disraeli's letter that a breach did not exist, Peel expressed himself as being satisfied. Again, the Prime Minister had gotten the better of the exchange. For the moment, at least, both were prepared to accept a truce.

Disraeli was in a difficult position. To continue to criticize Peel in the House was to risk being ostracized from the Tory Party. Disraeli had no illusions about his strength in the Commons, and recognized the likely consequences of an open break. To remain silent, however, was to accept a continuing exclusion from the Front Bench. Disraeli understood the urgency of clarifying his differences with the Prime Minister. While he knew those differences to be largely personal, he recognized the political disadvantage of permitting them to appear so. His task was to make them seem ideological. Characteristically, he turned to write a novel; his purpose in *Coningsby* was to give an authoritative statement to the principles which he believed were central to the Tory position. Peel's neglect of these principles would be made the issue between them. Disraeli constructed an improbable moral homily, larded it with satire, and prepared to see how his Tory readers responded.

The novel's plot was simple, unimportant, and may be quickly disposed of. The hero, Coningsby, an orphan and grandson of the richest man in England, Lord Monmouth, is first encountered at Eton. He is preparing to meet his grandfather for the first time; years earlier Monmouth disinherited Coningsby's father because he objected to his marriage. When, later, his daughter-in-law, widowed and impoverished, comes seeking help, it is offered on two conditions — that she give up the boy and go to live in one of the more remote counties of England. In no position to reject the offer, hard though it is, she hands over the boy and goes to die in her exile. Coningsby is dispatched to Eton; his life is closely regulated by Rigby, Monmouth's principal adviser. In his first meeting with his grandfather, the boy is frightened and makes an unfortunate impression. Only gradually does the old man begin to see that Coningsby resembles him; his interest is immediately engaged. While there can never be a close relation between the two, it is generally assumed that Monmouth's liking for his grandson will assure his being made his heir. This possibility is destroyed however when Coningsby refuses to contest an election which the old man insists that he fight. Rigby and others tell Monmouth that Coningsby is in love with the daughter of the man whom he would have to defeat, and that this is the reason for his refusal. Coningsby suffers the penalty of his disobedience; when the old man dies, a natural daughter, Flora, is discovered to be his heir. Fate, however, always close at hand in Disraeli's novels, intervenes to kill off Flora; her heir is none other than Coningsby. The novel ends with Coningsby's marriage.

Had Disraeli wished only to entertain, *Coningsby* would have begun to gather dust soon after its publication. As a novel, it showed the faults characteristic of other of Disraeli's literary efforts; an improbable plot, insubstantial character portrayal, and an excessive romanticism. However, Disraeli's purpose was not to entertain; he wished to use the novel to communicate certain political ideas and to render ridiculous, by irony and satire, certain political types. Monmouth, copied after the third Marquis of Hertford, was more than an old roué of iron will who looked upon men and women as purchasable. Disraeli intended a more subtle criticism; Monmouth, for all his power and intelligence, was irresponsible. By not giving any time to politics, he had no knowledge of its nature. Depending on Rigby and others for information, he gathered only rumor and scandal. His philosophy — the Tories are good and the Whigs be damned — Disraeli thought contemptible. It was not that Disraeli disagreed with that view but he understood its insufficiency. Monmouth was not a thinking creature; he simply felt. When things went well, he exulted; when they went badly, he packed his bags and embarked for the continent. His was not a political life; it was a life in which politics figured as one of several pleasures, and by no means the principal one. He controlled seats, but he did not control minds, except those of men who were willing to act as his lackeys. He was irresponsible in the most absolute sense because he failed to understand the dignity of the office which he occupied. The word "duty" had no place in his vocabulary.

Given the extraordinary power that Monmouth wielded, Disraeli could not fail to be fascinated by his character. Monmouth possessed size, though he did not begin to contend for greatness. He commanded men, but for purposes too petty to interest Disraeli. For Rigby, Monmouth's "counsellor," Disraeli felt no regard. He was a purchased man, prepared to serve for an ample wage. If Monmouth was indolent and a voluptuary, Rigby was neither, but infinitely more immoral. Rigby was a "fixer," without principles, who managed men and affairs in his patron's interest. He had no mind of his own; no will of his own; he was a "servant" in the literal sense.

Taper and Tadpole, two of Disraeli's most expertly drawn characters, expressed the emptiness of back-bench parliamentary existence. They were members of that class of politicians who believed the country was saved if they were guaranteed twelve hundred pounds a year. Disraeli implied that the Tory Party was too largely composed of such men. Without great powers of intrigue, they lived in a world where it was constantly thought of and looked for. To speak of them as good or bad made no sense; their sins were malice and self-seeking, small faults appropriate to small men. Disraeli intended that they should be seen as silly, almost contemptible, who by their banalities made a mockery of politics.

Millbank, Sr., was the only representative of the "older generation" for whom Disraeli indicated respect. A model employer, Millbank had created outside Manchester an industrial village which expressed the power of the machine, without hinting at its harsher possibilities. He represented the new and rising class of industrial property owners who were alienated by a Toryism which seemed incapable of appreciating their contribution to the national life. The implication was clear; men like Millbank would not remain Whigs if men like Monmouth, Rigby, Taper, and Tadpole did not determine Tory policy. A new policy was needed, one which would attract such men.

Coningsby, in visiting Manchester, is overwhelmed by the energy of the city. Dining with Millbank, the father of one of his school friends, he says: "I know, sir, from your son that you are opposed to an aristocracy," to which Millbank, in a phrase reminiscent of Burke, replies, "No, I am not. I am for an aristocracy; but a real one, a natural one." Coningsby, surprised, asks whether the English do not have a real aristocracy. The reply is that an aristocracy must be based on some real distinction, and that those who call themselves Earls and Dukes in England do nothing to merit the respect they ask. Coningsby says that political stability depends upon honor being shown those who claim ancient lineage. "Ancient lineage!" Millbank says; "I never heard of a peer with an ancient lineage. The real old families of this country are to be found among the peasantry; the gentry, too, may lay claim to some old blood. I can point you out Saxon families in this county who can trace their pedigrees beyond the Conquest; I know of some Norman gentlemen whose fathers undoubtedly came over with the Conqueror. But a peer with an ancient lineage is to me quite a novelty."

Disraeli, in these comments, expressed a view on the English aristocracy which he was to repeat many times in his later works. Charmed neither by the supposed antiquity of the peerage nor by the attention it gave to its responsibilities, Disraeli saw little reason to flatter the privileged. In distinguished men, willing to give of their time and experience, Disraeli placed his confidence. In his portrayal of Millbank, he hoped to suggest that great industrialists, believing in progress and proud of their accomplishments, were not necessarily men lacking in taste, feeling, or a sense of history. Millbank's style of life was simple but not without dignity. His house, while not rivaling those of the great landed men of England, showed refinement and discrimination. Millbank — a Whig, active, intelligent, and industrious — was much to be preferred to the Tapers, Tadpoles, Rigbys, and Monmouths of the world.

Disraeli intended *Coningsby* to serve a political purpose. If this required him to interrupt his narrative to launch a political idea or deliver an assault on Peel, he did so with little hesitation. Thus, speaking as the unidentified narrator, Disraeli asked whether the Reform Act of 1832 might not in the long run have unexpected consequences. In destroying the "Venetian constitution" and the Whig oligarchy in the House of Lords, it had transferred power to the House of Commons. He asked whether, in the new situation where there were no longer any "magnificoes," the Sovereign might not cease to be a Doge.

"It is not impossible," he wrote, "that the political movements of our time, which seem on the surface to have a tendency to democracy, may have in reality a monarchical bias." At another point, in commenting on Peel's Tamworth Manifesto of 1834, he called it "an attempt to construct a party without principles." "Its basis," he said, "was necessarily Latitudinarianism; and its inevitable consequence has been Political Infidelity." Disraeli condemned a policy which claimed to be conservative but compromised on every principle as soon as sufficient pressure was exerted. In this, as in other remarks, he made no attempt to conceal his hostility to Peel.

Since his principal hero, Coningsby, could not serve for all purposes, Disraeli introduced a second hero, Sidonia, to utter those things which might have seemed strange when expressed by even the most gifted of youths. Sidonia, a Jew of immense wealth and influence, meets Coningsby in an inn where both are taking shelter from a storm. On learning that the stranger knows the Mediterranean, Coningsby expresses the hope that he may one day see it, and most particularly, Athens. Sidonia replies: "I have seen it and more wonderful things. Phantoms and spectres! The Age of Ruins is past. Have you seen Manchester?" Coningsby replies that this is his first experience of travel, and expresses the fear that the age of adventures, like the age of ruins, may be past. "Adventures are to the adventurous," the older man answers. Later Coningsby remarks: "I perceive that you have great confidence in the influence of individual character. I also have some confused persuasions of that kind. But it is not the Spirit of the Age." The stranger replies: "The age does not believe in great men, because it does not possess any. The Spirit of the Age is the very thing that a great man changes." "But what," Coningsby asks, "is an individual against a vast public opinion?" "Divine," the stranger answers; "God made man in His own image; but the Public is made by Newspapers, Members of Parliament, Excise Officers, Poor Law Guardians." The stranger mentions individual men who have changed the whole course of history. To this Coningsby replies: "But when men are young they want experience, and when they have gained experience, they want energy." "Great men never want experience," the stranger answers. "But everybody says that experience —"; Coningsby's reply is interrupted by the stranger who adds: "Is the best thing in the world, a treasure for you, for me, for millions. But for a creative mind, less than nothing. Almost everything that is great has been done by youth." Later in the conversation the older man is even more specific when he says: "The history of Heroes is the history of Youth." To this Coningsby replies: "Ah! I should like to be a great man." "Nurture your mind with great thoughts," the stranger answers. "To believe in the heroic makes heroes."

The stranger is not identified until a later point in the novel when Coningsby again encounters him, this time as a guest in his grandfather's house. Sidonia destroyed whatever plausibility the novel may have had as a literal description of political life in Britain. While some have seen in Sidonia an idealized representation of Disraeli himself, this is true to only a limited extent. In his Jewish birth, and in his ideas, Sidonia resembled Disraeli; otherwise, he assumed almost superhuman proportions. Born into the greatest wealth of a Spanish family whose members had remained secretly Jewish for centuries while pretending to be Christian, members of the family had served the Church in roles as high as that of Archbishop and Grand Inquisitor. Sidonia was a man without equal in all of Europe. No one knew more; no one was more objective in his judgments; no one was so lacking in cares and duties. Sidonia was represented as the perfectly objective man who needed never to compromise his beliefs in order to gain the good opinions of others. "The only human quality that interested Sidonia was Intellect. He cared not whence it came; where it was to be found: creed, country, class, character, in this respect were alike indifferent to him." Disraeli might delude himself in many things; he could never imagine that such a figure was a representation of himself, even of his ideal self.

Disraeli invented Sidonia because he required him as a spokesman for ideas which could not be entrusted to callow youths, and which, because of their novelty, required the authority of a man whose critical and prophetic powers transcended what was common to the world of British politics. Sidonia, in his historical interpretation, in his estimate of the importance of race, and in his prophecy, served as the oracle whom Coningsby then interpreted. It is in a conversation between the two that the idea is broached that power is always distrusted in England, and that its overthrow follows the creation of weighty combinations formed to oppose it. Thus, Sidonia sees the power of the great barons destroyed by the Church, which uses the King as its instrument. Clerical power, in turn, is destroyed by the King, who uses Parliament as his agent. Royal power falls victim to Parliament's aggressions, the People being called in to aid in this assault. If parliamentary power is not to be overthrown, Sidonia warns, then England as a *community* must be strengthened. This, he assures the youth, cannot be accomplished by rationalizing English government. "Man is only great," Sidonia says, "when he acts from the passions; never irresistible but when he appeals to the imagination." That "Mormon counts more votaries than Bentham" is a fact which no politician will wish to ignore. Sidonia tells Coningsby that "man is made to adore and obey, but if you will not command him, if you give him nothing to worship, he will fashion his own divinities, and find a chieftain in his own passions."

More than anywhere else in his writings, Disraeli expressed in this brief exchange the bases on which he founded his political philosophy. He knew that the individual needed to believe, and that the man of political acumen responded to this need in the ideas that he expressed. The idea of "community" would appeal to men; the idea of "rationalizing" government would never have the same appeal. Sidonia's remarks had an immediate relevance to the English political scene; Coningsby could ponder them, realize their implications, and seek to incorporate them into his own political thinking.

Benjamin Disraeli: The Romantic Egotist

It is difficult to understand why Disraeli charged Sidonia with another teaching mission — to instruct Coningsby in the greatness of the Jewish race. Coningsby is told by Sidonia that Jews are by nature monarchical and religious, and that only a stupid English policy makes them the allies of levelers and latitudinarians. If the government ceased its persecutions, the deeply conservative strain in the Jewish race would reveal itself, and Jews would emerge as principal defenders of established institutions. While this may be construed as an effort by Disraeli to speak for a reform long overdue, the context of Sidonia's remarks suggests that Disraeli's intentions were almost certainly greater than that. Many of his statements make an explicit appeal to the reader's tolerance. Disraeli seemed intent on instructing his readers on the character of the race to which he belonged. If he appealed to their understanding, he was not above showing a certain bravado. "Do you think," Sidonia asks, "that the quiet humdrum persecution of a decorous representative of an English university can crush those who have successively baffled the Pharaohs, Nebuchadnezzar, Rome, and the Feudal ages?" The Jew was capable of resisting his enemies; that was his whole history. Disraeli needed to believe that such resistance had meaning for his own life. Try as he would, he could not divorce himself from a concern with his own particular problems.

Coningsby, under Sidonia's tutelage, emerges as a thoughtful Conservative. Repeating many of the historical constructions which Disraeli first expressed a decade earlier, Coningsby speaks of his contempt for a Tory Party which has lost its principles. While Tories pretend to be interested in keeping things as they are, and speak as if they are devoted to the prerogatives of the Crown, the constitution of the Church as established by law, and the independence of the House of Lords, they know, in fact, that none of these things exist. The choice, he says, is between a Destructive Creed, such as the Whigs proclaim, and Political Infidelity, such as the Tories practice. If Democracy encounters no foe more formidable than that represented by

Peelite Toryism, then its triumph is inevitable. In such a victory, one class will come to dominate, and the freedom and security of all others will be jeopardized. It is only the restoration of an authority above class that can save the nation. The Sovereign, Coningsby insists, must be regarded as the leader of the whole people; the office of the king must again be revered. The Church, also, must be infused with this new spirit.

In the final encounter between Lord Monmouth and his grandson, when Coningsby refuses to contest a seat as Conservative candidate, the young man tries to explain why he cannot support the party which is guilty of political infidelity. To his complicated arguments Monmouth replies: "All this is fine but I see no means by which I can attain my object but by supporting Peel. After all, what is the end of all parties and all politics? To gain your object. I want to turn our coronet into a ducal one, and to get your grandmother's barony called out of abeyance in your favour. It is impossible that Peel can refuse me." To this Coningsby answers: "What we want, sir, is not to fashion new dukes and furbish up old baronies, but establish great principles which may attain the realm and secure the happiness of the people. Let me see authority once more honoured; a solemn reverence again the habit of our lives; let me see property acknowledging, as in the old days of faith, that labour is his twin brother, and that the essence of all tenure is the performance of duty; let results such as these be brought about, and let me participate, however feebly, in the great fulfilment, and public life then indeed becomes a noble career, and a seat in Parliament an enviable distinction." Lord Monmouth's answer to this is characteristic: "I tell you what it is, Harry, members of this family may think as they like, but they must act as I please."

Coningsby, published in 1844, expressed the discontent which Disraeli at that moment felt with Peel. That such a novel would never have been produced if Disraeli had been given a place in the Tory Ministry of 1841, no one can seriously doubt. Disraeli's contempt for the Tapers and Tadpoles would have been considerably less if he had been viewing them from the Front Bench in the House of Commons. Disraeli's anger with the "moderation" of Peel was exaggerated to serve his political purposes. The political program which he advocated really amounted to very little. The reestablishment of the influence of the Church, for example, while perhaps desirable, could never be achieved by the crude devices suggested by Disraeli. It was not simply a matter of having a more conscientious clergy or seeing to it that the House of Commons did not tamper with existing Church powers. Disraeli spoke eloquently about the true principles which ought to dominate the Tory Party, but these principles, when enumerated, were ephemeral and obscure.

Disraeli's situation was an almost impossible one. Unless he could prove that Peel's government violated Tory traditions and relied for its success on dubious policies and tactics, his outbursts in the House of Commons could only be interpreted as the outraged pique of a rejected suitor. But, to distinguish between his policies and those of Peel's, he had to create a romantic image of man and society which bore little relation to what existed, had existed, or might exist. An aristocracy acknowledging its responsibilities, a monarchy exercising real power, a Church pursuing its holy mission — these were goals which no political party could hope to legislate. If a Tory tradition existed, Peel was not as faithless to it as Disraeli pretended. A decade of Whig Party rule could not be undone simply by the decision of an individual, even if he happened to reside in Number 10 Downing Street. Disraeli must have recognized the emptiness of many of his recommendations, but his own political career depended upon the illusion being maintained that a substantial gulf separated him from his rival. Knowing the difficulty of his position, Disraeli required encouragement. In Sidonia, he created a character calculated to reassure himself. Sidonia, confident about the role of race, and the possibilities of the individual's making progress against what was commonly thought to be the spirit of the age, provided a reassurance with which Disraeli may have lulled himself. If he abandoned this belief, he would have to admit defeat.

In 1845, Disraeli tried again, in a second novel, *Sybil*, to explore the differences between himself and Peel. In this instance, he used the effects of the Industrial Revolution on English society as his principal theme. Believing that British life had been fundamentally transformed by economic change, Disraeli hoped to develop a policy which would take account of that change and provide a program for the Tory Party. He had no fear of large-scale manufacturing, and no interest in seeing England return to its agrarian past, or to its romantic image of what that past had been. If the machine was to be accepted, however, it could not be admitted as a master. It had already produced too great a cleavage between social groups; the nation had been split asunder by its force. Disraeli argued that the Tory Party's principal responsibility was to heal that breach, and bring to an end the suffering which it had caused.

No injustice is done to *Sybil* if it is described as a fairy tale set in the context of nineteenth-century England. The story, simply told, concerns the love of Egremont, younger brother of an English lord, for Sybil, daughter of an English Chartist. Egremont, afraid that the "daughter of the People" will spurn him if she knows his identity, assumes a false name and position before her. When his true identity is revealed, a breach follows, which is healed only when Sybil comes to understand that Egremont's sympathies do lie with the people. Egremont proves this by his speeches in Parliament, and even more, by his efforts to save Sybil's father from arrest as a Chartist agitator. The two are finally united when Sybil, chancing to be in the house of an English lord which comes under attack by a mob, is rescued from her assailants by Egremont. Among the consequences of this fateful incident, one is especially important: papers are discovered in the castle which prove that Sybil is the descendant of its first proprietors, and is, by law, its rightful owner. The "daughter of the People" is proved to be noble after all.

Any attempt to judge *Sybil* by standards of reasonableness is doomed to certain failure. The bizarre elements in the story were intentional; Disraeli never imagined that anyone would require him to defend the tale by arguing for its plausibility. That Sybil was entirely the creation of his imagination, and that no woman like her existed in fact, Disraeli knew. He also knew that in Victorian England class and religious barriers (Sybil was Catholic) were more formidable than his tale suggested. The improbability of the story in no way affected its truth, since the author, in this, as in all his novels, was asserting the reality of a truth which depended on the acceptance of mystery and chance in human affairs. Only a Romantic could believe in Disraeli's romances.

Sybil was written with a serious political purpose. Disraeli intended that the book should be read as a commentary on the England of his day. While the social question, created by the pauperization of large segments of the population as a result of the Industrial Revolution figured prominently in the novel, this was only one of his concerns. In his portrayal of individual characters, and in their relations with each other, Disraeli explored the thought and habits of the governing class, and criticized them mercilessly. He felt little enchantment with an aristocracy which lacked both spirit and conscience; even more than in *Coningsby*, he lashed out at its irresponsibility. The Marney family, to which Egremont belonged, showed all of the characteristic failings. The Marney claim to nobility was ancient, going back nearly three centuries, and originating in the seizure of religious houses in the reign of Henry VIII.

If the Marneys represented one sort of aristocratic family for whom Disraeli felt little respect, the de Mowbrays represented another. Disraeli gloried in the genealogy of this connection; it all started with one John Warren who, a few years before the American Revolution, served as a waiter in a club in St.

James's Street. Engaged as a valet to a man leaving for Madras, he emerged as private secretary before the six-month voyage to India was over. Some years later, Disraeli explained, "A Mr. Warren, of whom no one had ever heard except that he was a Nabob, had recently returned from India, and purchased a large estate in the North of England, was returned to Parliament one of the representatives of a close borough which he had also purchased; a quiet, gentlemanlike, middle-aged man, with no decided political opinions; and, as parties were then getting equal, of course much courted." A vote for the Ministry in a crucial debate led to Warren being made a baronet; marriage with the daughter of an Irish Earl further improved his social standing. The secret of his origins was soon discovered, but Pitt, who cared nothing about such matters, valued Warren's support, and made him an Irish baron. He now figured as Lord Fitz-Warene; the Norman origin of the family had been discovered. Men laughed, but the new baron was unmoved; as Disraeli explained, he "cared nothing for ridicule, for he was working for posterity." Before his death, he achieved the ultimate object of his ambition; his Irish barony was converted into an English peerage. His son and heir, "most fully, entirely, and absolutely believed in his pedigree; his coat of arms was emblazoned on every window, embroidered on every chair, carved in every corner." Married to the daughter of a ducal house, his sole ambition was to gain an earldom. This, he finally achieved when Canning was made Prime Minister; he emerged as Earl de Mowbray of Mowbray Castle.

Disraeli's mockery of the pedigree and services of those who claimed noble birth indicated no hostility to men so happily circumstanced. It served only to remind his readers of what had already been made abundantly clear in *Coningsby*, that the English nobility was *parvenu*, and that its aggressions could be justified only if it chose to act in a way that commanded respect. Otherwise, there was nothing to be said for such an element in society.

The education of Egremont, Disraeli entrusted to a stranger,

Sybil's father, who is represented as an individual of humble birth. The first encounter between Walter Gerard and Egremont occurs in the ruins of Marney abbey. The conversation begins with the older man speaking of the poor monks who had been evicted from the abbey. Egremont suggests that "they would hardly have forfeited their resting-place had they deserved to retain it." The stranger replies: "They were rich. I thought it was poverty that was a crime." "But they had committed other crimes," Egremont answers. "It may be so; we are very frail," the man answers, but "their history has been written by their enemies; they were condemned without a hearing; the people rose oftentimes in their behalf; and their property was divided among those on whose reports it was forfeited." "At any rate, it was a forfeiture which gave life to the community," Egremont answers; "the lands are held by active men and not by drones." To this the stranger answers: "A drone is one who does not labour, whether he wear a cowl or a coronet, 'tis the same to me." Pursuing this argument, the stranger suggests that the monks were easy landlords, and that they provided a permanent security to those who were their tenants. Egremont says: "You plead their cause with feeling." "It is my own," the stranger answers; "they were the sons of the people, like myself."

A new note is introduced into the conversation when a second stranger appears; it is obvious that he has overheard the talk of the other two. He suggests that the destruction of the monasteries meant the disappearance of the only community that England ever knew. As he explains, "There is no community in England; there is aggregation, but aggregation under circumstances which make it rather a disassociating than a uniting principle." As between association and aggregation, there is no question of which is to be preferred. The second stranger, a younger man than the first, says: "It is a community of purpose that constitutes society; without that, men may be drawn into contiguity, but they still continue virtually isolated." "Christianity," he says, "teaches us to love our neighbour as ourself; modern society acknowledges no neighbour." Struggling to meet the criticism implicit in all these remarks, Egremont says, "but say what you like, our Queen reigns over the greatest nation that ever existed." "Which nation," the younger stranger asks, "for she reigns over two." The look of bewilderment on Egremont's face brings a further explanation. "Yes, two nations; between whom there is no intercourse and no sympathy; who are as ignorant of each other's habits, thoughts, and feelings, as if they were dwellers in different zones, or inhabitants of different planets; who are formed by a different breeding, are fed by a different food, are ordered by different manners, and are not governed by the same laws." Egremont says hesitatingly: "You speak of —." "The Rich and the Poor," is the answer. At this moment, the conversation is interrupted by a beautiful voice singing the evening hymn to the Virgin. Egremont perceives a young woman dressed in the garments of a Religious, but obviously not a nun. Sybil makes her appearance in the novel.

The education of Egremont is thus opened. In the months that follow, when Egremont comes to know the strangers, Walter Gerard, his daughter Sybil, and Stephen Morley, the education is continued. The themes are almost always the same. Sybil, parroting her father, tells Egremont that "there is more serfdom in England now than at any time since the Conquest." She speaks of having two great ideas, one gained from living in a Convent, the other acquired from living in a Cottage. The first has taught her the degradation of her faith, the second the degradation of her race. Her thoughts, she explains to Egremont, are entirely concentrated on the Church and the People. When Egremont suggests that there may be other ideas equally entitled to her thought, she answers: "I feel these are enough."

Out of these encounters, Egremont emerges with something of a social philosophy, at least one which permits him to voice the demands of the working class in Parliament. He speaks of the necessity of protecting the rights of labor — these being no less vital than property rights. Egremont argues "that the social happiness of the millions should be the first object of a statesman, and that, if this [is] not achieved, thrones and dominions, the pomp and power of courts and empires, [are] alike worthless." Moved by a genuinely humanitarian impulse, Egremont wishes to improve the condition of the laboring people of Britain. Disraeli's problem, however, was to discover some formula by which this might be achieved. He knew that Chartism provided no answer, and he demolished its arguments easily. However, the construction of a positive and precise alternative eluded the author as much as it eluded his age. Disraeli fell back on the empty rhetoric which had characterized so much of his complaint in *Coningsby*. Interrupting his narrative, he embarked on a renewed criticism of Peel, but always in terms which had almost no relevance to specific problems as they existed at that moment. Condemning Peel for his failure to take office in 1839, Disraeli claimed that this permitted the Whigs, who had always been the enemies of monarchy, to retain power through the support of the Crown. This, he implied, would never have happened if the Tory Party had remained faithful to its traditions.

Disraeli's chief complaint was against a political situation in which the lines between political parties were blurred, and in which the Tories had ceased to identify themselves with principles manifestly different from those which the Whigs expressed. His views on the Whigs had undergone no major transformation since his youth. In *Sybil*, as in his other works, he wrote of them as the oligarchs; they were the defenders of the "Venetian Constitution," which they had created. In *Sybil*, he paid one of his rare tributes to Burke, saying that he accomplished for the Whigs what Bolingbroke in an earlier day had done for the Tories. In Disraeli's words, "he restored the moral existence of the party. He taught them to recur to the ancient principles of their connection, and suffused those principles with all the delusive splendour of his imagination. He raised the tone of their public discourse; he breathed a high spirit into their public acts." But, what was the final result of all this effort? According to Disraeli, "when the hour arrived for the triumph which he had prepared, he was not even admitted into the Cabinet, virtually presided over by his graceless pupil." Disraeli viewed this as an intolerable humiliation, but gloried in the fact that Burke had had his revenge. "Hard necessity made Mr. Burke submit to the yoke, but the humiliation could never be forgotten. Nemesis favours genius; the inevitable hour at length arrived. A voice like the Apocalypse sounded over England, and even echoed in all the courts of Europe. Burke poured forth the vials of his hoarded vengeance into the agitated heart of Christendom; he stimulated the panic of a world by the wild pictures of his inspired imagination; he dashed to the ground the rival who had robbed him of his hard-earned greatness; rent in twain the proud oligarchy that had dared to use and insult him; and, followed with servility by the haughtiest and the most timid of its members, amid the frantic exultation of his country, he placed his heel upon the neck of the ancient serpent." One cannot avoid the impression that Disraeli, in writing about Burke, was thinking of himself. There is no reason to believe that Burke felt the humiliation which Disraeli suggested, or that he viewed his attacks on his former Whig colleagues as an act of revenge.

This sympathy for Burke, as expressed in *Sybil*, was the sympathy of one injured man for another who had been ill-treated by his party. He expressed little sympathy for Burke's ideas. When Disraeli searched for political principles, it was never to the Whig Party or to its adherents that he looked. In the Tory Party, and particularly in Bolingbroke and Shelburne, he found his heroes. He regarded Shelburne as Bolingbroke's chief disciple; he explained: "Lord Shelburne adopted from the first the Bolingbroke system; a real royalty, in lieu of the chief magistracy; a permanent alliance with France, instead of the whig scheme of viewing in that power the natural enemy of England; and, above all, a plan of commercial freedom, the germ of which may be found in the long-maligned negotiations of Utrecht, but which, in the instance of Lord Shelburne, were soon in time matured by all the economical science of Europe, in which he was a proficient." Shelburne, who was regarded in his own time with suspicion by many, was "reserved, deep, adroit, brave, firm, and even profound." George III, according to Disraeli, selected

Shelburne as his champion against the Venetian party. Later, when Shelburne was replaced by Pitt and removed from the Cabinet, a mistake was made. His "unrivalled knowledge and dexterity" ought to have been made use of. In the first years of Pitt's Prime Ministership, Shelburne's influence was still felt. In the later years, less glorious ones in Disraeli's view, that influence was no longer exerted. Disraeli's glorification of Shelburne affords additional evidence of the extent to which he identified himself with talented men who suffered political exclusion at the hands of mediocrity. In Shelburne's lifetime, no one denied his knowledge or intelligence; his reliability, on the other hand, was frequently questioned; this fact, Disraeli never mentioned. Disraeli, in writing about Burke or Shelburne, wrote about himself; he could not view their careers except in the light shed by the problems of his own.

While Disraeli intended that *Sybil* should be read as an indictment of the effects of the Industrial Revolution on the people of England, his efforts to achieve this fell short of success. Disraeli tended always to exaggerate; in treating the rich, he made their homes more magnificent than any human habitation can be, their women eternally beautiful, and their men, when they were his heroes, almost unhuman in their excellence. In his treatment of the poor, he went to the opposite extreme. Charles Dickens' descriptions pale by comparison with those constructed by Disraeli in *Sybil*. In describing an impoverished household, he spared no detail; the furniture was nonexistent, the room cold and dank, the wife ailing, the small children starving, the father unemployed, and the older daughter, who might have helped, a runaway stray. Characteristically, only the happy arrival of Sybil brought relief to all this suffering. Disraeli could not conceive a larger and more permanent solution for his problem.

The picture of Wodgate, a squalid and depraved community without park or church, filled with impoverished workers inhabiting filthy lodgings, showed an industrial center which was sufficiently common in the 1840's to be almost typical. Disraeli, not satisfied simply to describe the foul place, introduced other macabre elements to heighten the drama. The "Bishop of Wodgate," a master locksmith, subsequently revealed to be the brother of a famous antiquary, Disraeli depicted as a tyrannical monster who surveyed his apprentices with an eye which made a crime of any inattention to work. He would beat an apprentice as readily as speak to him. "Bishop" Hatton is no worse than Master Joseph Diggs, proprietor with his father of a company store in which the miners of a colliery near Wodgate are compelled to buy their provisions. Receiving goods instead of wages, these people are mauled, cheated, insulted, and beaten. The events of a typical shopping day include the near-death of one small boy and the maiming of an infant. The scene is grim; Master Joseph Diggs is shouting: "Order there, order; you cussed women, order, or I'll be among you. And if I just do jump over this here counter, won't I let fly right and left! Speak out, you idiot! do you think I can hear your muttering in this Babel? Cuss them; I'll keep them quiet." Diggs leans over the counter and hits people with a yardstick to the right and left of him. Suddenly a woman is heard to cry: "Oh! You little monster! You have put out my babby's eye." "Whose baby's hurt," Diggs asks. "Mine, sir, Mary Church" is the answer. "Oh! Mary Church, is it!" Diggs says; "then I'll put Mary Church down for half a pound of best arrowroot; that's the finest thing in the world for babbies, and will cure you of bringing your cussed monkeys here, as if you all thought our shop was a hinfant school." Disraeli would have been more convincing if he had curbed his tendency to exaggerate.

Disraeli, in 1845, was fighting for his political life. Denied a position commensurate with his talents, aware that he would not enjoy such a place until Peel was pushed from the leadership of the Tory Party, he felt compelled to formulate some idea or principle which would distinguish him and his friends from the Tapers, Tadpoles, de Mowbrays, and Marneys of the political world. He imagined that he found this idea in the notion that a conspiracy existed against the nation. He wrote: "The written history of our country for the last ten reigns has been a mere phantasma; giving to the origin and consequences of public transactions a character and colour in every respect dissimilar to their natural form and hue. In this mighty mystery all thoughts and things have assumed an aspect and title contrary to their real quality and style; Oligarchy has been called Liberty; an exclusive Priesthood has been christened a National Church; Sovereignty has been the title of something that has had no dominion; while absolute power has been wielded by those who profess themselves the servants of the People. In the selfish strife of factions, two great existences have been blotted out of the history of England, the Monarch and the Multitude; as the power of the Crown has diminished, the privileges of the People have disappeared; till at length the sceptre has become a pageant, and its subject has degenerated into a serf." Disraeli's aim, in short, was to raise the Crown and the People. How he proposed to do this, he never explained. Obviously, the first step was the revival of the Tory Party. The times were too serious for small men to hold great posts. Whether England boasted a sufficient number of "great men" to achieve the desired ends, Disraeli never stopped to inquire. It was enough for him to know that he and his friends were such men.

Sybil would almost certainly never have been written if Peel had recognized Disraeli's services in 1841. Smarting under wounds magnified by his own imagination, Disraeli responded as he imagined Burke had done in a similar situation a half century earlier. He sought his revenge on those who had misused him. The Tory Party, he insisted, was becoming, under Peel, an organization lacking in both principles and ideals. Both had once existed, and Disraeli took upon himself the task of reeducating the Party in its historic mission. While he showed the greatest skill in documenting the evils of his day, he showed less talent in discovering possible remedies. Disraeli used rhetoric and a very original historic interpretation to conceal the absence of a valid social policy. Philanthropy seemed the solution to problems which resisted other treatment.

Sybil emerged at a moment when Disraeli's reputation in the

House of Commons was growing. His persistent attacks on Peel, and the latter's discomfiture before these criticisms, had begun to have their effect. While the absence of a large issue hampered Disraeli in his effort, the spectacle delighted an assembly which always admired exhibitions of verbal prowess. The "small boy" Disraeli appeared to be flooring the "big boy" Peel; even if nothing came of these encounters, they provided a diversion at a time when Chartist agitation made politics seem somber and serious. And then, suddenly, in the autumn of 1845, an event occurred which transformed the whole situation. The failure of the potato crop made an Irish famine an imminent possibility. Peel and his Cabinet began to consider a temporary abandonment of the Corn Laws, and the introduction of new legislation to modify permanently the duties on the importation of wheat. This struck at one of the fundamental dogmas of the Tory Party: defense of the agricultural interest had long figured as its principal economic doctrine. Peel, unable to secure the consent of his full Cabinet to these changes, submitted his resignation. In the circumstances, he saw no other solution to the problem. The Queen asked Russell, the Whig Party leader, to form a Government, but divisions in that Party compelled him to abandon the attempt. Peel was recalled, and a new Tory Government formed. Stanley, who had been recalcitrant in the earlier Cabinet, was replaced by Gladstone. Early in 1846, Peel presented a bill in Parliament to abolish the Corn Laws.

It is difficult to conceive of any situation that would have played more completely into Disraeli's hands. The evidence of treachery, of which Disraeli had spoken in two novels and numerous speeches, was now apparent for all to see. How could anyone have so mistaken Peel's character? Had Disraeli not warned that Peel was a man without respect for the past, who had no feeling for Tory tradition, and bent before every adverse wind? Could any better proof be given of his disloyalty than his willingness to sacrifice the interest of the group on which the Tory Party relied, and on which the nation's prosperity depended? Disraeli, joining forces with Lord George Bentinck, a younger son of the Duke of Portland, prepared to organize the Tory squires against Peel's policy. Bentinck, given his social position, was leader of the opposition; Disraeli, delighted at being a member of the company, was prepared to act as his principal lieutenant. In the months that followed, the two, supported by others, maintained a steady fire on the Government. Their success was sufficient to disassociate from Peel a substantial number of Tory members, thereby creating the nucleus of a new Tory Party. Peel won his Corn Law repeal, but on the very night of his victory in the House of Lords, a combination of Protectionist Tories and Whigs defeated him in the Commons on an Irish Coercion Bill. Peel surrendered his seals of office; a Whig ministry under Russell was formed. The rebellious Tories took their revenge. The Prime Minister had his way on protection, only to be brought down by those who argued that he had abandoned their interest, which was bad enough, but also, a pledge of his own, which was worse. Disraeli, at that moment, was riding high. Peel's neglect of him had been amply repaid. A new Tory Party was in the making; Lord George Bentinck would be its leader, and he would be Bentinck's chief aide. The protectionists, though few in number, represented Tory tradition, and sentiment for their cause would certainly grow. The Tory Party required careful tending, and Disraeli prepared to give both time and effort to a cause from which his own future was not divorced. At last, he belonged to an instrument which might serve to secure for him the position and power he sought.

His new responsibilities placed severe limits on the time available for writing; in any case, the principal reason for writing had passed. *Tancred or the New Crusade*, which appeared in 1847, was a work started before the corn law crisis broke. Its first chapters seem only incidentally connected with what follows, suggesting the gulf between a concern still dominated by the accidents of British politics and one liberated from those problems. Tancred, the hero, when in England, speaks of faith as Coningsby or Egremont might have done. He talks of a monarch without power, an aristocracy without prestige, and a people without rights. Suddenly, there is a break with this whole idiom, and Tancred, seeking wisdom in the East, emerges as a critic of the decadent European world he has abandoned. The plot makes almost no sense; the hymn to "the great house of Israel," rendered in a confused score, suggests that "unhappy Europe" may yet be saved by Asia. Disraeli never stopped to explain what that salvation would be or how it might be achieved. It is apparent that Europe, "amid its false excitement; its bustling invention, and its endless toil," is hopelessly confused, and that it has sought to resolve its confusion by calling its "tumult" progress.

While in *Sybil*, Disraeli had suggested that England's malady was too grave to be cured by political devices only, he had never suggested that the whole of Europe was sick and cried for a remedy. In *Tancred*, he showed such confusion about the ailment, and also, about the cure, that his meaning was almost entirely buried in his prose. The voice on Mount Sinai seemed to be arguing against the principles of the French Revolution, but also, against the democratic aspirations which it had engendered. How far back in history would Europe need to go to recover its faith? Disraeli began *Tancred* when Peel was still Prime Minister; he completed it when Peel was no longer a threat to his own future. By these incidents, Disraeli achieved a new freedom; it was no longer necessary for him to write about British politics. He addressed himself to other more urgent concerns. Whether his ideas about Europe were as confused as *Tancred* made them seem, it is impossible to say. Disraeli did not know what to do with his hero once he had launched him on his travels. Inevitably, the work became increasingly autobiographical. Disraeli thought again about the conditions making for success. The idea of race, always appealing, seemed again to command his allegiance. Disraeli was not of the Anglo-Saxon race which he aspired to govern, but his beliefs about the nature of the Hebrew genius encouraged him in his belief that he might yet achieve that objective. He reflected on Europe's condition, found it discouraging, but offered no remedy; the "Asian mystery," which was to free Europe of its bondage to material and insubstantial things, remained a mystery. In the end, Disraeli had no message for Europe, just as he had no message for Great Britain. He seemed to be speaking to himself, reminding himself that as a Jew his powers were unusual, and his prospects excellent.

By harping on the Jewish theme, Disraeli risked giving offense to many who believed neither in the virtue of that race nor in its distinctive contributions to the welfare of mankind. Lord George Bentinck actually came to grief with the Tory Party principally because of his support of the Jew Bill, which would have relieved Jews of remaining civil disabilities. Bentinck, in resigning as Leader of the Tory Party in the House of Commons in late 1847, gave ill-health as his reason, but everyone understood that criticism of his stand on the Jew Bill had figured in his decision to step down.

The problem of a successor immediately engaged the attention of the Party. While Disraeli's claims were obvious, and his contributions admitted and recognized, there was a genuine reluctance to elevate him to the first place in the Commons. Disraeli, for all that he had done in their behalf, continued to be distrusted by the Tory squires. He was too alien; too unlike them; too intellectual. In one of his many assaults on Peel, he formulated what he thought to be the qualities of a statesman; he said: ". . . my conception of a great statesman is of one who represents a great idea — an idea which may lead him to power; an idea with which he may identify himself; an idea which he may develop; an idea which he may and can impress on the mind and conscience of a nation." Disraeli contrasted such a man with one "who never originates an idea — a watcher of the atmosphere, a man who, as he says, takes his observations, and when he finds the wind in a certain quarter, trims to suit it." Peel, Disraeli said, belonged to the second group; he, Disraeli, obviously preferred to belong to the first. The Protectionist Tories were not persuaded that they wished to be led by a man of such opinions. Insofar as they understood his ideas, they distrusted them. Disraeli alarmed and unsettled them, for reasons they could rarely explain. The result was a decision not to appoint him as Leader. For a year the Tory Party lacked a Leader in the House of Commons; during the whole of the 1848 session makeshift arrangements prevailed. Finally, in February 1849, the Party had to admit that Disraeli was its principal force in the Commons, and that he could no longer be denied first place. The Party made him Leader because it had need of him.

It would be difficult to exaggerate the importance of this success. Starting with almost no advantages in 1832, when he emerged from a period of troubled isolation, Disraeli had managed to negotiate a course by which a lesser man would certainly have been defeated. His romantic impulse led him, in the beginning, to advocate the founding of a new political party, which would appeal to both Tories and Radicals, but the indifference of his electors persuaded him to abandon such grandiose schemes, and to concentrate on getting into Parliament as a Tory. Although this proved an uncommonly difficult task, it was finally accomplished in 1837. Disraeli, at that moment, must have realized that his trials were only beginning. Peel, in denying him an office in 1841, delivered a blow which could not be easily countered. To oppose the Prime Minister openly was hazardous; to accept the exclusion, and seek to make a record as a backbencher, might lead only to new frustrations. For a time, Disraeli sought to negotiate a path between all extremes, but events led him finally to open opposition. In Parliament, and in his novels, he sounded the attack. He took a calculated risk, which the accident of the Irish famine converted into a stroke of great good fortune. At the moment of Peel's apostasy, Disraeli emerged as the prophet who had foretold it. With the greatest number of Peel's friends removed from leading posts in the Tory Party, the path to Disraeli's advance lay open. In association with Bentinck he took hold of the Tory reins in the House of Commons. It was only a matter of time before the Whigs, who had come in on Peel's defeat, would themselves go; then, Disraeli's chance would come.

Benjamin Disraeli: The Romantic Egotist

As leader of the Tory Party in the House of Commons, Disraeli made a concerted effort to appease his followers. He could not convert himself into a Tory squire; physiognomy, physique, philosophy — all these defeated him. He could, however, moderate his ways and appear as the substantial middle-aged citizen whose deftness in debate gave courage to those behind him. Disraeli, always capable of great self-discipline, learned the necessity of mastering the data on which he spoke, even when they related to matters of no great interest to him. William Beresford, who was staying with him at Hughenden in September 1849, remarked on this quality in a letter to Stanley; Beresford wrote: "I am writing to you from Disraeli's. . . . He is living here very quietly, and working very hard. He is reading up all the Blue Books of the past Session, having divided them into classes, and separated them so that each group should comprehend different subjects. He attributes Peel's great power and effect in the House to having always had Blue Books by heart, and having thereby the appearance of a fund of general knowledge greater than he really possessed." Disraeli was no longer the backbencher, concerned only to get ahead. He had come into a prominent position, and needed to develop habits which would enable him to conduct the affairs of that office with dignity and effect. In order to maintain his self-confidence, he needed the confidence of others. If this required him to adopt a less flamboyant pose, or to become even more inscrutable in his ways, this was a small price to pay for a large prize.

In the House of Commons, he relied on wit and fact to defeat his opponents. He gave little attention to instructing either his fellow members or his constituents. The prophecy with which he had filled so many novels he now reserved for his correspondents. In December 1849, he wrote Lady Londonderry of his fears about the situation in England and on the Continent. He explained that, "tho' nobody talks of foreign affairs," there was reason for concern. "The fact is," he wrote, "the elements of government do not exist in the greater part of Europe — and we are destroying them pretty quickly in England. Russia alone developes herself, and will develope herself still more in the great struggle, which is perhaps nearer than we imagine. Once destroy the English aristocracy, and enthrone the commercial principle as omnipotent in this island, and there will be no repelling force which will prevent the Sclavonians conquering the whole of the South of Europe. I look upon France as quite exhausted; insolvent in purse and soul: no republic can restore it, for there is no plunder left to support a Republic — and plunder was the inspiration of the great movement of the last century." Such thoughts Disraeli reserved for his intimates; in parliamentary speeches he was no less eloquent, but considerably less frank.

Disraeli, after the publication of *Tancred*, abandoned fiction almost entirely; for two decades, he busied himself with other sorts of writing. Most of it was strictly political, prepared for particular debates in the House of Commons. In 1851, however, he found time to compose a biography of his late chief, Lord George Bentinck, who had died in 1848. His decision to produce this work needs to be interpreted as something other than a disciple's effort to honor a friend and patron. The biography was conventional in many respects, but where it ceased to be conventional, it became a vehicle for the elaboration of Disraeli's rather singular views on Jews. Recalling Bentinck's efforts to relieve British Jews of the last disabilities under which they suffered, Disraeli used the opening provided by this as a way of treating the question of Jewish persecution more generally. The notion that Jews were persecuted because they committed a crime in crucifying Jesus, Disraeli said was both historically and dogmatically unsound. The dispersal of the Jewish people preceded rather than followed Christ's advent, and could not therefore be regarded as a divine judgment on them. Moreover, many Jews remained in Palestine, adopted Christ's teaching, and went forth to convert the heathen. Without the Jews, Disraeli wrote, there would have been no preachers to communicate the tale of Christ's suffering and death. Some men, Disraeli wrote, argued as if the Scriptures enjoined a persecution of the Jews. This, he thought preposterous; brotherly love, and not persecution, was the message preached by Christ. Disraeli reminded his readers that in the crucifixion, both the victim and his persecutors were Jews, and that God had preordained these events. Forty years ago, he said, "the two most dishonoured races in Europe were the Attic and the Hebrew, and they were the two races that had done most for mankind." The Greek genius had dried up, but the Jewish one prevailed, as all who "yield themselves to the full spell of a Mozart[sic], a Meyerbeer, or a Mendelssohn" must know. Disraeli, in this biography, as much as in any of his volumes of fiction, expressed his unconventional views on the importance of race and racial character. There was never a question in his mind about the integral connection between race and artistic achievement. More important for his purpose, however, was a development of the notion already suggested in *Coningsby*, that the Jews were by nature a conservative people. Disraeli wrote enthusiastically about the "Semitic principle," which emphasized the spiritual element in man and repudiated all ideas about natural equality. While other races might be seduced by false doctrines, the Jews accepted with confidence a truth which was hallowed by tradition, which expressed their genius, set them aside from others of lesser insight, and in which they willingly placed their faith. Conscious that they were a superior race, they made no attempt to mingle with others. This, Disraeli wrote, was part of their greatness. "What would be the consequence on the great Anglo-Saxon republic," he asked, "were its citizens to secede from their sound principle of reserve, and mingle with their negro and coloured populations?" The result, he said, would be that "in the course of time they would become so deteriorated that their states would probably be reconquered and regained by the aborigines whom they have expelled, and who would then be their superiors." Disraeli saw in the Jewish love of wealth, and in the acquisitive instinct, further evidence of conservative leanings. As he explained: "Their bias is to religion, property, and natural aristocracy: and it should be the interest of statesmen that this bias of a great race should be encouraged, and their energies and creative powers enlisted in the cause of existing society."

Disraeli traced the disasters of modern states to their rebellion against the Semitic principle. France's rebellion at the end of the eighteenth century led to a time of great troubles. The United States, faithful to the Semitic principle, prospered, as did England. Disraeli went very far when he wrote: "Austria would long ago have dissolved but for the Semitic principle and if the north of Germany has never succeeded in attaining that imperial position which seemed its natural destiny, it is that the north of Germany has never at any time been thoroughly converted."

Disraeli's decision to make so aggressive a defense of the Jewish race in a work which would be read by many who were hostile to such an idea must be seen as a calculated move. He knew that if his progress in the Party was not to be impeded, it was absolutely essential that he assume the offensive. So long as it was possible to say that the Party chose Disraeli only because no other choice existed, Disraeli would be in the position of the unwanted but tolerated Leader. In the Bentinck biography, which was written for a Tory audience, Disraeli explained why the Jewish people were naturally conservative, and why, by implication, he, as a Jew, should be regarded not as an interloper but as the most natural person to lead the Tory Party. Disraeli offered no excuses for being a Jew; he imagined that none was required. England, he implied, ought to recognize its good fortune in having Jews; other countries, such as Spain, were not equally fortunate. Modesty prevented him from going one step further to suggest that the greatest part of England's good fortune was to have one particular Jew, himself, to turn to.

Disraeli, by the middle of the century, had realized at least a few of his youthful ambitions. While Number 10 Downing Street remained a distant objective, some progress had been registered even toward this goal. In any future Tory government, Disraeli knew that he would occupy a prominent place. His father's death in 1848 gave him additional income which he used to purchase a country house, Hughenden Manor, near High Wycombe. Disraeli, while never adopting the manners of the country gentleman, and never participating in the English passion for sport, settled into the country as an eccentric but affable property owner. In London, he pursued politics; in the country he found time to make his plans and meditate on the future.

In 1851, the Whig ministry fell; the Queen summoned Stanley, the Tory leader in the House of Lords, and commissioned him to form a government. After prolonged negotiations, Stanley concluded that he could not find among the members of his own Party a sufficient number to satisfy his judgment of what a ministry should be. The Peelites, in refusing to join the government, gave Stanley the excuse he required. Reluctantly, he informed the Queen that he could not accept her invitation. Victoria had no recourse but to recall Russell. Disraeli, shocked by his chief's timidity, knew the advantage of holding his tongue. While he had condemned Peel for a comparable act, he understood the danger of criticizing Stanley publicly. Disraeli's position in the Tory Party was still not one which permitted him that sort of freedom. As an outsider, admitted on sufferance, loyalty and acquiescence were expected of him. Disraeli performed as the rules required him to. In 1852, he had his reward. A second crisis led the Queen again to summon Stanley, now the Earl of Derby, and in this instance, he succeeded in forming a ministry. Disraeli was appointed Chancellor of the Exchequer; his address at last was Downing Street; he had moved one door away from the place which he most wished to inhabit.

Disraeli remained as Chancellor of the Exchequer for less than a year. The ministry was formed in late February; on July 1 Parliament was prorogued, and the following day dissolved. In the General Election that followed, the Tories failed to make the gains they had hoped for; they returned about 310 in a House of more than 650 members. The Whigs and Peelites, together with the Irish members, constituted a majority. When Disraeli offered his budget in December, it was easily defeated. His first term of office ended, he returned to his old seat on the Opposition side.

The 1850's were filled with political surprises; a few, at least, produced by the Crimean War into which the country drifted. The Whig-Peelite coalition showed itself remarkably inept in the prosecution of the war, and its support began to disintegrate. In early 1855, the ministry was defeated in the House of Commons, and submitted its resignation. The Queen asked Derby to form a new government. He gave his usual careful consideration to the offer, but finding the Peelites unwilling to support him, decided against attempting to form a ministry of Tories only. Disraeli, shocked by Derby's hesitation, complained privately to friends, but otherwise kept silent. The Queen summoned Palmerston, the aged parliamentarian who had served first in the reign of George III. Given his years, few expected that he would retain power for long. In this, Palmerston confounded all the prophets; except for one brief interlude, he served as the Queen's Prime Minister for almost a decade.

No one foresaw this situation; it destroyed every forecast about what the enfranchisement of the middle classes would mean. Palmerston, an old-fashioned Whig, proud of British arms, and determined to protect Britain's interest against any incursion, enjoyed a remarkable and almost persistent popularity. While his critics ridiculed his bombast, the electors showed considerably greater tolerance, thinking it a proof of British power. Hostile to all proposals for political or economic reform, uninterested in the extension of the franchise, and disinclined to make any fundamental social reforms, he governed during a period when England's prosperity reached new dimensions, and the "hungry forties" disappeared in memory. Laissez-faire principles seemed to triumph on every front. In the 1857 General Election, the Whigs won easily; Palmerston's party controlled 370 seats in the House of Commons. Such a majority generally sufficed for the whole of a Parliament's natural life. In this instance, however, a political accident destroyed it. The attempt on Napoleon III's life by Italian members of the Carbonari Society led to disclosures that the bombs were of English manufacture and that the plot had been laid in London. The excitement in Paris was intense; Palmerston, believing that some gesture should be made to calm the French, let it be known that changes would be made in the British laws affecting conspiracy. The British public, while initially sympathetic to Napoleon III, now believed that Palmerston was capitulating to French pressure. The situation was complicated by a dispatch from the French Foreign Minister, Walewski, which in its anger went beyond what diplomacy or politics dictated. The House of Commons, reacting to these various pressures, showed its displeasure by defeating the Government. Palmerston resigned immediately, Derby was called for, and, within the week, Disraeli was again installed in Number 11 Downing Street.

This second Derby administration survived for a year. Defeated on a bill to reform parliamentary representation, it went to the country confident that its strength in the Commons would be increased. In this, both Derby and Disraeli were disappointed; the General Election of 1859 saw the Whigs again victorious, and Palmerston resumed his place on the Government Front Bench. Disraeli, in opposition, maintained a steady fire on Palmerston, and, even more, on his Chancellor of the Exchequer, William Gladstone. While these efforts merited praise, Disraeli soon discovered that the Tory Party was growing restive. Excluded from office, except for two brief occasions, for almost fifteen years, it began to search for a scapegoat. Disraeli appeared as a legitimate target. In the beginning, the talk was limited to the smoking rooms of the Commons and the great country houses, but in 1860 the *Quarterly Review*, the principal Tory journal, published an article which took Disraeli to task for his ineffective leadership. He was described as a "favourite of misfortune" who showed "unrivalled powers of conducting his party into the ditch." The article was unsigned; its author, Lord Robert Cecil, would, in a later day, serve as Foreign Secretary in a Disraeli administration. In 1860, however, he represented the voice of the younger generation sounding the attack on its elders. Disraeli felt the wound deeply; he went so far as to contemplate resigning his position as Leader of the Party. To Sir William Miles, a leading Tory, he wrote: "So long as they [the Tories] were in distress, I have borne without a murmur the neglect, the desertion, the personal insults that I have experienced; so long even as these were confined to our own ranks, and not the scandal of the world, I would, for party sake, have been silent. But the Tories are no longer in distress — they have abundance of friends; and, with respect to the privacy of their feelings towards me, they chalk the walls in the market-place with my opprobrium. . . . I must resign a leadership which I unwillingly [*sic*] accepted, and to which it is my opinion that fourteen years of unqualified devotion have not reconciled the party." In the end, reason prevailed, the storm blew over, and Disraeli remained.

Had Disraeli chosen this moment to reflect on what he had accomplished since assuming the leadership of the Tory Party in the House of Commons in 1849, he would have been less than totally satisfied. In his struggle with Peel, whom he had invariably characterized as the defender of expediency, Disraeli had emphasized his own preference for principle. With Peel's defeat, however, the reason for dwelling on Tory principles seemed to disappear, or at least lose some of its relevance. In the 1850's, political circumstance precluded the possibility of making the party struggle appear as a contest between two approaches to political truth. The confusion of parties, symbolized by Tory-Peelite divisions and Whig-Radical dissensions, rendered politics more a contest of personalities than of clearly defined principles. In such a period, the skills of the energetic party manager and negotiator were called for; it was not a time for striking poses. The issues were lacking, and even the most ingenious mind could not invent them. Disraeli did what he could to stir the fires of political warfare, but in the absence of agricultural distress or industrial unrest, the opportunities for party agitation were severely limited.

Benjamin Disraeli: The Romantic Egotist

In December 1861, the Prince Consort died. Disraeli's relations with Victoria and Albert had grown increasingly cordial during the 1850's. As Leader of the House of Commons during the two brief Tory ministries, he had exhibited a particular, almost excessive concern to inform the Queen of everything that occurred in Parliament. These attentions did not go unnoticed, and Disraeli, at the time of Albert's death, enjoyed a high reputation at Court. The Queen was much moved by the eloquent tribute that he rendered her late husband in the House of Commons in February 1862. Reading Disraeli's words today, one is struck by the extent to which, in lauding the Prince, he dwelled on qualities which he imagined were his own; also, by the fact that he seemed no less a romantic in middle age than when he wrote *Coningsby* and *Sybil*. It was the voice of Young England that the House of Commons heard say: "Sir, it is sometimes deplored by those who admired and loved him that he was thwarted occasionally in his undertakings, and that he was not duly appreciated. But these are not circumstances for regret, but for congratulation. They prove the leading and original mind which has so long and so advantageously laboured for this country. Had he not encountered these obstacles, had he not been subject to this occasional distrust and misconception, it would only have shown that he was a man of ordinary mould and temper. Those who improve must change, those who change must necessarily disturb and alarm men's prejudices. What he had to encounter was only a demonstration that he was a man superior to his age, and therefore admirably suited for the work of progress." The English-born alien said of the German-born Prince that he had grasped the deficiency of English national character, which was a failure to appreciate the importance of culture. Albert's greatness, Disraeli said, was not only to "detect a want," but to "resolve to supply it." Disraeli, even in the most solemn moments, could never quite free himself of a tendency to view men and events in a light cast by the limits of his own experience.

Palmerston, in his last years as Prime Minister, seemed to live a charmed existence. Though crises befell the ministry in the usual number, and evidences of inadequacy multiplied, public opinion remained remarkably faithful. Nothing that the Tories could say or do seemed to make an impression on the nation. Only in 1866, some six months after Palmerston's death, did Russell's government fall as a result of dissension within its ranks on the question of parliamentary reform. Derby, though lacking a majority in the House of Commons, formed a Tory ministry, and Disraeli returned to his old place as Chancellor of the Exchequer.

For almost two decades, Parliament had been besieged with requests for electoral reform. As early as 1852, Disraeli expressed himself as opposed to parliamentary reform. In a speech which he was to vary but repeat many times, he emphasized the Tory Party's receptiveness to reform, but insisted that this could not be thought synonomous with approval of an extension of the franchise to persons without property. The Tory Party, he insisted, would welcome a measure which gave the vote to "deserving artisans" who understood the importance of maintaining the nation's institutions. As late as May 1865, Disraeli was speaking in the same idiom. He refused to accept any proposal which would "re-distribute political power in the country" or sanction any "step that has a tendency to democracy." A concern for consistency, if not for principle, might have led a man with this record to move slowly, fearing lest a precipitous step be judged a betrayal.

In 1867, however, Disraeli showed that he had no intention of being imprisoned by his own past utterances. The thing which he had condemned Peel for doing two decades earlier he proceeded to do himself. Pressed by a growing public sentiment for reform, and a parliamentary situation which suggested that the Tory Party might gain from sponsoring a large and comprehensive measure, Disraeli took the plunge. He began by introducing innocuous resolutions detailing the need for reform, all the time working to compose differences within the Cabinet so that a major reform bill might be offered. On the very day that he intended to lay such a measure before the House of Commons, three ministers — Cranborne, Carnarvon, and Peel — indicated that the presentation of such a bill would cause them to resign. In a last-minute effort to maintain unity in the Cabinet, Disraeli substituted a more moderate measure. Its reception in Parliament, however, convinced him that the consequences of three ministerial resignations were less grave than those which would follow any attempt to defend the bill in its various stages. Disraeli persuaded Derby that a more comprehensive measure was needed. He won the Prime Minister's consent, and, on March 2, the three ministers resigned; sixteen days later a new bill was offered.

Earlier in the year, Disraeli published *Speeches on Parliamentary Reform* to show that he had always supported such a measure, and that this policy was entirely consistent with Tory principles. While such an interpretation of his speeches could not be declared absolutely inadmissible, a skeptic might be forgiven for noting the caveats and reservations that Disraeli generally employed when speaking of an extension of the suffrage. Actually, until 1867, no one in Parliament thought of Disraeli as a parliamentary reformer, in spite of the fact that the Conservative ministry of 1858 had introduced a moderate reform measure. It was only in 1867 that Disraeli emerged as a major proponent of reform. For those in the Tory Party who regarded the prospect of admitting workers to the franchise with apprehension and distaste, Disraeli's act assumed the character of apostasy. In 1867, however, these die-hards were few in number and constituted no threat to Disraeli's position; they had neither the fervor nor the ambition of those other "young men" who had brought Peel down for a comparable submission to popular pressure.

If the country was surprised by the extent of the Tory Party's willingness to contemplate and sponsor parliamentary reform, it was dumbfounded by what Disraeli proceeded to do as the bill passed through its various parliamentary stages. One radical amendment after the other, pressed by members of the Opposition, was permitted to pass, until the bill assumed a shape totally different from what it had in the beginning. Disraeli made a calculated and hazardous gamble; believing that the Tory Party would receive credit for the legislation, and that it represented no ultimate threat to the Party's future electoral success — in fact, that it might be the condition of a new sort of success — he determined that the Opposition should not be permitted to steal a march on him. The days of Palmerston were over; in the new political age, the Tory Party would need to appear as the national party, standing above class and private interests. Disraeli refurbished his old ideas to serve a new purpose; the weapons which he had used to such little effect with Melbourne he prepared to use against the "new" Whigs. While no person could claim credit for the Reform Act of 1867, it was Disraeli's work as much as any one else's. In negotiating the bill through the Commons, and in persuading Tory backbenchers to accept the many amendments, Disraeli showed his immense parliamentary abilities. In bowing to circumstance, which an unfriendly critic might have called expediency, he revealed himself as a superb political conjurer. He knew how to use "principle" and pretend to consistency when the situation required him to. The workingman gained the vote, and Disraeli recalled that he had always spoken of the natural alliance between squire and worker. The idea of Tory Democracy, first developed in the 1830's, took on a new meaning; it was no longer a personal philosophy; it had been adopted by the Party for whom it had been invented.

Early in 1868, Derby's health, which had long given the Tories concern, took a turn for the worse. Two decades previously, the Party had squabbled for a year before it agreed to have Disraeli as Leader of the Party in the Commons; in 1868, not a voice was raised against his elevation to the Prime Ministership. Derby wished it, and the Queen, who had come to know Disraeli through the detailed reports he rendered on House of Commons debates, accepted the choice with pleasure. Finally, after three decades of parliamentary struggle, and after several major defeats, Disraeli achieved the object of his ambition — he was the Queen's first minister.

Disraeli held the office for only a brief time. The returns of the General Election of 1868, in which he had expected the workers to express their gratitude to the Party which had enfranchized them, showed that he had misjudged the popular mood. The Liberals emerged with a substantial majority. Realizing that he would be defeated as soon as the new Parliament assembled, Disraeli tendered his resignation to the Queen. Reluctantly she accepted it and summoned Gladstone to take his place. As he reflected on these months, Disraeli must have felt a keen satisfaction. He had achieved the object of his ambition and won the confidence and admiration of his sovereign. In taking leave of her, he asked not for an honor for himself, but for his aged wife, who had supported him through so many of his troubles. Disraeli left office knowing that he had realized his own ambitions and those of the woman who would subsequently be known as Lady Beaconsfield.

Another man of Disraeli's age and infirmities might have thought the moment had arrived to lay aside his political burdens. Disraeli did not even consider that possibility. He remained as active as ever at Westminster, and began, very secretly, to make plans for a new novel. Former prime ministers were not in the habit of writing novels on their retirement from office, but, then, they rarely began life as novelists. Disraeli had no need for money, and fame was no longer a problem. He was pulled to his novel, *Lothair*, by the need of finding a vehicle for expressing thoughts which could not be voiced in Parliament. Political life, with all of its opportunities for talk, restrained the individual. Disraeli felt that he had something important to say, and knew no other way to say it.

Lothair, published in 1870, is the tale of a youth, an orphan, an only child, who on attaining his majority inherits enormous wealth. The Catholic Church is determined to achieve his conversion, and an intricate plot is laid to effect that end. Though captivated by the Church and its ritual, Lothair turns for instruction to a mysterious older woman who is finally revealed as a leader in the movement for Italian independence. The Church persists in its efforts, but the influence of the lady, Theodora, proves too great. Lothair embarks for Italy to fight on the Italian side against the Papal armies. Wounded, he is found and nursed back to health by Catholic friends. They concoct and circulate the story that Lothair suffered his wounds while fighting on the Papal side, and that his recovery is a sign of divine intervention. A great mass is arranged to celebrate the miraculous event. Realizing too late what his Catholic friends intend, namely, his conversion, Lothair flees from their grasp. After extensive travels he returns to England where he marries a conventional Disraelian heroine. The story, told in bare outline, seems as improbable as any of the efforts of Disraeli's youth. Its dialogue, however, shows a peculiar fascination with problems which had never previously concerned him.

It is in conversation with Cardinal Grandison, a Catholic convert, that Lothair says: "I wonder if England will ever again be a religious country." "I pray for that daily," the prelate answers. "I know not a grander or a nobler career for a young man of talents and position in this age, than to be the champion and asserter of Divine truth. It is not probable that there could be another conqueror in our time. The world is wearied of statesmen, whom democracy has degraded into politicians, and of orators who have become what they call debaters. I do not believe there could be another Dante, even another Milton. The world is devoted to physical science, because it believes these discoveries will increase its capacity of luxury and self-indulgence. But the pursuit of science leads only to the insoluble. When we arrive at that barren term, the Divine voice summons man, as it summoned Samuel; all the poetry and passion and sentiment of human nature are taking refuge in religion; and he whose deeds and words most nobly represent human thoughts, will be the man of this century." "But who could be equal to such a task?" Lothair asks. "Yourself," is the answer.

This is characteristic of the flattery and pressure to which Lothair is subjected. But Lothair chooses to fight not for the Catholic Church, but for its enemies. In doing so, he takes sides with the power which the Church recognizes as its principal foe. Disraeli constructed a scene in which a reflective Monsignore is made to say: "After all, it is the Church against the secret societies. They are the only two things in Europe, and will survive kings, emperors, or parliaments."

In the Jesuit Church of St. George of Cappadocia in Rome, on the day set for the celebration of Lothair's rescue from death, Disraeli wrote, there was a scene without equal; "the arcades were festooned with tapestry and hangings of crimson velvet and gold. Every part was crowded, and all the rank and fashion and power of Rome seemed to be there assembling. There had been once some intention on the part of the Holy Father to be present, but a slight indisposition had rendered that not desirable. His Holiness, however, had ordered a company of his halberdiers to attend . . . The Princess Tarpeia-Cinque Cento was there, and most of the Roman princes and princesses and dukes and duchesses. It seemed that the whole court of Rome was there; monsignori and prelates without end." As Lothair leaves the Church, he is surrounded by the faithful, on their knees, asking a blessing from him, and seeking to kiss the hem of his garment.

The Cardinal and his friends have overplayed their hand. When Lothair reads the official account of the celebration, it is hard for him to contain his anger. To the Cardinal he expresses the indignation and disgust that he feels. The Cardinal pretends to be surprised. "It is a tissue of falsehood and imposture," Lothair says, "and I will take care that my opinion is known of it." The Cardinal urges Lothair to "do nothing rashly." The journal, he explains, written by pious men, and an official organ of the Church, may be guilty of misstatement or exaggeration, but of nothing more. Lothair claims that the whole thing is founded on falsehood; "Good God!" he says; "Why! take the very first allegation, that I fell at Mentana fighting in the ranks of the Holy Father. Every one knows that I fell fighting against him, and that I was almost slain by one of his chassepots." The Cardinal answers: "I know there are two narratives of your relations with the battle of Mentana. The one accepted as authentic is that which appears in this journal; the other account, which can only be traced to yourself, bears no doubt a somewhat different character, but considering that it is the highest degree improbable, and that there is not a tittle of confirmatory or collateral evidence to extenuate its absolute unlikelihood, I hardly think you are justified in using, with reference to the statement in this article, the harsh expression which I am persuaded, on reflection, you will feel you have hastily used." Lothair answers: "I think that I am the best judge of what I did at Mentana." "Well, well," the Cardinal replies, "you naturally think so; but you must remember you have been very ill, my dear young friend, and labouring under much excitement. If I were you, and I speak as your friend, I hope your best one, I would not dwell too much on this fancy of yours about the battle of Mentana. I would myself always deal tenderly with a fixed idea; harsh attempts to terminate hallucinations are seldom successful. Nevertheless, in the case of a public event, a matter of fact, if a man finds that he is of one opinion and all orders of society of another, he should not be encouraged to dwell on a perverted view; he should be gradually weaned from it."

When Lothair refuses to be convinced by the Cardinal's argument, he hears the Cardinal say: ". . . this statement . . . officially communicated to the whole world, and which in its results will probably be not less important even than the celebration of the Centenary of St. Peter, is established by evidence so incontestable, by witnesses so numerous, so various, in all the circumstances and accidents of testimony so satisfactory, I may say so irresistible, that controversy on this head would be

[156]

a mere impertinence and waste of time." To all this Lothair says: "I am not convinced." The Cardinal answers "Hush! The freaks of your own mind about personal incidents, however lamentable, may be viewed with indulgence, at least for a time. But you cannot be permitted to doubt of the rest. You must be convinced, and on reflection you will be convinced. Remember, sir, where you are. You are in the centre of Christendom, where truth, and where alone truth resides. Divine authority has perused this paper and approved it. It is published for the joy and satisfaction of two hundred millions of Christians, and for the salvation of all those who unhappily for themselves are not yet converted to the faith. It records the most memorable event of this century. Our Blessed Lady has personally appeared to her votaries before during that period, but never at Rome. Wisely and well she has worked in villages and among the illiterate as at the beginning did her Divine Son. But the time is now ripe for terminating the infidelity of the world. In the eternal city, amid all its matchless learning and profound theology, in the sight of thousands, this great act has been accomplished, in a manner which can admit of no doubt, and which can lead to no controversy. Some of the most notorious atheists of Rome have already solicited to be admitted to the offices of the Church; the Secret Societies have received their death-blow; I look to the alienation of England as virtually over. I am panting to see you return to the home of your fathers and reconquer it for the Church in the name of the Lord God of Sabaoth. Never was a man in a greater position since Godfrey or Ignatius. The eyes of all Christendom are upon you as the most favoured of men, and you stand there like St. Thomas."

Lothair's answer to all this is: "Perhaps he was as bewildered as I am." The Cardinal replies: "Well, his bewilderment ended in his becoming an apostle, as yours will. I am glad we have had this conversation, and that we agree; I knew we should. But now I wish to speak to you on business, and very grave. The world assumes that being the favoured of Heaven you are naturally and necessarily a member of the Church. I, your late guardian, know that is not the case, and sometimes I blame myself that it is not so. But I have ever scrupulously refrained from attempting to control your convictions; and the result has justified me. Heaven has directed your life, and I have now to impart to you the most gratifying intelligence that can be communicated by man, and that the Holy Father will tomorrow himself receive you into the bosom of that Church of which he is the divine head. Christendom will then hail you as its champion and regenerator, and thus will be realised the divine dream with which you were inspired in our morning walk in the park at Vauxe."

Lothair, shaken by this revelation, and realizing that to accept its implications is to deny all that Theodora has meant to him, passes through the "darkest hour" of his life. He thinks of himself as a renegade, faithless to himself and to the woman he so much admired. There is only one solution to his problem; he must seek to escape from the place in which the Catholics hold him prisoner. This he manages to do. Like so many of Disraeli's novels, *Lothair* continues after its story is told. Lothair's travels are uneventful, and the conclusion, Lothair's marriage with Lady Corisande, is suggested as soon as the escape from Rome is effected.

Leslie Stephen, who wrote admiringly of Disraeli's abilities as a novelist, and deplored his abandoning literature for politics, thought *Lothair* one of the least successful of his novels. Stephen thought it comprehensible only if interpreted as "a practical joke on a large scale" or as "a prolonged burlesque upon Disraeli's own youthful performances." It is difficult to understand why Stephen should have selected this novel as the one which played "a practical joke on a large scale." It was no more improbable than *Tancred*, which Disraeli wrote more than two decades previously. As for it being a "prolonged burlesque" on his earlier works, the remarks which Disraeli wrote for the General Preface to his novels, published in 1870, contained no suggestion that those works deserved to be burlesqued. Except for *Vivian Grey*, he made no apology for any of them. Why Disraeli should have wished to burlesque them, Stephen never explained.

Given what we know of Disraeli, there is no reason to believe that *Lothair* was written for any except a serious purpose. The defects of the novel were those of which Disraeli was often guilty. The plot became too complex, and the story ended before the last page was written. The whole tale smacked of exaggeration. Wherever one turned — to the celebrations of Lothair's majority, the habits of the Cardinal and his entourage, the activities of Theodora — one found evidences of excess. However, even the best of Disraeli's novels — *Coningsby* and *Sybil* — suffered from these same defects. If Disraeli's serious purpose is admitted, then an attempt must be made to explain that purpose. Given the understanding which Disraeli habitually showed for Catholics, *Lothair* cannot be thought simply to express an anti-Catholic prejudice.

In *Lothair*, Disraeli introduced the notion of the Church and the secret societies as the two great forces of Europe, contending for mastery. A decade later, when he wrote *Endymion*, he was still preoccupied with this problem. Disraeli had no experience which would tell him how the secret societies operated or how they gained their adherents; he knew almost as little about the Catholic Church, but in this his imagination worked more easily. He presented in *Lothair* a new picture of Europe, one in which Parliaments and political parties did not figure. His own prophecy was that this would be the way Europe appeared in the future. The Church and/or the secret societies would exist when kings and parliaments were gone. It would be perhaps too much to suggest that Disraeli, in constructing the Cardinal's argument with Lothair, imagined that the same argument might occur in the secret societies. Disraeli seemed to be saying that Europe, in the future, would be governed by one of two absolutisms. The Church, confident of its truth, was arrayed against the secret societies, equally confident of theirs. Lothair chose, because of a woman, to fight for the secret societies. In the end, he returned to London to take his place in British political life. But the struggle which he had witnessed would go on.

Disraeli, in publishing *Lothair*, showed a continuing fidelity to the romantic ideas characteristic of his youth. He seemed unwilling to accept restraints imposed by his prominence. As Gladstone proceeded to make the record of his "great ministry," Disraeli maintained a steady attack on him. Men, watching the titans in their combat, imagined that the eighteenth century had known something of the same struggle. Disraeli's reputation soared, but his interest in politics declined. The death of Lady Beaconsfield in 1873 plunged him into a deep melancholy from which nothing seemed to rouse him. In his friendships he found some small solace, but it was not till the General Election of 1874 that the old enthusiasm was rekindled. The Tories made impressive gains, and a month after the returns were in, Disraeli was again residing in Downing Street, where he remained as Prime Minister for the next six years. His health, which was bad from the beginning, compelled him to take special precautions; there were periods when he was entirely incapable of work. His acceptance of a peerage in 1876 — which made him the Earl of Beaconsfield — proved what everyone suspected; he wished to remain in office but knew that he could do so only if he husbanded his strength. The Queen, always solicitous for the counselor who had taken the place once occupied by Melbourne, and later by Prince Albert, assisted him in every way that she could.

The 1874–1880 ministry was filled with accomplishment, in the foreign field even more than in the domestic. In 1872, in two important public speeches, one at Manchester, the other at the Crystal Palace, Disraeli had outlined the Conservative program which he now sought to incorporate in legislation. Toryism, rechristened Conservatism, was a political philosophy pledged to the preservation of the established order. The rights of the Crown, Lords, Commons, and Church needed to be defended. Conservatism, Disraeli claimed, aimed at protecting the Empire and "elevating" the condition of the people. Against Liberal principles, variously described as Jacobin, cosmopolitan, and Continental, he enunciated another set which he thought were national and Imperial, in short, English. Disraeli, in his "great ministry," came close to fulfilling at least the promise contained in these ideas. On the domestic front, in association with Cross and Northcote, he sponsored social reform legislation which suggested that the Tories were sincere in their claim of having the interest of the workers at heart. While the achievement was small, it indicated a direction which Tories never again entirely abandoned.

In the area of foreign policy, Disraeli made a more remarkable contribution. Even when one recalls that his ministry ended with wars, not always brilliantly conducted, against the Afghans and the Zulus, and that these ill-managed affairs contributed to his defeat in 1880, there is no denying the fact that on balance the success of the Disraeli ministry in foreign affairs was considerable. His greatest triumph, perhaps, was achieved at the Congress of Berlin in 1878. Russia, in imposing the Treaty of San Stefano on the Turks, effected changes in Europe and Asia which the British government thought dangerous in the extreme. Disraeli insisted that the treaty be submitted to a general congress of European powers. In the Cabinet he fought for military measures that would indicate to the Russians that no other solution was acceptable. In insisting that the reserves be called out and that troops be returned from India to take up stations in the eastern Mediterranean, Disraeli caused the Foreign Secretary, Derby, the son of his late chief, to resign. Undeterred by this, he chose Salisbury to replace him, and proceeded to take steps which conveyed a clear message to Russia — the alternatives were a general congress or war. Complicated secret negotiations followed, and, in the end, a formula introduced by Bismarck satisfied both parties: the powers agreed to meet in Berlin to discuss "the entire content of the Treaty of San Stefano."

The Congress opened in Berlin on June 13, 1878; Disraeli and Salisbury led the British delegation. This was a peace conference in which the principal victors were the British. In almost every instance, their demands were satisfied, and where they were not, there were other compensations to offset any sense of loss. By the Cyprus Convention, negotiated with the Sultan before Berlin and kept secret till the last days of the Congress, Britain was to occupy Cyprus if Russia kept Batum, Kars, or Ardahan; theoretically, this was intended to increase Turkey's protection against any future Russian attack. Although the other powers sought equivalent advantages, few gained anything quite so concrete. In reducing the size of Bulgaria, which was expected to become a Russian client state, and in gaining Cyprus, which provided a new link with its Eastern possessions, Britain achieved through diplomacy what it might have considered a reasonable prize in war. Russia, having beaten Turkey, emerged with a considerably smaller gain than she had anticipated. Whatever faults a later generation would find with the peace, they were scarcely apparent to the Britons who welcomed the Prime Minister home as a returning hero. The Queen, ever grateful to her devoted Disraeli, awarded him the Garter, and pressed him to accept a marquisate or a dukedom. A sense of proportion told Disraeli to refuse these additional gifts. He seemed satisfied; after all, had he not brought "peace with honour"? Only a few of his contemporaries would have thought to question that claim or suggest that it was an improper or excessive boast.

Disraeli's European fame was established by his actions at Berlin in 1878. Even earlier, in 1875, when he saw fit to press for British purchase of shares in the Suez Canal which would otherwise have gone to a syndicate of French capitalists, Disraeli showed the sort of daring which could never be thought common. The story of his borrowing some four million pounds from Baron Lionel de Rothschild, with the only security being his pledge that Parliament would honor the engagement, could not fail to capture the imagination of even his most severe critics. The Suez purchase had as its object, among others, the securing of the commercial and military route to India. Disraeli's interest in India, frequently demonstrated, was never more impressively shown than when he achieved by act of Parliament a change in the Queen's title which made her Empress of that vast realm. These achievements, when taken together, were not inconsiderable. When one reflects that Disraeli headed a ministry only twice — once briefly — and that his great period as Prime Minister came when he was over seventy and in failing health, the accomplishment takes on additional luster.

The swing of the political pendulum, however, in 1880, suggested that the nation was not entirely satisfied with Disraeli's leadership or with the Conservatism preached at the Crystal Palace. Finding his Party reduced in number, Disraeli resigned almost immediately. Even more than in 1868 he must have meditated on the fickleness of public taste and the injustice of its decisions; yet he accepted the situation without a protest. Again, in his beloved Hughenden, he turned to write a novel. Ill with asthma, bronchitis, and the gout, Disraeli knew that his life was ebbing away. Still he felt the necessity of producing some final testament. *Endymion,* which appeared late in 1880, only a few months before his death, repeated themes introduced in *Lothair.* The novel was clearly the work of an old man, who, if not cynical, was at least no longer prisoner of illusions of a certain sort.

The story of *Endymion* may be briefly told. Endymion and Myra, twin children of William Ferrars, are born into great wealth. Their parents live lavishly in London, and are the center of an admiring Tory society. A major political mistake and the habit of living beyond their economic means bring disaster to the family. Compelled to abandon London and their fashionable circle, the Ferrars move to a modest establishment in the country. The death of Endymion's mother and the suicide of his father leave the boy with only one support in the world, Myra. This, actually, is a very considerable support; Myra, strong and determined, has pledged her life to Endymion's success. Her marriage with a man who becomes Foreign Secretary, and, in time, Prime Minister, leads to various advancements for Endymion. At critical moments, other women intervene to help Endymion in his quest for high political office. Particularly important is the assistance of the Duchess of Montfort, who, after her husband's death, becomes Endymion's wife. In the end, Endymion is Prime Minister. Together with Myra, married a second time to a foreign monarch (her first husband, Lord Roehampton, having died), he recalls the dark hour when they first learned their father was ruined.

The weakness of the chief character, Endymion, who is simply negotiated into his success by the efforts of others, has often been commented on. Endymion, as insipid a hero as Disraeli ever created, served to emphasize a fact already apparent in *Lothair*, where the central figure boasted scarcely larger dimensions: Disraeli, in his old age, was moving away from a concern with the hero to a concern with the heroic. In *Endymion*, the heroic was represented by Myra, Florestan (who insisted on becoming a king, and whom Myra eventually married), and the Duchess of Montfort. In these persons, and in their efforts, Disraeli represented the heroic possibilities open to those prepared to aspire to great things.

Disraeli used *Endymion* as he had used his earlier novels — to convey ideas which he thought important. When it is realized that the work emerged after a lifetime of political activity, its comments take on some significance. Disraeli wrote the first part of the novel before the beginning of his last ministry. Interested in establishing the mood of the 1820's and early 1830's, he created a scene in which a foreign dignitary, Baron Sergius, in conversation with William Ferrars, attempts to predict the future. The Baron suggests that the concerns which seem paramount at that moment will soon be seen to be ephemeral. He says: "You are a young man and will live to see what I can only predict. The world is thinking of something else than civil and religious liberty. Those are phrases of the eighteenth century. The men who have won these 'three glorious days' at Paris, want neither civilisation nor religion. They will not be content till they have destroyed both. It is possible that they may be parried for a time; that the adroit wisdom of the house of Orleans, guided by Talleyrand, may give this movement the resemblance, and even the character, of a middle-class revolution. It is no such thing; the barricades were not erected by the middle class. I know these people; it is a fraternity, not a nation. Europe is honeycombed with their secret societies. They are spread all over Spain. Italy is entirely mined. I know more of the southern than the northern nations; but I have been assured by one who should know that the brotherhood are organised throughout Germany and even in Russia." The Baron adds: "[— The Whigs —] tell me that there is only one specific, and that a complete one — constitutional government; that with representative institutions, secret societies cannot co-exist. I may be wrong, but it seems to me that with these secret societies representative institutions rather will disappear." Disraeli had not abandoned the theme which he first developed in *Lothair*. He used Baron Sergius several times in the novel to express ideas which most faithfully reproduced his own.

Disraeli, having himself tasted all the joys that power could bring, constructed a scene between Endymion and Baron Sergius in which Endymion wonders whether success, which is so rare in life, will come to him. Endymion says to the baron: "I should like to have power." The baron's answer is an interesting one; he says: "The most powerful men are not public men. A public man is responsible, and a responsible man is a slave. It is private life that governs the world. You will find this out some day. The world talks much of powerful sovereigns and great ministers; and if being talked about made one powerful, they would be irresistible. But the fact is, the more you are talked about the less powerful you are." The baron adds: "As an Englishman, you will have difficulty in avoiding public life. But at any rate do not at present be discontented that you are unknown.

It is the first condition of real power. When you have succeeded in life according to your views, and I am inclined to believe that you will so succeed, you will, some day, sigh for real power, and denounce the time when you became a public man, and belonged to any one but yourself."

It is again the baron who expresses Disraeli's views on race. Having listened to a great deal of talk about the greatness of the Latin race, he says to Endymion: "You have heard to-day a great deal about the Latin race, their wondrous qualities, their peculiar destiny, their possible danger. It is a new idea, or rather a new phrase, that I observe is now getting into the political world, and is probably destined to produce consequences. No man will treat with indifference the principle of race. It is the key of history, and why history is often so confused is that it has been written by men who were ignorant of this principle and all the knowledge it involves. As one who may become a statesman and assist in governing mankind, it is necessary that you should not be insensible to it; whether you encounter its influence in communities or in individuals, its qualities must ever be taken into account." Having spoken about the importance of race generally, the baron turns next to consider the role of the Jews; he suggests that "there is no race gifted with so much tenacity and such skill in organisation." "As you advance in life," he says, "and get experience in affairs, the Jews will cross you everywhere. They have long been stealing into our secret diplomacy, which they have almost appropriated; in another quarter of a century they will claim their share of open government. . . . Language and religion do not make a race — there is only one thing which makes a race, and that is blood."

Endymion's success is finally achieved through the support of women like Lady Montfort, who informs him, quite casually: "I am now going to your sister to consult with her. All you have got to do is to make up your mind that you will be in the next parliament, and you will succeed; for everything in this world depends upon will." To this, Endymion replies: "I think everything in this world depends upon woman." "It is the same thing," Lady Montfort replies. When a hero is so manipulated by the women who admire or love him, the chances of his emerging as a person of consequence are not very great. Disraeli had no interest in creating an imposing image of Endymion. He gained his power, as he won his wife, by waiting. There was nothing splendid or remarkable in his victory, and Disraeli intended the matter to be seen in this way. Myra and Lady Montfort were heroic because they knew what they wanted and proceeded to achieve it, against all obstacles. Florestan, who won a kingdom, was also a hero. He understood men and knew how to use them.

Endymion was not the greatest of Disraeli's novels but it expressed certain things unmistakably. Four and a half decades of political experience had not converted Disraeli from the opinions which he held as a youth. He was a romantic in the end as in the beginning. He knew that reality was stranger than fiction, and that history did not tell the whole tale of man's activity on earth. He knew that, though the achievement of one's ambition never provided the satisfaction that the anticipation of success had promised, this gave no excuse for abandoning the effort to succeed. To live was to fight, though for illusory ends. The only man who knew how little it meant to be Prime Minister was one who had been Prime Minister. Disraeli saw the world as one of flux. Not only men, but states, empires, and kingdoms all perished. Disraeli never imagined that it was possible to fix permanently that which could only be transient. He refused to be surprised by anything. It was not strange to him that men of humble origins should end their lives leading empires. How could it be strange to one who was himself an outsider, had attained the highest political office, and was the favorite of a Queen whom he resembled almost not at all?

The unusual character of Disraeli's career emerges from even the most casual narration of its principal events. The success of such a rank outsider, who lacked so many of the conventional graces which might have recommended him, and who made so little effort to acquire them, makes his accomplishment seem all the more remarkable. In youth, a gaudily dressed dandy, whom one might regard as an oddity, in middle age, an aloof and forbidding politician, with whom one did not tangle without reason — neither was a figure for whom one could feel an immediate warmth. Disraeli was never chosen by the Tory Party; he forced himself upon it. He made his way by overcoming obstacles which others, more favored by fortune, would not have encountered. He gave no quarter and asked none; he rarely thought himself ill-used, though there were many occasions when he might legitimately have believed this. Disraeli, absolutely confident of his abilities, and of his understanding of the world, seemed untouched by the failures which seemed to thwart his ambition at so many critical junctures. He maintained his reserve in the company of all except his intimates. In an age which was becoming increasingly democratic, Disraeli refused to appeal to the mob. He spoke before large public assemblies but preferred to speak in Parliament. He seemed impervious to the new demands which politics made on those who wished to serve the greatly expanded electorate.

Disraeli's ambition, fed by sources deep within himself, could not have secured its ends if it had not been grounded in some deep faith. That such a faith existed, there is every reason to believe. Disraeli left a record of it in his numerous novels. These books, which Disraeli began writing when money and fame were his youthful ambitions, became in the end the most complete expression of his true nature. In the novel, more than in a parliamentary speech or in a letter to an intimate friend, Disraeli felt liberated. In the novel he could say openly all that his romantic imagination conjured up. Disguised as simple tales, they gave unmistakable evidence of the depth of his emotions and of the extraordinary confidence he felt in himself and in his race. The novel provided the release which Disraeli's nature demanded. For so great a satirist, the House of Commons offered too limited a field. Political satire, necessarily limited to a few subjects, did not even begin to exhaust his interests. He yearned to comment on more sacrosanct subjects. The novel provided him with the opportunity he sought.

It is not without significance that Disraeli chose the novel as the vehicle for his thought. No other form would have given him such freedom to interpolate his romantic images into a setting which retained always a link with reality. Only rarely did he produce novels without political overtones. As a young man, Disraeli had some interest in consorting with others who earned a living by writing, but as he grew older this interest declined; he preferred to spend his days in the company of other sorts of people. The extent of his divorce from literary society may be judged by a letter written to Lady Londonderry in 1857, in which he said: "I wish, like you, I could console myself with reading novels, or even writing them; but I have lost all zeal for fiction, and have for many years. I have never read anything of Dickens, except an extract in a newspaper, and, therefore, I cannot help to decide on the merits of Little Dorritt." This, however, did not mean that Disraeli had lost his appreciation of the man of letters. In 1874, he recommended to the Queen that she award the G.C.B. to Thomas Carlyle, a man who years earlier had spoken of him as "a conscious juggler" and "a superlative Hebrew conjurer." Disraeli, in his old age, could forgive such slights, for, as he explained to Carlyle, "a Government should recognize intellect." Carlyle refused the honor, but Disraeli showed by the offer his continuing fidelity to genius.

If Disraeli was capable of generosity and independence, he also knew the subtle art of flattery. With the Queen, perhaps more than with any other person, he negotiated in this currency. Disraeli's romantic disposition made his excessive deference to the monarch seem entirely natural, but many resented it and imagined that they saw deception in it. When the Queen made his wife Viscountess Beaconsfield, Disraeli responded with a note almost Oriental in tone, but not without its personal flavor; it read: "Mr. Disraeli at your Majesty's feet offers to your

Majesty his deep gratitude for your Majesty's inestimable favor and for the terms — so gracious and so graceful — in which your Majesty has deigned to speak of his efforts when working under a Sovereign whom it is really a delight to serve."

While such flattery may be dismissed as the hypocrisy of a man who understood its probable advantages to him, to view the matter in such a light would be to miss its real meaning. Disraeli liked to flatter; it was in his nature to flatter; he wished to make life appear more gallant and more gracious than the facts warranted. If this involved him in some specious sport, there was no loss to anyone. Disraeli flattered for other than reasons of personal advantage. When circumstance recommended firmness, no man could be more rigid and less forgiving. In 1858, his friend Bulwer-Lytton sought release from his duties as Colonial Secretary, and offered as a reason the counsel of his physician. Disraeli responded with: "I have no opinion of Dr. Reed, or of any Doctors. In the course of my life I have received fifty letters from physicians like that which you enclosed to me, and which I return. Had I attended to them I should not be here, Chancellor of the Exchequer, and in robust health. . . . I say nothing of the effect on the position of the Government by the retirement of any of its members at this moment. The true motive will never be credited. Whatever your illness may be, your secession will be a paralytic stroke to the Ministry." Disraeli, when he needed to be hard, knew how to be so, even with friends.

To ignore this element of hardness in Disraeli is to miss one of his principal qualities. This was the man capable of responding to one of Palmerston's more blustering effusions with the remark that it was unworthy of one "who is not only leader of the House of Commons — which is an accident of life — but is also a gentleman." Disraeli did not place small value on his own reputation as a gentleman. It delighted him, in 1868, that the political world thought well of his decision to resign as soon as the results of the General Election were known. He was not the man to hang on to office, or to ignore the opinion of others in questions affecting his conduct. In all these matters, he chose to conform as the standards of the day indicated.

Disraeli remained a romantic till the end of his life. Budgets and Reform Bills were a penance to be paid for the chance to participate in a sport which he found engrossing. However, he never made the mistake of becoming entirely dependent on either politics or society. So long as he knew that he might return to them, he was happy to abandon both and seek his pleasures at Hughenden. There, in the quiet of a house which had already begun to bear the stamp of its new proprietor, Disraeli worked on his novels, as, at an earlier time, he used his father's house for the same purpose. Disraeli never told everything about himself. He kept back much that would have interested those who came after him. He did, however, tell enough to suggest how original were the powers of his very singular imagination. He left a record of his mind. Whether it was, as he once suggested, a "revolutionary mind" depended on what one cared to read into that phrase. If the "revolutionary" is the creator of a great myth, which is more real for him than anything which is commonly thought real, then Disraeli deserves to be thought of in such a light.

WINSTON CHURCHILL

✤ *Critic and Cassandra* ✤

Winston Churchill started life with almost too many advantages; born in 1874, the son of Lord Randolph Churchill, grandson of the seventh Duke of Marlborough, and heir to a family tradition which never ignored the glories of Blenheim, he joined the clan at a moment when its fortunes seemed to prosper. Between the "Great Duke" in the seventeenth century and Winston Churchill's grandfather, the family had produced its share of weak and ineffectual men, but its patrimony remained virtually intact. His grandfather, while not wealthy by the standards set by the Dukes of Westminster, Bedford, or Norfolk, controlled properties with an annual income of some forty thousand pounds a year. In 1874, Disraeli recommended the Duke to the Queen as Lord Lieutenant of Ireland. The expenses of the post were so heavy that Marlborough felt it necessary to refuse the honor. By 1876, however, the situation had changed; rivalry between the Prince of Wales and Lord Randolph's older brother for the affections of a lady led to a nasty quarrel in which Lord Randolph became involved. Taking his brother's side, he lost the friendship of the prince, and was for a time ostracized from London society. Disraeli, sympathizing both with the father and his unfortunate son, renewed the offer of 1874. The Duke accepted, went over to Dublin, and took Lord Randolph along as his private secretary.

Winston Churchill's first memories were of the Viceregal Lodge in Dublin. There, as at Blenheim, the family lived in the midst of impressive luxury. Irish violence only occasionally threw a shadow across the prevailing calm. The boy grew up in a world of great parks, immense houses, lavish dinners, perpetual entertainments, and endless sport. Irish hospitality had always been famous, and Churchill's parents, installed in the Little Lodge, not far from the Viceregal Lodge, worked hard to maintain the tradition. The Marlboroughs knew or were related to practically every person of consequence in the realm. Whether in Dublin, in London, in Oxfordshire, or on the continent, they moved with a sureness which suggested that they knew everyone and everything. The governing class formed a family — part Conservative, part Liberal — but essentially united. Winston, by right of birth, belonged to that class. Even as a child he must have been conscious of its rules and habits. In the nursery, in school, at home, the Marlborough name summoned up a historic legend, and gave a "cachet" which neither money nor achievement could ever purchase.

At the time dictated by convention, Winston was sent off to public school. At Harrow, he achieved little distinction and gave his family real cause for worry. He seemed remarkably incapable of study, and his masters held out little hope for his future. Lord Randolph, then at the height of his powers, was naturally distressed; he had hoped that his son would follow him in politics. At the end of the nineteenth century, no other career commanded a comparable prestige, and no other was deemed so worthy of the talents of the well-born. Given Churchill's incompetence, however, some other occupation needed to be found for him. Lord Randolph concluded that he might be suited to a military career. This was not an unpleasing prospect for Winston, and plans were made for his admission to Sandhurst. These plans were almost frustrated by the youth's academic backwardness; Churchill tried on three separate occasions before he succeeded in passing the required examinations. The services of an accomplished "cram school" were required in the end. Coming in near the bottom of his class, Churchill was compelled to prepare for the cavalry. His father would have preferred that he train for an infantry regiment, but this was impossible. At Harrow, Churchill had been generally unhappy; at Sandhurst, he enjoyed himself immensely. He became an accomplished horseman, showed industry in his studies, and even acquired some degree of competence in drill.

Churchill's years at Harrow and Sandhurst coincided with the rise, fall, and final eclipse of his father's political fortunes. The decade 1885–1895 opened with Lord Randolph safely installed as Chancellor of the Exchequer; it ended with his death, a broken man conscious of his great gifts having been wasted. For the young Churchill, who never knew his father intimately, but who always felt respect and awe before the mysterious presence whose personality raised such conjecture in his time, the event was a tragedy. A youthful dream — of standing by his father as a political ally and colleague — was shattered. While Churchill could not at that moment understand all that had passed to account for his father's ruin, the problem was not one permanently to elude him. He buried his grief in the busy preparations associated with entering on his military duty; he had been accepted by a cavalry regiment, the Fourth Hussars.

Had Churchill been born in the middle of the century, his career in the Army would have included agreeable periods in London and equally congenial tours of duty in India, where British society maintained as pleasant an existence as heat and distance permitted. After the Crimean War, Great Britain found little use for its military, except to stand guard over its large and growing empire. Military engagements were rare — almost unknown — and young officers had no experience of battle.

Given Churchill's temperament, such a situation would almost certainly have proved intolerable. His wish was for action, on the drill field, in polo matches, but, most particularly, in battle. Coming out of Sandhurst in 1895, he must have wondered whether fate would be kind, and reward him with the action he craved. He had no need to fear; what the century did not do for him, he did for himself. In India with his regiment, in Cuba as a "private observer," and in the Sudan as an uninvited correspondent, Churchill saw war as his century knew it. The recapture of Omdurman, the defeat of the Dervish armies, the vindication of General Gordon's memory, and the pacification of the Sudan were chapters in his personal life. While Kitchener, the commanding officer, had no wish for him to be in the Sudan, Churchill treated the objection as an obstacle to be overcome. Employing the same aggressive methods that had enabled him to participate in fighting on the North West frontier, in which his own regiment had no part, he witnessed the Sudan operations, and wrote of them in *The River War*, published in 1899.

The book was an immediate success. Widely read and favorably reviewed, it suggested horizons to Churchill that had not previously existed. His education, by his own admission, had been defective. It was not till he had come to live in India that he began to be interested in history. His acquaintance with the works of Gibbon and Macaulay — which he owed to this period in his life — sharpened his interest in the past and also in writing. Churchill took pleasure in the tales he read, and admired the skill of those who understood the art of historical narration. While in no way unhappy with his Army life, he began inevitably to think also of other things. Politics seemed to beckon; if he could combine a political career with active writing, he might have money from the second to finance the first. By 1899, Churchill made his decision; he resigned his commission and presented himself in a bye-election for a seat at Oldham. In this, his first experience of parliamentary combat, he failed to make the impression he sought. Defeated, he began to think of how he might earn his living.

Winston Churchill: Critic and Cassandra

These thoughts were interrupted by the outbreak of the Boer War. Churchill could not imagine remaining at home when so much was happening at the other end of the world. He thought immediately of going as a newspaper reporter; the *Morning Post*, recognizing the advantages of having a man on the spot, fell in with his plans. Before the year was out, Churchill had landed in South Africa. In the months that followed, adventure pursued him with its usual recklessness. Participating in a reconnaissance effort, which made use of an armored train, he came under Boer attack. He helped free the train but was himself captured. Detention in a Boer prison camp followed. Churchill, restless and determined, could not abide his confinement. In a hazardous escape, made all the more remarkable by the determination of the Boers to recover him, dead or alive, he made his way to freedom. For several days, England was saturated with rumors of his recapture. Finally, it learned what it was most anxious to hear: Churchill had eluded the enemy and had made his way back to the British forces. The nation, war-weary and distressed by a whole series of humiliating defeats, took him to its heart; the courage and ingenuity which had always been expected of British arms was at last represented in the bold act of an individual, who refused to accept the notion of even temporary surrender. For some days, the jubilation was universal; then, quite suddenly, men began to ask what Churchill, a reporter, was doing in a military action. Had he any right to be so involved? Churchill disregarded the criticism but recognized the necessity of regularizing his role. He applied for readmission to the Army, but insisted on retaining his position as journalist; he would be both combatant and scribe. Churchill remained in this role long enough to participate in the relief of Ladysmith and the taking of Johannesburg and Pretoria. In the Khaki Election of 1900, he presented himself again at Oldham. This time, he had no difficulty in winning. The Tory Party, appearing as the architects of a major military victory, emerged with an impressive majority; Churchill took his place in its ranks.

[177]

Churchill's career, to this point, had turned out very differently from what Lord Randolph had feared. By an extraordinary combination of good luck and gall, Churchill had removed himself from the military backwater, and had begun to swim in the swifter channels of politics. While his inexperience as a speaker and a slight speech impediment served to reduce the impact made on the House of Commons in his first parliamentary performances, there was no little interest in the son of the now legendary Lord Randolph. Men were curious to see whether the son would prove more stable than his father, more faithful to his Tory allegiance, and more congenial to direction from above. These questions did not long remain unanswered. Winston resembled his father in many ways, not least in his independence; by 1902, it was obvious to many of his colleagues that he was uncomfortable in the Party, and unhappy with many of its policies. His differences with the Party were never spelled out, but they extended beyond the immediate issue, that of protection. Writing many years later about his decision to abandon the Tories and join the Liberals, Churchill said: "Even apart from the Free Trade quarrel, I was in full reaction against the war and they [the Tories] in full exploitation in the political sphere of the so-called victory. Thus, when the protection issue was raised I was already disposed to view all their actions in the most critical light."

Why had Churchill come, in so short a time, to be suspicious of his Tory associates, and uncomfortable in their company? To answer that question, attention must be directed to his personality even more than to his beliefs. While little disposed to question the values of his society, Churchill craved an independence which permitted him to live free of the more stultifying conventions of his age. Just as he thought it entirely proper, as kinsman of the Duke of Marlborough, to choose journalism as an occupation, so he found it natural to associate with persons of birth and position foreign to the aristocracy in which so much of his activity centered. Churchill, even as a young man, showed the qualities of an adventurer; he felt no reluctance to seek out others of similar disposition. The Tory Party, conscious of its success — it had governed, except for brief periods, for almost two decades — had no interest in innovation. Joseph Chamberlain, forced out of the Liberal Party because of Irish Home Rule, had been the last radical element to penetrate the Tory Party. His conversion, while important in the 1880's, did not permanently deflect the Tory Party from its traditional path. Tory Democracy, as Lord Randolph Churchill had spoken of it, made only slight progress in the long and tranquil years when Salisbury presided over successive governments. Born into Toryism, Churchill's nature rebelled against its quiet conformities; he much preferred the company of people like himself; at that moment their political home was the Liberal Party. It was this, as much as anything else, that influenced his decision to abandon Toryism for Liberalism.

The Liberal Party could not fail to be impressed by the convert. The accession of a prominent member of the Marlborough clan was gain enough, but even more important was the fact that Churchill seemed to be in sympathy with Liberal impatience over too long deferred reforms. Clearly, Churchill possessed exceptional powers, and these were now made available to a Party which had every intention of using them. After the great Liberal victory in 1906, Churchill received an initial token of the esteem in which his new friends held him — he was appointed Under-Secretary of State for the Colonies; with his chief, Lord Elgin, in the House of Lords, Churchill had an admirable apprenticeship to high office. The death of Campbell-Bannerman, the Liberal Prime Minister, in 1908, led to a reorganization of the Cabinet. Churchill emerged as President of the Board of Trade; his predecessor in that office, Lloyd George, had just been made Chancellor of the Exchequer. This was a totally satisfactory arrangement, but in 1911, an even greater plum fell to him: Asquith asked him to serve as First Lord of the Admiralty. From October 1911, Churchill sat at the head of the defense arm whose chief responsibility was to guard Britain against the possibility of a German attack. During these years, he had little time for writing. His duties consumed the whole of his energies. The crises of the period 1909–1914 — domestic and international — made it necessary for Churchill to stand with the other Liberal leaders in a constant crossfire. Ireland, House of Lords reform, suffragette agitation, labor unrest, German rearmament — these were only a few of the problems that kept Liberal ministers permanently occupied.

In 1906, before the pressure of official life became too heavy, Churchill completed a large two-volume biography of his father. This was a work of love, produced by a devoted son to honor a man little known or understood in his day. Churchill's own acquaintance with his father had been slight; he depended on documents made available to him, and also, on the memory of those who had known him well. He hoped to make intelligible the act of resignation that had ruined Lord Randolph's career in 1886. He sought to vindicate the memory of a man sorely used by his colleagues, who had died in full knowledge of his failure. The resignation, which had seemed so ill-advised and impetuous in 1886, was not made any more reasonable by the efforts of his son to explain it. Churchill's concern to show that the issue was really Tory Democracy did not conceal the plain fact that the resignation arose over a difference on relatively small military expenditures, and that Lord Randolph's objections on this score were carping and excessive. Lord Randolph's abilities and energies were never denied; it was only his judgment that men questioned. Even after the meticulous researches of his son, the suspicion about this flaw in his character remained.

Lord Randolph's early death, at forty-six, made the story of his life poignant and tragic; it could not make it heroic. Winston Churchill struggled valiantly to give this dimension to his story, but the facts refused to support such an estimate. *Lord Randolph Churchill*, a careful and heavily documented biography, testified to the industry of the young man who felt more than a conventional filial affection for his hero. As biography, it compared favorably with others produced at the time, and suggested again the extraordinary talents of the new recruit to Liberalism.

After 1906, Churchill did not write another major work till 1923. In the interim, much happened to change the character of his life and of the society into which he had been born. The years as First Lord of the Admiralty — among the happiest of Churchill's life — stretched from October 1911 to May 1915. It was during this time that he shared in the effort to prepare the Navy for the war that threatened, and from which Britain was spared great harm by its naval defenses. Churchill's responsibility for the Gallipoli campaign of 1915 — a disaster for British arms — made him a principal target for all who believed that the prosecution of the war required more stable and responsible leadership. Churchill was given up to the attack, which had its center in the Northcliffe press. In the Coalition Government formed in 1915, over which Herbert Asquith presided, Churchill was given the post of Chancellor of the Duchy of Lancaster. An honorific office, without responsibilities affecting the conduct of the war, Churchill healed his wound with a brief period of service at the front. Lloyd George, aware of Churchill's abilities and anxious that they be used, felt by the middle of 1917 that his own position was strong enough to make his Tory colleagues accept Churchill as head of the Ministry of Munitions. Churchill held this office till after the Armistice. In 1919, after the victory of the Coalition forces in the Khaki Election, he became Minister of War. As the person responsible for regulating demobilization, and as one of the chief organizers of the effort to defeat the Bolsheviks in Russia, Churchill gained new fame, but became an even more controversial figure. The animus against him in Labour and Radical circles increased immensely; among Conservatives, he remained unpopular. In October 1922, the Conservative Party, under Bonar Law's leadership, elected to remove itself from the Coalition. This decision destroyed the Government, and Churchill joined his other Liberal colleagues on the Opposition benches. In the General Election that followed, Churchill lost his seat at Dundee; he wrote of this experience some years later; "in an instant," he said, "I found myself without portfolio, without a seat, without a party, and without an appendix." The last, which caused his hospitalization during the campaign, was the least of his worries.

For the first time in over two decades, Churchill was without a seat in the Commons. In the 1923 General Election, when Baldwin introduced Protection as an issue, Churchill ran as a Liberal for one of the Leicester seats; he was defeated again. The events of the months that followed shocked him profoundly; he felt that Asquith made a terrible mistake in helping the Labour Party to form a ministry. Whatever the differences between Liberals and Conservatives, they were as nothing compared to those which divided both from Labour — such, at least, was Churchill's view. In a bye-election at Westminster, he ran as a Constitutionalist, believing that the Liberal label no longer defined his position. Churchill was now moving very purposefully in a Tory direction; when, in October 1924, Liberal and Tory votes brought the Labour Party down in a House of Commons defeat, he decided that he would throw his lot once again with the Tory Party. At that moment, its policies seemed closer to his own than those proclaimed by the Liberal Party, split between its Asquith and Lloyd George factions. Churchill found it difficult to forgive Asquith for what he had done in bringing the first Labour Government into being; in the years since the war, he had moved away from Lloyd George. The Tories accepted their prodigal son, and, in the fight for Dundee, Churchill won.

Stanley Baldwin, the new Prime Minister, estimating with his habitual shrewdness the challenge that Churchill might present to his Cabinet if he did not have a place in it, decided to ask him to be Chancellor of the Exchequer. The offer — considerably more elevated than any that Churchill in his wildest moments had imagined possible — was quickly accepted. Moving into Number 11 Downing Street, Churchill was soon absorbed in his ministerial responsibilities. The years of political exclusion were ended, but he had no reason to regret them. During this time, he had written and published the first volumes of a history of the World War. The first volume, *The World Crisis*, appeared in April 1923. As a principal architect of British policy in the immediate prewar and early war periods, Churchill thought it necessary to give an account of his stewardship of an office which touched so closely the security of the nation. He realized that his history would be in great part autobiographical, but this only increased his interest in telling the tale as he recalled it. He expected that others would have a different story to tell, and hoped that they would also write, that the public might choose between the several testimonies. Of one thing he was certain: if men read his book, they would understand that "perhaps after all Britain and her Empire have not been so ill-guided through the great convulsions as it is customary to declare." By 1923, the British public, or at least a great part of it, must have been anxious to forget the war and the unredeemed pledges and promises which had kept the nation faithful to that herculean effort. Churchill, however, had no intention of letting the events of the recent past disappear from the national consciousness. There was a story to tell, tragic in its main lines, but also glorious in the reflection it shed on British purpose.

Churchill opened his history with an account of the crises which increased tension in Europe in the years before Sarajevo. Germany, by deed and word, gave evidence of an ambition which could only frighten those who were commissioned to safeguard Great Britain's position in the world. Churchill told of the efforts made in the Admiralty to prepare the Navy for any eventuality. In the end, Germany forced Great Britain to go to war. By attacking Belgium, she threatened the area which Britain could never permit to be controlled by an unfriendly power. Geography, sentiment, treaty obligations bound Great Britain to Belgium's defense. "Having let Hell loose," he wrote, Germany "kept well in the van of terror; but she was followed step by step by the desperate and ultimately avenging nations she had assailed." In the end, the war became more horrible than

[183]

any the world had ever known. Terrible weapons were employed; if torture and cannibalism were shunned, it was only because they were of doubtful utility.

Given the character of the 1914–1918 War, it is not surprising that Churchill thought to dwell on its violence. He knew the consequences of Armageddon only too well to ignore them. His purpose, however, was not simply to express his horror at what had happened; he intended a more profound and less emotional response to the problem. Recalling a luncheon with Sir William Harcourt in 1895, he was reminded of the old Liberal's words: "My dear Winston, the experiences of a long life have convinced me that nothing ever happens." That may have been true of the nineteenth century; it was not true of the twentieth. Churchill said that since that moment "nothing has ever ceased happening." The age was violent, and its beginning, for England, he set in 1896, the year of the Jameson Raid. From that moment, national and international crises had multiplied steadily, threatening not simply a temporary dislocation of affairs but a permanent transformation of Europe. There were optimists, of course, men who spoke reassuringly that "the interdependence of nations in trade and traffic, the sense of public law, the Hague Convention, Liberal principles, the Labour Party, high finance, Christian charity, common sense" would in the end save Europe. But even optimists could not feel certain about their facts. As First Lord of the Admiralty, Churchill worked to make certain that if war came, Great Britain would not be defenseless before its enemy.

There was never any question as to who that enemy would be. Germany, with the most powerful land forces in Europe, was constructing a navy calculated to rival Britain's; this was the threat against which Churchill imagined the most careful preparations needed to be made. Churchill never doubted that the Germans made a fundamental miscalculation in embarking upon their large naval-building program. Admiral von Tirpitz, in Churchill's eyes a foolish and wrongheaded old man, believed that the new German navy would frighten Britain; actually, it only reenforced her will to stand closer to the other members of the Entente. When the final crisis came, following on the assassination of the Archduke at Sarajevo, the British Cabinet was deeply divided. The German ultimatum to Belgium proved to be the decisive factor. A regard for treaty obligations and a sense of military necessity dictated Britain's entry into the war. Churchill claimed that everything possible was done to avoid war, but that in the end Germany "had rushed with head down and settled resolve to her own undoing."

Churchill's narrative of the events leading up to the war, particularly those involving himself, communicated the keen excitement which he felt at being associated with so important a venture. In the first days of the war, everything moved in accordance with long-laid plans; the harmony was unbroken. "Had all our action been upon this level," Churchill opined, "we should to-day be living in an easier world." By the end of 1914, however, it was obvious to all the belligerents that repeated optimistic forecasts of early victory were not destined to be realized. The war was certain to continue, and no one could say for how long. For Churchill, 1915 was the year of tragedy. At that moment, the slaughter might still have been curtailed. Victory in the East, which would have indicated to the Central Powers the impossible position which they held, might have led to a demand for a negotiated peace. The Gallipoli campaign, had it succeeded, would have altered the relative strength of the contending forces. It might have precluded the years of trench warfare in France, with the consequent saving of millions of lives. Churchill opened the second volume of *The World Crisis* with the somber words: "The year 1915 was disastrous to the cause of the Allies and to the whole world. By the mistakes of this year the opportunity was lost of confining the conflagration within limits which though enormous were not uncontrolled. Thereafter the fire roared on till it burned itself out. Thereafter events passed very largely outside the scope of conscious choice. Governments and individuals conformed to the rhythm of the tragedy, and swayed and staggered forward in helpless violence, slaughtering and squandering on ever-increasing scales, till injuries were wrought to the structure of human society which a century will not efface, and which may conceivably prove fatal to the present civilization. But in January, 1915, the terrific affair was still not unmanageable. It could have been grasped in human hands and brought to rest in righteous and fruitful victory before the world was exhausted, before the nations were broken, before the empires were shattered to pieces, before Europe was ruined. It was not to be. Mankind was not to escape so easily from the catastrophe in which it had involved itself. Pride was everywhere to be humbled, and nowhere to receive its satisfaction. No splendid harmony was to crown the wonderful achievements. No prize was to reward the sacrifices of the combatants. Victory was to be bought so dear as to be almost indistinguishable from defeat. It was not to give even security to the victors."

These words were written with the advantage of historical hindsight. Churchill felt the need to set the Gallipoli venture in a context which would explain why he had agitated so insistently for it. Unless a later generation could see why, to use Churchill's favorite image, "the turning of the flanks" could have been achieved by this campaign, its defeat would appear always as a final judgment on it. Churchill knew that, in describing Gallipoli as he did, he was taking issue with other opinions, and he showed a becoming modesty in the claims made for his own interpretation. He wrote: "I must therefore at the outset disclaim the position of the historian. It is not for me with my record and special point of view to pronounce a final conclusion. That must be left to others and to other times." Having warned his readers, he felt free to tell his story as he remembered it.

The tale was not a happy one. A campaign which started as a purely naval attack, with limited costs and risks, became in time an offensive of a very different character. In the beginning, Kitchener claimed that no men were available for a military assault. Two months later it became evident that at least ten divisions might be spared for the attack. A limited operation was suddenly transformed into a major military undertaking, on the success of which everything depended. The errors of judgment, naval and military, extending over a period of many months, meant in the end the loss of thousands of lives and the failure to make any of the gains anticipated. Before that occurred, however, the effects of the first failures had been felt at the center of British government. The resignation of Fisher as First Sea Lord indicated what many already suspected; the old Admiral would not go along with a plan to commit additional forces to a campaign which he imagined was doomed.

To Churchill, a friend, Fisher wrote: ". . . I find it increasingly difficult to adjust myself to the increasing daily requirements of the Dardanelles to meet your views." Churchill tried to recall Fisher to his duty; it was characteristic that he should begin his own letter to him with the words: "The only thing to think of now is what is best for the country and for the brave men who are fighting. Anything which does injury to those interests will be harshly judged by history, on whose stage we now are." The appeal fell on deaf ears; Fisher would not heed the call, even in the name of history.

The resignation of Fisher, coming at a time when rumors about shell shortages were widespread in Conservative Party circles, created a major political crisis. Asquith, acting on the recommendation of Lloyd George, saw no way out of his difficulties except in the establishment of a Coalition Government. Churchill argued that Asquith made a fundamental error in acceding so easily to these various pressures. Had the Prime Minister laid his case before Parliament in a secret session, Churchill wrote, he would almost certainly have won a vote of confidence. With such a vote, he would have been in a position to secure Conservative Party cooperation on his own terms. Instead, giving way to pressure, he seemed to be asking the Conservatives to come in as a rescue party, on terms chosen by themselves. The result, Churchill said, was a Coalition Ministry with many heads, much recrimination, and no possibility of real union. The consequences of this mistake were many, including further and more costly errors in the Gallipoli campaign. As Churchill explained, "Those who had knowledge had pasts to defend; those free from war commitments were also free from war experience." The new team brought Great Britain no closer to victory. Churchill, made the scapegoat of the Dardanelles adventure, was given no place in the new Government.

Churchill never doubted that the failure of the Turkish campaign meant a prolongation of the war, and in the end, a loss of the sort of peace that might still have been made in 1915. The Allied victory, when it came in 1918, owed more to the mistakes made by the Germans than to the ingenuity revealed by the Allies. Churchill was convinced that the Germans, in adopting a policy of unrestricted submarine warfare, sealed their own fate.

In the first two volumes of *The World Crisis*, Churchill wrote about that period of the war when he stood at the center of affairs, seeing everything from his Admiralty quarters. All the excitement which he felt in those difficult days, he communicated to his readers. When he issued two additional volumes in 1927, covering the years 1916–1918, a new spirit dominated the work. The change was not simply the result of Churchill's loss of office. In the second of these volumes, Churchill discussed matters which occurred in the period after his return to the Cabinet as Minister of Munitions in July 1917. And yet, both volumes conveyed the same sense of fatigue, frustration, and tragedy. The war, after 1916, became in Churchill's words, "a blood test." The opportunity for brilliant maneuver was lost; Europe was caught in a nightmare of its own making. Churchill, in *The World Crisis*, as in all his histories, concluded each volume with appendices containing relevant documents; for the volume which covered the period January 1916–May 1917, there was only a single appendix — it listed British, French, and German casualties. The volume was dedicated "To All Who Endured."

These later volumes, like the earlier ones, described in some detail the various land and sea engagements in which British forces participated. Churchill, always temperate in criticism of his countrymen, indicated in no uncertain manner the reservations he felt about both Kitchener and Jellicoe. Each gave a great deal to his country, but neither carried forward what Churchill called the "audacious and conquering traditions of the past." As for Britain's political leaders, while Churchill avoided a detailed criticism of Asquith, he indicated that he could not acquit the Prime Minister of the responsibility for having failed to halt the murderous Allied offensives in France.

The German General Staff, and the errors it made, finally brought victory to the Allies; Churchill wrote: "The total defeat of Germany was due to three cardinal mistakes: the decision to march through Belgium regardless of bringing Britain into the war; the decision to begin the unrestricted U-boat war regardless of bringing the United States into the war; and thirdly, the decision to use the German forces liberated from Russia in 1918 for a final onslaught in France. But for the first mistake they would have beaten France and Russia easily in a year; but for the second mistake they would have been able to make a satisfactory peace in 1917; but for the third mistake they would have been able to confront the Allies with an unbreakable front on the Meuse or on the Rhine, and to have made self-respecting terms as a price for abridging the slaughter. All these three errors were committed by the same forces, and by the very forces that made the military strength of the German Empire. The German General Staff, which sustained the German cause with such wonderful power, was responsible for all these three fatal decisions. Thus nations as well as individuals come to ruin through the over-exercise of those very qualities and faculties on which their dominion has been founded."

Churchill showed a particular concern to emphasize the contribution made by President Wilson in the final Allied victory. Of Wilson, he said, ". . . it seems no exaggeration to pronounce that the action of the United States with its repercussions on the history of the world depended, during the awful period of Armageddon, upon the workings of this man's mind and spirit to the exclusion of almost every other factor; and that he played a part in the fate of nations incomparably more direct and personal than any other man." While unstinting in his praise, Churchill could not help reflecting on how different Europe's fate would have been if Wilson had done in May 1915 what he finally chose to do in April 1917. If only the President had been more prescient, Churchill mused, "how different would be the shattered world in which victors and vanquished alike are condemned to live!"

While Churchill's principal concern was to delineate Europe's suffering in the war, he did not neglect the adverse effects produced on Great Britain. Among the unhappy consequences, the one that rankled most in Churchill was the power gained by the popular press. Churchill's disdain for Northcliffe, while never explicitly stated, was implicit throughout. Asquith, who ignored Northcliffe's power, suffered the consequences of not understanding the realities of the situation. The power of the press, in time of war, was irresponsible in the most absolute sense. Possessing unusual authority, and being able to dwell on every ministerial error or failure without fear of contradiction, there was almost no limit to what the press might not claim. Ministers were seldom in a position to reply. For Churchill, one of the most nefarious aspects of this persistent newspaper propaganda was the unmerited elevation of generals and admirals, and the habitual deprecation of political men. He thought, naturally, of the criticism which he and others suffered for their so-called "interference" in military matters. Churchill, without saying so, believed that war was too serious a matter to leave to generals and others who were merely technicians. Churchill's contempt for the British military command was never more outspoken than when he wrote of Passchendaele and the military actions of that period. Reviewing the Allied infantry offensives of 1915, 1916, and 1917, he indicated that none of these ought ever to have taken place. The development of the tank ought to have occurred earlier. Other sorts of actions ought to have been conceived; they would have been, Churchill wrote bitterly, "if only the Generals had not been content to fight machine-gun bullets with the breasts of gallant men, and think that that was waging war."

Winston Churchill: Critic and Cassandra

In *The World Crisis*, Churchill wrote mournfully of a war badly mismanaged by military and political men who lacked the imagination to do those things which, while securing victory, would also have saved Europe. The failure was too large for any one man to be held responsible for it. General Robertson on the English side, General Nivelle on the French, Kitchener and Joffre, and dozens of lesser men, all contributed to the tragedy. The politicians showed no greater sagacity, and no one man could safely point a finger at another and argue that the fault lay there. The war, eventually won by the Allies, brought victory to no one. Its heroes were the countless millions who had fought in those desperate days when hope was nearly extinct.

In *The Aftermath*, published in 1929, Churchill continued his melancholy tale. From the first pages, his theme was obvious. "The war of the giants has ended; the quarrels of the pygmies have begun." Out of such a war, nothing but disillusionment could come; the victors, Wilson, Lloyd George, and Clemenceau "were soon to follow into retirement or adversity the Kings and Emperors they had dethroned." Again, the blame was to be placed at no one door; it grew out of regrettable but understandable mistakes, and most of all, out of lost opportunities. Men simply did not possess the vision to see things as they were.

How could they be blamed? Everything had changed in such unexpected ways since the calm August day when Europe's peace was shattered. Few of the old familiar landmarks remained; travel was necessarily difficult. In place of Russia, Churchill wrote, there was "a state without a nation, an army without a country, a religion without a God." Lenin, transported into Russia by the Germans "in a sealed truck like a plague bacillus," had done his work. "A thousand years," Churchill wrote, "will not forget it." Lenin, he regarded as the Grand Repudiator, who "repudiated God, King, Country, morals, treaties, debts, rents, interest, the laws and customs of centuries, all contracts written or implied, the whole structure — such as it is — of human society." In the end, Churchill explained, he repudiated himself. In his

New Economic Policy, Lenin admitted the defeat of his communist hopes. But shortly after that he died. "The Russian people," Churchill wrote, "were left floundering in the bog. Their worst misfortune was his [Lenin's] birth: their next worst — his death." Churchill left no doubts as to what he believed the Allies ought to have done in Russia. This, they did not do. The aid which they were prepared to give to "Admiral Kolchak and his Associates" in June 1919, they ought to have offered in January. In June, it was too late. The Supreme Council had given the Bolsheviks time to raise armies, consolidate their power, and appear as the representatives of a new Russia. In Russia, as in so much else, opportunity was lost through Allied procrastination and indecision.

The Aftermath was dominated by this single theme. At the moment of victory, when the Allies might have done anything, when they stood to gain so much from their unbroken unity, they did nothing. This was the tragedy of 1918–19. "The hour was fleeting," and men did not understand that what was left undone at that moment could never be done again. For this and other reasons, Wilson's decision to participate personally in the Peace Conference was a serious, possibly fatal, error. It only served to add one more force making for delay.

Churchill, who had spoken well of Wilson in his earlier volumes, thought his Paris performance a deplorable one. Wilson, self-righteous and adamant, with all the right feelings and all the wrong ideas, intervening where he ought to have left matters alone, ignoring that which he ought to have attended to, ended by destroying the very things that he wished to preserve. Churchill criticized not in anger, but in disappointment. So much would have been different if the President had been a little less certain of his complete understanding of Europe and a little more attentive to his obligations at home. If he had preached less and thought more, and trusted someone other than himself, so many errors could have been avoided.

Churchill wrote about a meeting on board the *George Washington*, where, three days before it came into Brest, Wilson spoke to those who would be his aides at the Peace Conference. Dr. Isaiah Bowman, who kept a record of his remarks, said that the President informed the group that "we would be the only disinterested people at the peace conference, and that the men whom we were about to deal with did not represent their own people." The first claim, Churchill chose to ignore; the second he thought a fundamental error. Insofar as Europe's representatives argued for a harsh treatment of Germany, he insisted, they expressed popular sentiment. The public demanded that Germany pay for the harm it had done Europe; reparations seemed a sensible and proper request. Wilson scarcely knew the "plain people," of whom he spoke so frequently. His ideas, Churchill wrote, were never theirs. For the "world democracy," about which he felt so deeply, they scarcely felt anything. At Paris, the United States President sought to represent the conscience of a stricken Europe; the result was that the United States Senate repudiated his handiwork. In a tone suggesting anger as well as disappointment, Churchill remarked: "After immense delays and false hopes that only aggravated her difficulties, Europe was to be left to scramble out of the world disaster as best she could; and the United States, which had lost but 125,000 lives in the whole struggle, was to settle down upon the basis of receiving through one channel or another four-fifths of the reparations paid by Germany to the countries she had devastated or whose manhood she had slain." On Wilson, Churchill was even more caustic; he wrote of him: "If Wilson had been either simply an idealist or a caucus politician, he might have succeeded. His attempt to run the two in double harness was the cause of his undoing. The spacious philanthropy which he exhaled upon Europe stopped quite sharply at the coast of his own country. There he was in every main decision a party politician, calculating and brazen. A tithe of the fine principles and generous sentiments he lavished upon Europe, applied during 1918 to his Republican opponents in the United States, would have made him in truth the leader of a nation. His sense of proportion operated in separate water-tight compartments. The differences in

Europe between France and Germany seemed trivial, petty, easy to be adjusted by a little good sense and charity. But the differences between Democrat and Republican in the United States! Here were really grave quarrels. He could not understand why the French should not be more forgiving to their beaten enemy; nor why the American Republicans should not expect cold comfort from a Democratic Administration. His gaze was fixed with equal earnestness upon the destiny of mankind and the fortunes of his party candidates. Peace and goodwill among all nations abroad, but no truck with the Republican Party at home. That was his ticket and that was his ruin, and the ruin of much else as well. It is difficult for a man to do great things if he tries to combine a lambent charity embracing the whole world with the sharper forms of populist party strife."

However angry Churchill might be with Wilson, he could never fail to be moved by the tragedy which overwhelmed the American President in the last years of his life. He was critical of Wilson's failures, intellectual and moral, but never lost respect for the essential magnanimity of the man. For Ray Stannard Baker, Wilson's biographer, Churchill felt no comparable respect, and no interest in moderating his criticisms. Baker showed a self-righteousness which came easily to one who had suffered not at all, and who knew nothing of the feelings of a Europe devastated by war. Baker criticized the Allies for their Secret Treaties, imagining that they proved the "inherent cynical wickedness and materialism of old-world diplomacy." Churchill described these treaties as being "in the main simply convulsive gestures of self-preservation." He went on to remark: "One has a right to stand on the bank; but if one has exercised the right for a prolonged and agonising period without even throwing a rope to a man struggling in the rapids, some allowance should be made for the swimmer who now clutches at this rock and now at that in rough or ungainly fashion. It is not open to the cool bystander, who afterwards becomes the loyal and ardent comrade and brave rescuer, to set himself up as an impartial judge of events which never would have occurred had he outstretched a helping hand in time." Churchill, in puckish scorn, ridiculed the shock which Baker felt at learning about the Secret Treaties: "no such effect had been produced since Fatima opened the secret chamber of Bluebeard." Baker, wishing to distinguish between the young American democracy, one hundred million strong, and old truculent Europe, created a tableau which Churchill felt was cheap melodrama. Churchill wrote: "Here young, healthy, hearty, ardent millions, advancing so hopefully to reform mankind. There, shrinking from the limelights, cameras and cinemas, huddled the crafty, cunning, intriguing, high-collared, gold-laced diplomatists. Tableau! Curtain! Slow music! Sobs: and afterwards chocolates!"

The mistakes made at the Peace Conference were many, and Churchill saw no reason to conceal them. In the early stages, the principals, Wilson, Lloyd George, and Clemenceau, never engaged in the sort of frank personal discussion which ought to have been their first order of business. These talks, when they did take place, in late March, came too late. The President's insistence that the League issue be settled before all others, was certainly not the best procedure. It left questions of immediate urgency untouched, and concentrated all attention on proposals which might have been discussed more profitably when Europe's open wounds — in Russia, for example — had been attended to. Churchill made a great point of destroying the canard that the League of Nations was Wilson's child. He emphasized the support given by the British at every stage and the role played by men like Smuts in its formulation.

Churchill expressed immense sympathy for the French position at the Peace Conference. Understanding the basis of French fears, he could not but feel that Clemenceau, in insisting on guarantees, expressed a view which any French leader in his position would have taken. Great Britain and the United States could afford to be lenient. Their geographic good fortune made self-righteous denunciations of French intransigence easy and safe. While Churchill refused to condemn the French for any of their demands, he deplored the Treaty as a whole. To Lloyd

George in March 1920, he wrote: "Since the Armistice my policy would have been 'Peace with the German people, war on the bolshevik tyranny.' Willingly or unavoidably, you have followed something very near the reverse."

The years after the war, Churchill found equally discouraging. He thought British diplomacy shortsighted, and concluded that, if the peace was kept, it would be only because war on a large scale had become too horrible. "Next time," Churchill wrote mournfully, "the competition may be to kill women and children, and the civil population generally, and victory will give herself in sorry nuptials to the diligent hero who organizes it on the largest scale." Modern war, he warned, could destroy the human race. "Mankind has never been in this position before," he wrote. "Without having improved appreciably in virtue or enjoying wiser guidance, it has got into its hands for the first time the tools by which it can unfailingly accomplish its own extermination. That is the point in human destinies to which all the glories and toils of men have at last led them. They would do well to pause and ponder upon their new responsibilities." On this note, Churchill closed *The Aftermath*.

Churchill, in his volumes on the First World War, told a tale which was grave in tone and tragic in meaning. It was characteristic of the man that he should turn from this mood almost immediately that he had completed his task. In 1930, he published an autobiography, *My Early Life*. Dedicated "To a New Generation," it told of a world which Churchill knew had entirely vanished. He recalled his Victorian youth with nostalgia, but not with regret. He knew the world too well to imagine that the past could be relived or regained. All that could be done was to offer testimony to its greatness, and hope that the tale would inspire a generation which knew no such security, but which might profit from learning about it. Politics, in that day, Churchill wrote, was "directed by statesmen of commanding intellect and personality. The upper classes in their various stations took part in them as a habit and as a duty. The working men, whether they had votes or not, followed them as a sport. They took as much interest in national affairs and were as good judges of form in public men, as is now the case about cricket or football." While that world had entirely disappeared, Churchill saw no reason to despair. Interrupting his narrative, he issued a call to youth to take their places "in life's fighting line." They were needed to "fill the gap of a generation shorn by the War." "Twenty to twenty-five," these were the golden years. They had certainly been "golden" in Churchill's case.

He recalled his life at twenty-one, as an officer in the Fourth Hussars. War, he wrote, was not at that time the horrible thing which it was to become. It was not directed by "chemists in spectacles" or "chauffeurs pulling the levers of aeroplanes or machine guns." "War, which used to be cruel and magnificent, has now become cruel and squalid. It is all the fault of Democracy and Science. From the moment that either of these meddlers and muddlers was allowed to take part in actual fighting, the doom of War was sealed. Instead of a small number of well-trained professionals championing their country's cause with ancient weapons and a beautiful intricacy of archaic manoeuvre, sustained at every moment by the applause of their nation, we now have entire populations, including even women and children, pitted against one another in brutish mutual extermination, and only a set of bleary-eyed clerks left to add up the butcher's bill. From the moment Democracy was admitted to, or rather forced itself upon the battlefield, War ceased to be a gentleman's game. To hell with it! Hence the League of Nations." Churchill wrote that as a young officer he often wondered why statesmen did not settle international disputes by a military engagement in which each side sent its best army units to compete with the other. The same principle which gave the athletic crown to the best national team in the Olympic Games would give the victorious army the military accolade. "The Victorian Ministers," he said "were very unenterprising; they missed their chance; they simply let War pass out of the hands of the experts and properly-trained persons who knew all about it, and reduced it to a mere disgusting matter of Men, Money and Machinery."

Churchill believed that no other generation had seen so much change as his own. "Scarcely anything material or established which I was brought up to believe was permanent and vital, has lasted. Everything I was sure or taught to be sure was impossible, has happened." He recalled hearing Paul Cambon, the long-time French Ambassador to the Court of St. James, say in 1920 that he had seen an English Revolution which in its effects was more basic than the French Revolution. In Cambon's words, "The governing class have been almost entirely deprived of political power and to a very large extent of their property and estates; and this has been accomplished almost imperceptibly and without the loss of a single life." Churchill's only comment was that he supposed this was true; however, none of this had yet happened when he was young. That was a time when privilege still counted and when birth mattered both in the responsibilities it imposed and the pleasures it afforded.

Churchill, with his regiment in India, told of a vanished world, in which the "serious purpose of life" was represented by polo. It was not, he argued, a bad world, and it was not lacking in moral purpose. The Government of India was patient and efficient. It had force behind it, but never thought to use it unless pressed beyond endurance. Occasionally, a "regrettable incident" would occur, and a military attack seemed the only solution. Such engagements had nothing in common with the battles of the World War. Men did not expect to be killed, and few were. War, at least in India, remained principally a game of skill, and, as Churchill explained, with its cavalry charges, was not too different from what war had been in the time of the Crusades. The life of the Army officer educated a man in the value of discipline and comradeship. Although regretting his lack of a university education, Churchill was not absolutely convinced that his own had been inferior. He would only go so far as to say that perhaps it would have been better if he had known both.

Winston Churchill: Critic and Cassandra

The autobiography told of the world which privileged Englishmen knew before the twentieth century. In the last part of the work, Churchill described the Boer War. This, for him, was an adventure, and he wrote about it in these terms. He did not stop to reflect on the ways in which it contributed to changing the easy world into which he had been born. However, it was obvious from his descriptions that the war which an aroused Boer nation fought against the British represented a departure from convention in both tactics and spirit. The methods employed on both sides were new, and, for an individual who continued to think of war as a sport entered upon by trained men, the novelty was not pleasing.

In the early 1930's, when Britain along with the rest of the world was caught in a vise created by economic depression, and when Churchill's political fortunes reached a new low, he began work on a history which, when completed, appeared as his chief claim to recognition as an historian. Churchill, in writing about the Duke of Marlborough, discharged several obligations; some, to himself, others, to his country. Naturally curious about the individual who had planted the seed of the Churchill fortune, and concerned that he should no longer be thought of in the terms created by Macaulay, Churchill wished to wipe the historic slate clean and begin anew. In a curious way, Churchill's decision to study his distinguished ancestor gave evidence of his own private concerns. At a time when his own political star seemed in hopeless decline, some new sources of energy were needed. By studying his ancestor's defeats and difficulties, and even more, by recalling the calumny and hate which followed Marlborough so frequently through his life, Churchill was able to place his own disappointments in a proper perspective, and see that victory could not be won without risking defeat, and that no great achievement could be permanently ignored. In the early 1930's, the British nation had little cause to feel proud or contented. Economic insecurity, military inadequacy, diplomatic passivity — these seemed to be the qualities of its national existence at that moment. Churchill, in producing *Marlborough*, reminded his countrymen of a more glorious age, when English armies, in defense of Europe's liberties, achieved victories of unparalleled magnificence. The age was filled with political intrigue and cowardice, and Marlborough suffered the consequences of both, but nothing could dim his accomplishment. He created an alliance which kept in check the formidable force with which Louis XIV sought to dominate the continent.

The first volume of *Marlborough: His Life and Times* appeared in 1933; it covered the years 1650–1688. Like his Victorian predecessor, Macaulay, with whom he disagreed on many matters, Churchill began by setting the scene as it appeared on the eve of the Revolution of 1688. Unlike Macaulay, he had no interest in comparing the England of that age with his own in order to suggest the progress that had since been made. Churchill saw Stuart society as essentially different from his own, and sought to define its qualities in terms appropriate to itself. England, he informed his readers, was not a despotism in the time of Charles II. Independent powers existed, and the Crown would have risked a great deal if it had thought to challenge or ignore these. The society, for all of its surface immorality, was essentially religious. It was a society of privilege, in which rank counted heavily, giving liberties and imposing obligations on those who were most advantageously circumstanced. It was not, Churchill said, a society ignorant of the problems of international politics. Reversing Macaulay's habit, which was to regard seventeenth-century England as the first expression of an achievement which was destined to grow and receive its highest statement in Victorian times, Churchill saw the seventeenth century as superior in many ways to what had developed since. Churchill wrote: "We must not imagine that our ancestors were as careless and ignorant about international politics as are the immense political democracies of the present age. Had they been absorbed or amused as we are by the inexhaustible trivialities of the day, had their sense been dulled by speed, sport, luxury, and money-making, they could never have taken consciously the dire decisions without which England would not have been preserved. There were many solid citizens, secure in their estates, who pondered deeply and resolved valiantly upon the religious and political issues of the times."

Churchill never doubted the importance of this age in the whole future development of England. For the House of Commons, dominated by its aristocracy and country gentlemen, for British power, on land and sea, Churchill expressed his respect. But most of all, he honored two men, without whom the victories would not have been won — William of Orange, and John, Duke of Marlborough. These men "reversed the proportions and balances of Europe. They turned into new courses the destinies of Asia and America. They united Great Britain, and raised her to the rank she holds today." A grave injustice had been done to Marlborough's reputation by Macaulay's history. Churchill sought to reverse the verdict. In doing so, he did not neglect to strike out at the Victorian who had so maligned his hero. Churchill wrote: "Macaulay's life-work lay in the region of words, and few have been finer word-spinners. Marlborough's life is only known by his deeds. The comparison is unequal, because words are easy and many, while great deeds are difficult and rare." While Churchill could deny neither Marlborough's avarice nor the various liaisons which occurred before his marriage, the prudery of Macaulay in emphasizing these offended Churchill. Macaulay had given such matters a weight out of all proportion to their importance.

In his second volume, where Churchill wrote of the period 1688–1702, he told of one of the more frustrating periods in Marlborough's life. It was a difficult time, and Churchill informed his readers that their political anxieties were nothing as compared with those which dominated life in the seventeenth century. As he explained, "All our fundamentals have been for many generations securely established. The prizes of public life have diminished; its risks have been almost entirely removed. High office now means not the road to riches, but in most cases financial sacrifice. Power under the Crown passes from hand to hand with smooth decorum. The 'Ins' and 'Outs' take their turn in His Majesty's Government and in His Majesty's Opposition usually without a thought of personal vengeance, and often without a ruffle of private friendship. But are we really so sure that the statesmen of the twentieth century are entitled to sit in judgment upon those of the seventeenth? The age is gentler, the personal stakes and the players themselves are smaller, but the standard is not always so far superior that we should watch with unshakable confidence our modern leaders subjected to the strains of Halifax, Shrewsbury, Godolphin, or Marlborough."

Churchill, in arguing in this way, sought to prepare his readers for the complexity of politics in the seventeenth century. This was an age when friendships, slowly formed, were quickly broken. At the time of the Revolution, Marlborough and William stood together, but it was not long before they fell out. The origins of the quarrel were obscure, but they involved objections made by Marlborough to the King's Dutch advisers. Also, Marlborough's closeness to Anne, who was next in line to the throne, offended both William and Mary. There were rumors also of Marlborough being involved in secret negotiations with the Jacobite Court at St. Germains. The King acted in January 1692, and dismissed Marlborough from all of his military and civil posts. Marlborough, accused in a forged document of plotting to rebel against William and Mary, was arrested and sent to the Tower. When no case could be proved against him, he was freed, but only after an imprisonment of six weeks. Out of favor at court, he spent the next six years in retirement. Only the start of the War of the Spanish Succession changed Marlborough's life, and gave him his opportunity. The King, understanding the danger posed by Louis XIV's ambition, and realizing that his own declining health prevented him from taking the field, saw the need of Marlborough. He enlisted his services, proclaimed him Commander-in-Chief of the English forces gathering in Holland, appointed him Ambassador Extraordinary to the United Provinces, and commissioned him to form an alliance capable of defeating Louis' ambitions.

Winston Churchill: Critic and Cassandra

In the first volumes of the life of Marlborough, Churchill depended on records which were scanty and contradictory. For the war period, the records were abundant, and the work showed a detail previously impossible. Churchill's aim was to explain Marlborough's genius in terms which would make sense to men living in the twentieth century. He hoped to demonstrate that Marlborough was not simply a great military leader, but a person of remarkable diplomatic skill, capable of fashioning the Grand Alliance which eventually humbled Louis. At the same time, he was a man of great political talent. The situation required all of these qualities. "To beat the French in the field," Churchill explained, was the easiest of his tasks. To gain support from "the crowd of discordant, jealous, and often incompetent or lukewarm allies," and to manage politics at home so that English military policy always followed a sane course required patience and imagination. Britain, Churchill explained, was ruled in the early eighteenth century by an oligarchy. Although the total population was only an eighth of what it was to become in the twentieth century, there were probably twenty persons of consequence in Anne's time for every one that existed at that moment. "On every side were magnates, authorities, and institutions conscious of their rights and duties, and resolute to defend them on every occasion." This was not a society easily flattered or quick to approve. "A vigilant and jealous patriciate" governed, as proud as the one that had ruled in Rome or Venice. It "brooded with jealous eye upon all exceptional personal power." Great military commanders were prevented from courting the populace. Churchill explained: "None of those sweeping effects with which the French Revolution and Napoleon have made us acquainted, none of those sudden mass-impulses by which dictators rise and are acclaimed today, were possible then. The common people were allowed no share in the high public opinion of the period; to court them would have been adjudged a crime. The names of Cromwell and of Monk were fresh and deep in the memories of the governing classes. Marlborough almost crept home after his victories to avoid any form of popular demonstration other than the formal thanksgivings prescribed by Parliament and the Crown."

To manage such a country was no easy matter, and Churchill sought to impress his readers with the special skills which it required. Scarcely less difficult was the problem of organizing an alliance capable of defeating the armies of Louis XIV. The Dutch would necessarily form the nucleus of any Allied force. In the dike, Churchill detected the symbol of the Dutch Republic. The dike served to keep back both the seas and the French invaders. While the Dutch were willing to make almost any sacrifice to protect their homeland, they were suspicious of any plan which asked them to go beyond their dikes to defeat the enemy. The Republic, with its many voices, looked suspiciously on an English leader who came to ask for large new efforts in lands far distant from Holland.

War, in the eighteenth century, was still conducted in accordance with a strict moral code. Certain behavior, Churchill explained, common in the twentieth century, was unthinkable then. This was not a world which arrested and threw into internment camps enemy nationals. Nor was it a world which left the enemy wounded to die in agony in a No Man's Land. Churchill wrote: "Although the great causes in dispute were stated with a robust vigour and precision which we have now lost, no hatred, apart from military antagonism, was countenanced among the troops. All was governed by strict rules of war, into which bad temper was not permitted to enter. The main acceptance of a polite civilization still reigned across the lines of opposing armies, and mob violence and mechanical propaganda had not yet been admitted to the adjustment of international disputes."

While Churchill dwelled on the differences between war in the two centuries, he did not ignore similarities. France and Spain in 1702, like Germany and Austria in 1914, occupied central positions, with interior lines of communication. Everything, for them, depended upon the efficiency of their military forces. For the Allies, then, as in the World War, relations were frequently strained and communications almost always slow. Diplomacy would necessarily play a large role in such a war. Then, as in the twentieth century, command of the seas rested with the Allies. The greatest land force in Europe was that of the King of France; two hundred years later, it was the German Army. The problem of defeating such a military force required a plan which showed the genius of its architect. Churchill wrote: "Nothing but genius, the daemon in man, can answer the riddles of war, and genius, though it may be armed, cannot be acquired, either by reading or experience. In default of genius nations have to make war as best they can, and since that quality is much rarer than the largest and purest diamonds, most wars are mainly tales of muddle. But when from time to time it flashes upon the scene, order and design with a sense almost of infallibility draw out from hazard and confusion." Marlborough, Churchill seemed to imply, was England's genius. He was not to be compared with a modern commander; his skills were infinitely greater. Churchill had no wish to belittle the military commanders of his own century, but he saw them as men "working in calm surroundings, often beyond even the sound of the cannonade." He went on to write: "There are no physical disturbances: there is no danger: there is no hurry. The generalissimo of an army of two million men, already for ten days in desperate battle, has little or nothing to do except to keep himself fit and cool. His life is not different, except in its glory, from that of a painstaking, punctual public official, and far less agitating than that of a Cabinet Minister who must face an angry Chamber on the one hand or an offended party upon the other. There is no need for the modern commander to wear boots and breeches: he will never ride a horse except for the purposes of health. In the height of his largest battles, when twenty thousand men are falling every day, time will hang heavy on his hands."

In Marlborough's day, military genius meant something else than a talent for organization. Churchill, in the greatest detail, outlined the preparations — military, diplomatic, and political — which went into making the great victories of the period 1702–

1706. The genius which conceived the operation that culminated in the victory at Blenheim was Marlborough's; a grateful nation praised him for his ingenuity and courage. In 1706, Churchill wrote, the war might have ended if the Dutch had permitted Marlborough to engage their armies in further battle. The "unfought Waterloo" caused the war to be continued; Holland was ruined by it, and politics snatched the victory from English arms. "The Dutch," Churchill wrote, "wore out Fortune with their sluggish precautions."

In the last volumes, Churchill wrote about a political situation which gradually sapped the energies of the English nation and, in the end, caused Marlborough to be removed from his command, and an invidious peace to be made. While Churchill gave the greatest attention to the domestic political happenings which affected the fortunes of war, he thought the military situation was the paramount issue. Writing about the Battle of Oudenarde, he said: "Battles are the principal milestones in secular history. Modern opinion resents this uninspiring truth, and historians often treat the decisions of the field as incidents in the dramas of politics and diplomacy. But great battles, won or lost, change the entire course of events, create new standards of values, new moods, new atmospheres, in armies and in nations, to which all must conform."

Again, a great opportunity existed for a knockout blow. Marlborough counseled an invasion of France, but neither Eugene nor the Dutch would agree. The supreme opportunity was lost, as it turned out, forever. In the years that followed, the acts of Harley and Bolingbroke, of Anne and Mrs. Masham, lost for England the services of Marlborough and the fruits of the victories he had won. But, in a more fundamental sense, Churchill seemed to say, those losses could never erase the gains the nation had made by its sacrifice and aspiration. Marlborough went into temporary eclipse, from which he returned only after the Queen's death. However, even if fortune had not been good to him in the end, England would in time have recognized the debt it owed to Marlborough.

Winston Churchill: Critic and Cassandra

Churchill's *Marlborough* needs to be read as history but also as autobiography. Its composition and publication coincided with the darkest period in Churchill's political life. From 1931 to 1938 (the last volume appeared in that year), Churchill experienced a political exile which wounded him deeply; a lesser man might have been led to despair. Physically and intellectually, he was at the height of his powers; the Tory Party was in office, first as partner in the National Government led by MacDonald; after 1935, alone, under Baldwin, and later, under Chamberlain. Churchill had no place in any of these governments. At times, in the quiet of Chartwell, he must have wondered whether destiny intended that he, like Lloyd George, should spend the best years of his life in opposition. Both men had been powerful in the first decades of the century; now, both were shelved. Churchill's difficulties with the Tory Party began in 1929. The Labour Government, with Liberal and Conservative support, seemed ready to award dominion status to India. Churchill regarded the prospect with deep distaste, and began, in 1929, to agitate against it. It seemed inconceivable to him that dominion status could be given a community which treated sixty million of its people as "untouchables," and where racial and religious strife would almost certainly follow any withdrawal of British protection. The political classes in India represented only an insignificant fraction of the people, and Churchill had little confidence in their ability to govern a realm which taxed even British ingenuity.

Since the Conservative Party showed little interest in supporting him in his fight against the Government, Churchill took it upon himself to organize an Indian Empire Society, pledged to the maintenance of India as an integral part of the British Empire. With the help of various die-hards, to whom he had rarely appealed in the past, Churchill began to propagate his views. In a meeting organized by the Indian Empire Society in December 1930, Churchill condemned the work of the Round Table Conference, which was just then beginning its secret sessions. This Conference would not, he assured his listeners, be able to form an agreement binding in any way on the British Parliament. If Great Britain saw fit to alter the status of India, then it must do so on the basis of its own understanding of the problem. The talk about India being "a great world power" and having "found her soul at last," seemed arrant nonsense. India was a vast territory in which the greatest number could neither read nor write, and where a Hindu despotism would almost certainly replace British control. Churchill did not blame India for the false information broadcast everywhere; the fault lay at home. In the last years, Great Britain had begun to talk as if it intended to terminate its control and establish some new form of government. It was time for Great Britain to halt all such talk, and proceed as if it intended to remain, in fulfillment of its obligations to the Indian people.

In January 1931, after the Round Table Conference had submitted a new Constitution for India, Churchill spoke in the House of Commons, as a Conservative, but not for the Conservative Party or its Leader, Stanley Baldwin. He repeated the views which had now come to be expected of him. The speech was less important than the fact that Baldwin chose to reply to it. Baldwin, in opening, remarked that he would not have intervened in the debate but for Churchill's speech. While he disliked disagreeing with an old and faithful colleague, he could not but express his own satisfaction with the work of the Round Table Conference. The nation had been excited, as he was, by the idea of a United States of India. While he recognized that many Conservatives — or at least a certain number — would sympathize with Churchill's reservations, he wished to remind them of two things. If Great Britain was to enter upon a period of strong and stable government, there had to be a certain continuity of policy and some unanimity between the political parties. In Ireland, Baldwin said, the absence of both had produced a chaos in which the alternatives seemed complete surrender or war. If India was to be governed at all, there had to be agreement about principles. In the last eighteen months, he had been working for such an agreement with the other parties. He intended to continue in that effort.

Churchill was trying to make the Labour Government appear as an irresponsible agent, undoing by its timidity the great and impressive achievements of centuries of British effort. In all of his speeches, he deplored the absence of will at home, which made certain men ready to compromise on their responsibilities; Churchill never forgot to mention the differences between Hindu and Mohammedan. To this, Baldwin had given his answer: "If anyone wishes to prevent any chance of agreement or settlement as we proceed, let him devote himself in this country to breaking down the Parliamentary unity, let him devote himself in India to making it impossible for agreement to take place." Churchill was being accused by his own Leader of obstructing a reform which the nation thought necessary and desirable.

Another man, listening to these words, might have thought that the time had come to halt. Churchill had done his best to alter Conservative opinion; he had failed. To continue to argue against Baldwin was only to risk harming himself. This, Churchill certainly understood, but in a speech at Manchester, sponsored by the Indian Empire Society, he showed his stubborn resolve. He began: "We have come here to Manchester to utter our solemn warning against the policy which the Socialist Government has pursued in India. It is our conviction that unless this policy is arrested it will bring a fatal disaster upon the British Empire and entail endless misery to hundreds of millions of harmless Indian subjects of the King. I feel obliged to claim complete party independence upon the Indian crisis, and I come here, where so much of my work has been done, to ask for your earnest attention upon matters which are the deep concern of the nation." Churchill had made his decision; he would risk his Party position to state what he conceived to be the truth about India. While Baldwin was seeking harmony among the British political parties, Churchill was spreading dissension.

Given this situation, Churchill could not have been surprised that MacDonald did not approach him in late 1931 when he chose other Conservatives to join him in the National Government.

Churchill, in taking on both Baldwin and MacDonald, engaged in a battle which he could not hope to win. At a time when "national unity" was on everyone's lips, men remembered his constant plea that "the Conservative Party regain its freedom" and that "there be no more co-operation with the Socialists." These words, uttered in March 1931, expressed a position which seemed outmoded by the end of the year. Baldwin's effort to achieve party unity on India was extended to economic and social issues as well. The Conservative policy was to work with those Labourites who were prepared to compromise on rigid Socialist doctrine. This was a time of unity, and Churchill, with his habitual disregard for those who spoke softly and calmly, sounded an alien note in the new House of Commons.

Soon, however, the Indian issue receded before an even more compelling cause. In the Reichstag elections of July 1931, the National Socialists polled 37.3 per cent of the vote, and a month later the German government demanded the right to rearm. Churchill saw that something more than equality of status was involved. As he explained in the House of Commons, "All these bands of sturdy Teutonic youths, marching through the streets and roads of Germany, with the light of desire in their eyes to suffer for their Fatherland, are not looking for status. They are looking for weapons, and, when they have the weapons, believe me they will then ask for the return of lost territories and lost colonies, and when that demand is made it cannot fail to shake and possibly shatter to their foundations every one of the countries I have mentioned, and some other countries I have not mentioned." Churchill believed that Great Britain was alone among the nations who had disarmed to its disadvantage, and he pressed the Government to admit the errors of the past and seek to repair them. He was tired of the constant criticism of the so-called "French ascendancy"; while not prepared to praise the French effort unreservedly, he asked his colleagues to admit that it did provide some measure of stability in Europe. Before Great Britain took upon itself the task of persuading the French to reduce their armament, Churchill asked that consideration be given to what security system would take its place.

In the months after the accession of Hitler, Churchill argued urgently for a sensible defense policy. In the improvement of Britain's air power lay the hope of creating an adequate force to withstand a foreign attack. MacDonald's efforts at the Geneva Disarmament Conference in March 1933 did not impress Churchill. He knew that MacDonald was making a fundamental error about the nature of the threat which Europe faced. It was not France's armament, but Germany's ambition that threatened the peace of Europe. Churchill refused to go along with those who believed that a Carthaginian peace had been imposed on Germany at Versailles. On the contrary, he argued that it was mild, infinitely more so than any which Germany would have imposed, had she won. Now, Germany, under a ruthless dictatorship, was demanding parity in arms. Churchill, when he looked at Germany, could not but be grateful that such a nation lacked tanks, heavy cannon, and airplanes.

By November 1933, Churchill's warnings had become even more insistent. While Lloyd George might seek to calm the House by suggesting that Germany's transgressions on the Versailles settlement involved nothing more than a few thousand more rifles and a few more Boy Scouts, Churchill understood that this was a caricature of the true situation. He thought George Lansbury's assurance that the Labour Party would never consent to the rearming of Germany encouraging, but he asked the Labour Party chief what made him so certain that the Germans would come seeking his consent before they rearmed. Churchill begged the Government not to weaken those powers who felt themselves endangered by the German menace. While it might be flattering to play the role of peacemaker, urging disarmament on one and all, Great Britain ought to recognize its own position more exactly. It was impossible, he said, to "be the saviors of Europe on a limited liability." The French were fortunate that they had not taken British advice in the past, or American advice, issued from the safe distance of 3000 miles. Had they done so, their position vis-à-vis Germany would at that moment be infinitely weaker, and the possibility of war infinitely greater.

In July 1934, after the Hitler purges, Churchill sought to explain the character of the Nazi regime to the House of Commons. There was reason for anxiety, he said; two or three men were in control of a country of seventy millions. "We must remember that there is no Parliament where anything can be discussed, that there is no dynastic interest such as Monarchy brings as a restraint upon policy, because it looks long ahead and has much to lose, and that there is no public opinion except what is manufactured by those new and terrible engines of broadcasting and a controlled Press." Churchill possessed information which suggested that the German air force was at that moment two-thirds as large as the British; he challenged the Government to contradict that statistic. If Great Britain did not make a substantially larger effort, by 1936 Germany would have surpassed her in the air. Baldwin, in replying, suggested that Churchill was excessively pessimistic, and that British superiority over Germany in 1936 would be almost 50 per cent. He refused to guess about what might happen in 1937.

In June 1935, the National Government was reorganized; Baldwin became Prime Minister and MacDonald took his place as Lord President of the Council. A General Election was clearly in the offing. In these circumstances, Churchill would have been wise to moderate his criticisms of the Government, and seek to ingratiate himself again with Baldwin. Neither of these possibilities recommended itself to him. If Baldwin needed his services, he would have to take him as an unregenerate critic. In October, attention was suddenly diverted from Germany to Italy and Ethiopia. The question of whether Great

Britain would support the League in imposing effective sanctions against Italy became a subject of universal concern. In everything that Baldwin and his Foreign Secretary, Sir Samuel Hoare, said, during the General Election campaign, it appeared that such was their intention. Only weeks after the Tory victory, however, the publication of the Hoare-Laval plan for the partition of Ethiopia suggested that the Government had interpreted its promises rather loosely. The national uproar which followed swept Hoare from the Foreign Office and installed Anthony Eden in his place. Churchill, while concerned with the Ethiopian problem, did not think it necessary to hasten home from his Continental vacation when news of the Hoare-Laval agreement broke. His eyes were wholly on Germany, and only as the Italian adventure affected Nazi power and Allied unity did it interest him.

With Germany's reoccupation of the Rhineland in March 1936, and her denunciation of the Versailles and Locarno Treaties, Churchill's prophecies seemed to gain credibility. As he reminded the House in April, he had given warning as early as 1933; to have accepted his counsel then would have been easy; in 1936, it was more difficult, but no less necessary. While a society may come to admire a Cassandra after the fact, it rarely embraces him when he is most alone. This was Churchill's plight throughout the 1930's. Men invented reasons — some of them, persuasive — to account for his continuing exclusion from power, but they all failed to explain the true situation. To his enemies, Churchill appeared an adventurer, who had led thousands of troops to their ruin in Gallipoli, had sought to continue the war after the Armistice in order to settle accounts with the Bolsheviks, had been hostile to all schemes for Indian reform, and had, in a dozen other ways, set Britain on wrong paths. Toward the end of 1936, critics found new evidence of his unreliability. Churchill, in taking the side of Edward VIII, and seeking to slow Baldwin in his effort to ease the King from his throne, showed once again the qualities of the adventurer. What could his purpose be? Only to gain power, split the country and have his own way about rearmament. So, at least, his enemies argued.

In fact, the situation was infinitely more complex. Churchill was not wanted because Churchill showed qualities which few in the Tory Party, and even fewer outside, admired or understood. He was too difficult; in the 1924–29 Cabinet, his interventions had slowed the work of the Cabinet. He was insufficiently loyal; his decision to oppose Baldwin on India showed that. He was too critical; he had not been kind to any of the governments which had not availed themselves of his services. And, perhaps, most of all, he was too frank. In 1933, in a speech before the Royal Society of St. George, he had said: "Historians have noticed, all down the centuries, one peculiarity of the English people which has cost them dear. We have always thrown away after a victory the greater part of the advantages we gained in the struggle. The worst difficulties from which we suffer do not come from without. They come from within. They do not come from the cottages of the wage-earners. They come from a peculiar type of brainy people always found in our country, who, if they add something to its culture, take much from its strength. Our difficulties come from the mood of unwarrantable self-abasement into which we have been cast by a powerful section of our own intellectuals. They come from the acceptance of defeatist doctrines by a large proportion of our politicians. But what have they to offer but a vague internationalism, a squalid materialism, and the promise of impossible Utopias?" To attack both intellectuals and politicians — groups known for their power of counterattack — showed a recklessness for which Churchill paid heavily. His leaders did not think him a sufficiently loyal Tory; the newspapers did not deem him reliable; other politicians were outraged by his schemes; the people, hearing these things, could not but conclude that he was a dangerous man, unsuited to the critical times through which they were living. Baldwin made the British people feel comfortable; Churchill upset them.

Because the times were so critical, Churchill could not permit his personal hurt to be reflected in his political utterances. The task of instructing, even if no one heard him, possessed him entirely. In 1937, he published a series of biographical sketches, *Great Contemporaries;* these had been written in the preceding eight years. They showed, as much as anything else, the qualities which Churchill prized, and the things which he deemed important. Also, even more than his political speeches, they revealed a deep wisdom about human nature and about the predicament faced by those who sought to govern others. In his likes, no less than in his dislikes, he spoke eloquently of himself. His values and opinions were not those which "democratic" Britain applauded.

Churchill wrote principally of British contemporaries who had been important in the first two decades of the century. These men, reared in the heyday of Victorian accomplishment, showed traits not common in the new and more democratic Britain of the postwar world. The Earl of Rosebery was presented as an aristocrat who had neither the wish nor the power to transform himself to suit a democratic electorate. So long as Gladstone lived, Rosebery was shielded from the knowledge of how distant in fact he was from ordinary men, with whom he sympathized but whom he could never hope to reach. As Churchill observed, "He knew what was wise and fair and true. He would not go through the laborious, vexatious and at times humiliating processes necessary under modern conditions to bring about these great ends. He would not stoop; he did not conquer." Rosebery, Churchill saw as "a child and brilliant survivor of the old vanishing, and now vanished, oligarchic world which across the centuries had built the might and the freedom of Britain." He lived in "an age of great men and small events." It was a peaceful world, vastly different from the one which Churchill inhabited.

Of all the Victorians, there was none for whom Churchill felt a greater respect than for John Morley. "The representative of great doctrines, an actor in historic controversies, a master of English prose, a practical scholar, a statesman-author, a repository of vast knowledge on almost every subject of practical interest," Morley fascinated Churchill and made him aware of how much had changed in Britain since the time of his father. "Such men are not found today. Certainly they are not found in British politics. The tidal wave of democracy and the volcanic explosion of the War have swept the shores bare. I cannot see any figure which resembles or recalls the Liberal statesmen of the Victorian epoch. To make head against the aristocratic predominance of those times, a Lancashire lad, the son of a Blackburn doctor without favor or fortune, had need of every intellectual weapon, of the highest personal address, and of all that learning, courtesy, dignity and consistency could bestow. Nowadays when 'one man is as good as another — or better,' as Morley once ironically observed, anything will do. The leadership of the privileged has passed away; but it has not been succeeded by that of the eminent. We have entered the region of mass effects." Morley could not survive intellectually the shock of the First World War. In the new age, his historical insights helped him not at all. He had no compass to guide him in the wreckage of the world which lay shattered about him.

For Arthur Balfour, another of the Victorians, Churchill expressed a more qualified but no less sincere respect. Balfour, like Rosebery, saw too much of life from afar, but his immense wealth gave him a large advantage and contributed to the development of his exquisite taste and lively mind. Knowing the value of manners, he also understood the necessity of duty. Calm and imperturbable, he showed himself the man in every crisis. For George Curzon, Churchill expressed a lesser regard. While incapable of defining the flaw which limited him, Churchill understood that he was a man who aroused admiration and envy, but rarely love or hatred. "Majestic in speech, appearance and demeanor, he never led. He often domineered; but at the center he never dominated." Why this was so, Churchill did not say.

Frederick Edwin Smith, the first Earl of Birkenhead, was a particular friend of Churchill's. He, alone among Churchill's intimates, enjoyed conversation in the way that Balfour, Morley, Asquith, Rosebery, and Lloyd George did. Churchill could not find sufficient words to praise him; "a sincere patriot; a wise, grave, sober-minded statesman; a truly great jurist; a scholar of high attainments; and a gay, brilliant, loyal, lovable being." Of humble origins, he exaggerated his early poverty, and gloried in the society which knew how to use his talents. Churchill admired him for his wit, but also for the rigor of his mind, and for the consistency of his opinion. "The opposite type of comrade or ally is so very common," Churchill wrote, "that I single this out as a magnificent characteristic."

Of his contemporaries abroad, Churchill drew particularly flattering portraits of Clemenceau and Foch. He saw that they possessed contradictory personalities, and understood why they ended by quarreling. Each, however, represented a sort of perfection, and Churchill admired them for this. Clemenceau, he saw as the representation of republican France — anticlerical, antimonarchist, anti-Communist, and anti-German. For Churchill, he was "an apparition of the French Revolution at its sublime moment." Foch, he saw in entirely different terms. He represented the older aristocratic France, with its chivalrous ideals, and its studied elegance. Churchill was able to appreciate the excellence of both.

If *Great Contemporaries* boasted portraits of men whom Churchill admired, it also included sketches of those whom he disapproved of. For George Bernard Shaw, he expressed a scarcely concealed contempt. Shaw wished to have the best of two worlds; while his spiritual home was Russia, his ancestral home Ireland, he chose to live in comfortable England. He was an acquisitive capitalist who insisted on the excellence of Communism, and bellowed when the state imposed an income tax. Churchill could not see that Great Britain had profited much from having Shaw in its midst. "When nations are fighting for life," Churchill wrote, "when the Palace in which the Jester dwells not uncomfortably, is itself assailed, and everyone from Prince to groom is fighting on the battlements, the Jester's jokes echo only through deserted halls, and his witticisms and commendations, distributed evenly between friend and foe, jar the ears of hurrying messengers, of mourning women and wounded men."

The ex-Kaiser William II, he treated more sympathetically. Since he had been taught to think only of his own importance, and of the role of the German Empire, it was not strange that he had developed as an egotistic militarist. Churchill thought him not a wicked man, but a blunderer. The German people were as responsible as their ruler; while their intelligence and courage were incontestable, so also was their love of power. They, as much as the Kaiser, erred in basic values. Reading the Kaiser's Memoirs, Churchill declared them a "disarming revelation of inherent triviality, lack of understanding and sense of proportion, and incidentally, of literary capacity."

Whatever sympathy Churchill felt for William II, he had none for Leon Trotsky. Showing a ferocious dislike for a man whom he thought beneath contempt, Churchill expressed the hope that he would long survive in exile to see the miserable work of his revolutionary hand. Of Trotsky, he wrote, "no trace of compassion, no sense of human kinship, no apprehension of the spiritual, weakened his high and tireless capacity for action." "Like the cancer bacillus," Churchill said, "he grew, he fed, he tortured, he slew in fulfillment of his nature." Trotsky's ambition finally defeated him, when it clashed with another, that of Stalin. "In vain," Churchill wrote, "he screams his protests against a hurricane of lies; in vain he denounces the bureaucratic tyranny of which he would so blithely be the head; in vain he strives to rally the underworld of Europe to the overthrow of the Russian Army he was once so proud to animate. Russia has done with him, and done with him forever."

Churchill published *Great Contemporaries* in 1937, the year that Neville Chamberlain succeeded Baldwin as Prime Minister. In Churchill's life, the change meant nothing. Chamberlain, like Baldwin, had no intention of introducing Churchill into his

Cabinet. Events now moved rapidly to the climax which Churchill foresaw and feared: a war for which Britain was inadequately prepared. The German invasion of Austria in February 1938, the Czech crisis in the late summer, and Munich in September only confirmed Churchill's dark expectations. The Government was drifting, lulled by popular approval, into a channel from which there was no safe return. The final occupation of what remained of Czechoslovakia in March 1939 shocked Chamberlain, but not sufficiently to make him think that the time had come to avail himself of Churchill's services. It was only in September, with the German attack on Poland and the imminence of war, that Chamberlain asked Churchill to return to his old post as First Lord of the Admiralty. The news was signaled to the Fleet: "Winston is back."

From this moment, events moved swiftly till the tragic days of May 1940 when Chamberlain laid down his charge, and Churchill took his place as Prime Minister. In the five years that followed, Churchill spoke frequently in the Commons, occasionally on the B.B.C., and, whenever possible, to civilian and military groups who everywhere clamored for him. The demands of war left no time for writing, and Churchill took leave of history and journalism. When, in July 1945, after the victory against Germany was secured, and that against Japan seemed assured, the British electorate voted, the decision went against the Tory Party. Churchill left Number 10 Downing Street and took up a new role, Leader of the Opposition. The defeat gave at least one advantage: it permitted him to write his war memoirs. These began to appear in 1948, with the publication of the first volume, *The Gathering Storm*.

In 1923, when the first volume of *The World Crisis* appeared, the joke was heard that "Winston has written an enormous book about himself and called it *The World Crisis*." In 1948, such witticism would have been meaningless and impossible. Churchill's position in the Second World War made his personal history and that of the nation indivisible; the presentation of one was the representation of the other. If the histories of the two wars are read as autobiographies, it is important to see how different they are. In his account of the 1914–1918 war, Churchill intended both to tell a story and draw a moral. In his Second World War history, he concentrated on the former and practically ignored the latter. Churchill expected that lessons would be drawn from his tale, but he did not make this his first concern. The drama was in the story, not in the moral.

If any volume was didactic, it was the first. Churchill recalled that he had once told President Roosevelt that he thought the war should be known as "The Unnecessary War." According to Churchill, "There never was a war more easy to stop than that which has just wrecked what was left of the world from the previous struggle." Churchill meant his words to be interpreted in a very specific way. He believed that the war had occurred because of the mistakes made by well-meaning but badly informed men who imagined that safety and quiet might be purchased by a policy of prudence and restraint. The totalitarian states — Germany, Italy, Japan — might have been stopped at any number of moments before 1939, but the West, divided in its counsel and unsure of its will, chose to take what it thought was the safe road, which in fact turned out to be the one that led straight to disaster.

Churchill wrote of the events leading up to the war with a certain Olympian detachment. Having had no governing responsibility during these years, and having constantly criticized successive governments for inadequate military preparations and for an unimaginative diplomacy, he felt that the record spoke for itself. The mistakes were serious, but the blame could not be placed on any one person or nation. If the trouble started in Europe, it was not Europe alone which was responsible. Churchill recalled with some feeling the American error in abandoning Europe after 1919. The Treaty of Versailles, with its complex security system, had relied on American participation, but after 1919 this was not to be expected. France sought to remedy the lack by a system of alliances with East European states. At Locarno, the effort to achieve some sort of stable order reached its greatest success. From that moment, and increasingly after 1929, the movement was all the other way. The growth of the Nazi Party in Germany, even before 1933, constituted a major threat to world peace, but few were prepared to admit that possibility. Instead, men gathered at Geneva to discuss disarmament plans which would only have weakened France and made her an easy prey to German aggression. Germany, undivided after the war, with a rapidly growing population, remained potentially the most powerful state in Europe.

After the rise of Hitler, mistakes of an even more serious character were made. Neither MacDonald nor Baldwin understood the nature of the German threat, and neither prepared the country adequately for it. Churchill issued his warnings, but these were dismissed as the uninformed views of a disappointed backbencher. Neville Chamberlain showed no greater sagacity. It was not only the mistake of Munich for which Churchill criticized him, but for much that had happened before. In January 1938, Roosevelt sent Chamberlain a secret and confidential letter in which he proposed to invite the representatives of various governments to Washington to discuss the causes of the deteriorating international situation. Eden was absent from London at the time, and Chamberlain replied to the letter without consulting him. While thanking the President for his offer, he thought it necessary to describe his Government's position. Great Britain, he explained, was prepared, with the League of Nations' approval, to recognize *de jure* the Italian occupation of Ethiopia. He mentioned this because he wondered whether the President's effort might not run counter to initiatives already taken by the British. Roosevelt, in replying, agreed to postpone his offer of intervention till the British negotiations had proceeded further. He expressed alarm, however, at the suggestion that Great Britain might soon recognize the Italian position in Ethiopia. This, the President explained, could not but have an adverse effect on American public opinion. It would also encourage Japan in its own aggressive policies. Other notes followed, but the Government failed to take advantage of the President's offer.

In these circumstances, the resignation of Eden was only a matter of time. When that happened, Churchill almost despaired. The Government was now composed entirely of men prepared to accept Chamberlain's lead. Outside the Government the situation was no better. Newspapers lulled their readers with reports which minimized the seriousness of Germany's aggression against Austria. The Tory Party, with few exceptions, supported the Prime Minister; the Labour Party did not seem to comprehend the nature of the threat. Chamberlain's initiative in visiting Hitler was universally applauded; when he returned, after a second encounter, with the Munich accord and the promise of "peace in our time," only a few voices broke into the symphony of praise and congratulation which greeted him.

Even after the events of March 1939, and the extinction of what remained of Czechoslovakia, the Government failed to show the imagination that the situation required. The talks with the Russians were entrusted to less than senior personnel and their slowness failed to sound any alarm in Whitehall. When war came, in September 1939, Great Britain's position, diplomatically and militarily, was considerably weaker than what it would have been a year earlier. Czechoslovakia, with its magnificent army and fortifications, was gone; Russia was pledged to neutrality; Poland would have to fight on its own territory with no hope of assistance from any quarter. Responsibility for these situations lay with Chamberlain and his Cabinet, but also on the British people, and on men who had made the wrong decisions in the period 1933–1937.

Churchill devoted a whole book to "The Twilight War" — the period from September 3, 1939 to May 10, 1940 — when Germany moved with ruthless purpose through Poland, Denmark, and Norway, and launched its attack on the Low Countries and France. The period was brief — too brief to remedy errors which went back to the time when MacDonald sat at the head of a National Government. In the end, Chamberlain paid for his mistakes but also for those made by others. After the Norway defeat, it was still possible to muster a parliamentary majority for the Government, but the demand for a new all-party ministry grew. Lloyd George begged Chamberlain to sacrifice his place and thereby serve the nation; the fact that over fifty Conservatives voted with the Liberal and Labour Opposition told Chamberlain that the time had come to go. The German attack on Holland caused him to reconsider his decision, but only momentarily. The nation required a National Government and the Labour Party refused to serve under him; the problem admitted of only one solution. On May 10 Chamberlain went to the king to give up his seals of office; that evening Churchill was summoned to Buckingham Palace and asked to form a Government.

In *Their Finest Hour*, the second volume of his World War II history, Churchill wrote of the most heroic period in the war. The defeat of France — with its grim tragic consequences for all of Europe — seemed to him a preventable disaster. While the military defeat was perhaps inevitable, this need not have been followed by the collapse of the state and the Armistice at Bordeaux. Churchill could not find sufficient words of praise for men like Paul Reynaud who wished to fight on. In the end, he was defeated by those whom he had introduced into his ministry — men like Pétain — who were defeatist from the moment that the German armies penetrated the Maginot defenses. The French fleet was saved, but otherwise the Germans acquired immense advantages by imposing an Armistice on a state which, in Churchill's mind, was only partially defeated. The debacle left Great Britain alone.

Out of such difficulties, Churchill seemed to say, the poet constructs his epic. The debarkation of the greatest part of the British Expeditionary Force from the beaches of Dunkirk was only the first act in a miracle which galvanized the nation and astonished the world. The achievement depended upon a close coordination of air, sea, and land forces, and the intervention of thousands of small civilian craft, making their way through hazards for which they were never constructed. If Dunkirk was the first act of the epic tale, the R.A.F. victory over the Luftwaffe was the second. Throughout July, August, and September, the Germans fought to gain mastery of the approaches to Britain, to destroy the air force which would impede its invasion attempt. In the battles which went on day after day, the British took heavy blows, but in the end succeeded in forcing the Germans to call off their offensive. Stopped in daylight, the Germans took to night bombing. From September 7 to November 3, an average of two hundred bombers attacked London every night. The German effort to bring Britain to its knees by causing a collapse of civilian morale worked no better than its plan to destroy the British air strength. Great Britain was not immediately able to reciprocate, but took confidence from the fact that her plight awakened sympathy in the New World, and that American destroyers and lend-lease were the rewards of her heroic ordeal.

Churchill was at his most lyrical in *Their Finest Hour;* in the next volume, *The Grand Alliance*, he turned to consider the events of 1941 which brought the Soviet Union and the United States into the war. Nothing was more characteristic of Churchill than that he should try, on the basis of his own Intelligence reports, to warn Stalin of the danger of a German attack. This, he did in a letter dispatched to Sir Stafford Cripps, the British Ambassador, on April 3, 1941. Later, within hours after news of the German attack on Russia was broadcast, Churchill took to the air to announce that Great Britain was prepared to give whatever help it could to the Russian nation. Churchill neither apologized for nor forgot any of the harsh things he had said about Russia in the past, but he recognized that the new situation required a new attitude. In a speech filled with an imagery which the nation had come to expect of its Prime Minister, Churchill said: "No one has been a more consistent opponent of Communism than I have for the last twenty-five years. I will unsay no word that I have spoken about it.

But all this fades away before the spectacle which is now unfolding. The past, with its crimes, its follies, and its tragedies, flashes away. I see the Russian soldiers standing on the threshold of their native land, guarding fields which their fathers have tilled from time immemorial. I see them guarding their homes where their mothers and wives pray — ah, yes, for there are times when all pray — for the safety of their loved ones, the return of the bread-winner, of their champion, of their protector. I see the ten thousand villages of Russia where the means of existence is wrung so hardly from the soil, but where there are still primordial joys, where maidens laugh and children play. I see advancing upon all this in hideous onslaught the Nazi war machine, with its clanking, heel-clicking, dandified Prussian officers, its crafty expert agents fresh from the cowing and tying-down of a dozen countries. I see also the dull, drilled, docile, brutish masses of the Hun soldiery plodding on like a swarm of crawling locusts. I see the German bombers and fighters in the sky, still smarting from many a British whipping, delighted to find what they believe is an easier and a safer prey."

On July 7, Churchill having had no communication from Stalin, sent a letter, hoping that it would elicit a reply. On July 18, Stalin answered; in this, his first direct message to Churchill, he wrote: "It seems to me therefore that the military situation of the Soviet Union, as well as of Great Britain, would be considerably improved if there could be established a front against Hitler in the West — Northern France, and in the North — the Arctic." Where Britain would find the men or material for such a front, Stalin did not bother to ask.

The formation of an alliance between Great Britain and the United States was more easily effected. The American contribution to the British cause, even before August 1941, was considerable. When, in August, Churchill met Roosevelt for the first time, in the Atlantic off Newfoundland, each held the other in high esteem. The Atlantic Charter, which emerged from this meeting, gave evidence that the United States intended to bind its fortunes ever more closely to those of Great Britain.

When, in December, the Japanese attack on Pearl Harbor forced the United States into the war, the strict neutrality of September 1939 seemed a distant thing, without much relevance to what had happened since. Churchill came to Washington full of hope, knowing that the war might be long, but more confident than ever that it could only end in Allied victory.

In *The Hinge of Fate,* the fourth volume of his history, Churchill told of the serious setbacks which the Allies suffered on almost every front in the first part of 1942. The Japanese overran Malaya, took Singapore, invaded and conquered the Dutch East Indies, captured Rangoon and all of Burma, and stood at the frontiers of India. In Africa, where the British had enjoyed great success against the Italians in 1941, the first months of 1942 saw German armies, under Rommel, recapture much of what had been taken. On the Atlantic, German submarines took a heavy toll of British and Allied shipping. The American defeats were only scarcely less serious, mitigated somewhat by naval victories over the Japanese in the Coral Sea and at Midway Island. The Russian situation was no better: the Germans continued to make a steady advance into that vast territory, and Stalin pressed increasingly for the Allies to open a second front immediately.

In the second half of the year, the situation improved in almost every theater of war. The Eighth Army, under Montgomery's leadership, resumed the offensive, and, in the battle of Alamein, defeated the Germans, taking over 20,000 prisoners, and immense amounts of equipment of every sort. Churchill saw the battle as the turning of "the Hinge of Fate." As he explained, it could almost be said that "before Alamein we never had a victory. After Alamein we never had a defeat." The Allied invasion of North Africa in the same month only served to reenforce the appearance of new strength. It was now only a matter of time before the Allied armies returned to Europe, to grapple with the Italian and German forces stationed there.

In *Closing the Ring,* Churchill recounted the tale of the defeat of Italy, which proved relatively easy, and the conquest of Italy, which proved, because of German resistance, considerably more difficult. Meanwhile, American strength was steadily growing and plans went forward for launching "Overlord," the Allied invasion of Western Europe. It was during this period that the Allied chiefs met for the first time jointly at Teheran. While relations between Roosevelt, Churchill, and Stalin were amicable, and the conference proceeded to agree on most important issues, Churchill's account of it suggested the development of some degree of difference between himself and Roosevelt. While there had been differences before, the most recent involving the question of whether all Allied actions against Germany, both from the Atlantic and the Mediterranean should be under a single commander, with the British chiefs of staff objecting to such a command, and the United States supporting it, these and similar problems had never caused ill feeling. In Teheran, however, the differences between the Western Allies seemed more acute. Churchill, in writing of them, said: "There have been many misleading accounts of the line I took, with the full agreement of the British Chiefs of Staff, at this Conference. It has become a legend in America that I strove to prevent the cross-Channel enterprise called 'Overlord,' and that I tried vainly to lure the Allies into some mass invasion of the Balkans, or a large-scale campaign in the Eastern Mediterranean, which would effectively kill it. Much of this nonsense has already in previous chapters been exposed and refuted, but it may be worth while to set forth what it was I actually sought, and what, in a very large measure, I got." According to Churchill, plans for the launching of "Overlord" were set for May or June 1944, the latest date being the opening days of July. A major landing in the south of France, along the Riviera, was planned, and Churchill insisted that some effort be made in the Eastern Mediterranean. He argued that six-tenths of the Allied strength should be sent across the Channel, three-tenths concentrated in Italy, and one-tenth made available in the Eastern Mediterranean. The capture of Rhodes, Allied control of the Aegean, and Turkey's entrance into the war on the side of the Allies seemed, to Churchill, the likely prizes of an Eastern Mediterranean operation. Roosevelt, acting on the advice of his military staff, refused to agree to the proposal. As Churchill explained: "Our American friends were comforted in their obstinacy by the reflection that 'at any rate we have stopped Churchill entangling us in the Balkans.' No such idea had ever crossed my mind. I regard the failure to use otherwise unemployable forces to bring Turkey into the war and to dominate the Aegean as an error in war direction which cannot be excused by the fact that in spite of it victory was won."

While such a difference of opinion about military strategy might dismay Churchill, it could not anger him. Other incidents, however, which occurred at Teheran, he found more difficult to accept. He recounted the tale of a dinner given by Stalin in which the Russian leader spoke of the necessity of liquidating some fifty thousand German officers and technicians at the end of the war. To this, Churchill answered: "The British Parliament and public will never tolerate mass executions. Even if in our war passion they allowed them to begin, they would turn violently against those responsible after the first butchery had taken place. The Soviets must be under no delusion on this point." Stalin insisted, as Churchill admitted, perhaps only in jest, that fifty thousand would have to be shot. The President then offered a compromise — might they agree on forty-nine thousand? Intended only as a jest, the President was followed by his son Elliott, an uninvited guest, who rose in his place and expressed himself as agreeing entirely with Stalin. He was sure, he said, that the American Army would support such a plan. At this, Churchill stalked from the room. In a minute, Stalin and Molotov had joined him, urging that he return, and declaring that they were only playing. Churchill's comment on the whole evening was, "although I was not then, and am not now, fully convinced that all was chaff and there was no serious intent lurking behind, I consented to return, and the rest of the evening passed pleasantly."

Churchill sensed an aloofness on the President's part, and became aware that Roosevelt was making a strenuous effort to impress Stalin with the fact that the United States and Great Britain were in no sense teaming up against their Soviet ally. Roosevelt, in playing up to Stalin, was undermining the British position; Churchill recognized this and sought to do something to correct it; as he explained: "The fact that the President was in private contact with Marshal Stalin and dwelling at the Soviet Embassy, and that he had avoided ever seeing me alone since we left Cairo, in spite of our hitherto intimate relations and the way in which our vital affairs were interwoven, led me to seek a direct personal interview with Stalin. I felt that the Russian leader was not deriving a true impression of the British attitude. The false idea was forming in his mind that, to put it shortly, 'Churchill and the British Staffs meant to stop "Overlord" if they can, because they want to invade the Balkans instead.' It was my duty to remove this double misconception." It was not necessary for Churchill to add that if the misconception existed, it was because the Americans had helped to implant it. Churchill never condemned the President or his advisers, but his meaning could not be misunderstood.

In the discussions on the future of Germany, the differences between Great Britain, on the one hand, and the United States and the Soviet Union on the other, were so obvious as to be incontestable. Churchill was being made to appear by the other two as the recalcitrant one. When the three came to discuss Germany, Stalin said that he would like to see Germany split up; to this, the President agreed. Stalin's answer was that he supposed Churchill would object. Churchill, in replying, denied any objection in principle. Roosevelt then proceeded to outline a plan which he and his advisers had evolved for a partition of Germany into five parts. Stalin remarked, with a grin, that Churchill was not listening because he had no interest in seeing Germany divided. To this Churchill answered that he thought the "root of the evil lay in Prussia, in the Prussian Army and General Staff." After Roosevelt finished explaining his plan, which called for five self-governing German areas, and two others, to be administered by the United Nations, Churchill said that the plan was new to him and would require study. He favored a solution which would treat Prussia differently from the rest of Germany. Prussia, he would treat sternly; the rest he would wish to see organized in some sort of new Danubian Confederation. Stalin said that he preferred some plan like Roosevelt's; one which would assure a weak Germany. All Germans, he said, were the same. After breaking up Germany it would be unwise to create any new combinations. The President agreed with this; the Bavarians, he said, were exactly like the Prussians; the American troops had already discovered that. Churchill insisted that the aim ought to be to create a new unit which would not be aggressive, but would have the strength to survive. Stalin insisted that Germany be broken up in such a way that it could never reunite. All agreed that the German question would need to be discussed again at further conferences.

While the theme of Churchill's fifth volume was certainly the growing power of the Allied force, and the imminence of an attack on the continent which would finally reduce Germany and compel her surrender, another theme also intruded. Without laying too much stress on it, Churchill was already showing the beginning of a separation between the United States and Great Britain. For reasons which he never examined, but which he must have suspected, Churchill knew that Roosevelt entertained dark suspicions about British intentions, and that these were widely held by American officials. He knew also that Roosevelt was making a particular effort to appear as the friend on whom Stalin might rely. The British, with their own peculiar interests, were gradually being pushed out of the innermost councils. Great Britain owed Roosevelt too great a debt for Churchill to admit that this was happening, but his description of the Teheran Conference suggests that he intended future generations to read the record in this light.

How else is one to explain the title of his final volume, *Triumph and Tragedy*? If the tragedy had simply been, as Churchill explained in his preface, that "the overwhelming victory of the Grand Alliance has failed so far to bring general peace to our anxious world," then why should his theme have been: "How the Great Democracies Triumphed, and so Were able to Resume the Follies Which Had so Nearly Cost Them Their Life"! Churchill did not use language loosely; when he spoke of "great democracies," he did not mean to include Russia in this company. The tragedy was not that the United States and Great Britain had been unable to maintain the alliance with Russia; that was probably inevitable. Churchill saw the tragedy in that the United States and Great Britain did not preserve the alliance among themselves. The unity of the first days of the war, when everything was going badly, did not survive into the period when huge Allied armies crossed the Channel and everything began to go exceedingly well.

The differences between Great Britain and the United States grew increasingly important after D-Day. In late June, the Chiefs of Staff differed over plans for the invasion of southern France. The British doubted the wisdom of a landing in the South and preferred that the Mediterranean forces be sent to assist in Eisenhower's campaign in the North. Roosevelt refused to consider this possibility; he insisted that "the grand strategy" worked out at Teheran be complied with. The American President, still suspicious of Churchill for his interest in what he chose to call "a Balkan campaign," wrote to suggest that he would not be able to "survive even a slight setback in 'Overlord' if it were known that fairly large forces had been diverted to the Balkans." Churchill, in his history, insisted that "no one involved in these discussions had ever thought of moving armies into the Balkans," but Istria and Trieste appeared as legitimate objectives. As Churchill noted, at one point the President suggested "that we should lay our respective cases before Stalin." Strategic differences continued to divide the two countries into August, with Roosevelt always insisting on the American plan. As Churchill explained, "There was no more to be done about it"; he was forced to comply.

Soon, an even more serious difficulty arose to create division between the two Western Allies. In May, the Soviet Ambassador approached Eden with the suggestion that the USSR should temporarily regard Rumania as its concern, while Great Britain took Greece as its own. In consulting the United States on this proposal, Churchill found the State Department cool. Hull did not wish to approve anything that "might appear to savour of the creation or acceptance of the idea of spheres of influence." Churchill wrote to Lord Halifax, in Washington, "There is no question of spheres of influence. We all have to act together, but someone must be playing the hand. It seems reasonable that the Russians should deal with the Rumanians and Bulgarians, upon whom their armies are impinging, and that we should deal with the Greeks, who are in our assigned theatre, who are our old allies, and for whom we sacrificed 40,000 men in 1941. I have reason to believe that the President is in entire agreement with the line I am taking about Greece. The same is true of Yugoslavia. I keep him constantly informed, but on the whole we, His Majesty's Government, are playing the hand, and have to be very careful to play it agreeably with the Russians." Churchill was too sanguine; Roosevelt was by no means in agreement with the line that the British were taking in Greece. A cable from Roosevelt on June 11 led the Prime Minister to respond immediately: "I am much concerned to receive your message. Action is paralysed if everybody is to consult everybody else about everything before it is taken. Events will always outstrip the changing situation in these Balkan regions. Somebody must have the power to plan and act." Churchill suggested that the plan be tried for three months. The President agreed, but warned that "we must be careful to make it clear that we are not establishing any post-war spheres of influence." In a later message, Roosevelt wrote: "We were disturbed that your people took this matter up with us only after it had been put up to the Russians." Churchill tried to reassure the President, but would not admit that the British had acted improperly. He made an effective countercharge in his own reply: "It would not be possible for three people in different parts of the world to work together effectively if no one of them may make any suggestion to either of the others without simultaneously keeping the third informed. A recent example of this is the message you have sent quite properly to Uncle Joe about your conversations with the Poles, of which as yet I have heard nothing from you. I am not complaining at all of this, because I know we are working for the general theme and purposes, and I hope you will feel that has been so in my conduct of the Greek affair." The President, in his reply, said: "It appears that both of us have inadvertently taken unilateral action in a direction that we both now agree to have been expedient for the time being. It is essential that we should always be in agreement in matters bearing on our Allied war effort." Churchill responded with a similar pledge, but noted in his history that "the Russians insisted on consulting the Americans direct."

In visiting Italy, Churchill realized again what a mistake had been made in taking away part of General Mark Clark's forces for the invasion of southern France. The forces that remained were insufficient to make any headway against the German defenses. Churchill wrote: "A very little more, half what had been taken from us, and we could have broken into the valley of the Po, with all the gleaming possibilities and prizes which lay open towards Vienna. As it was our forces, about a million strong, could play a mere secondary part in any commanding strategic conception. They could keep the enemy on their front busy at any cost and risk of a hard offensive. They could at least do their duty. Alexander maintained his soldierly cheerfulness, but it was in a sombre mood that I went to bed. In these great matters failing to gain one's way is no escape from the responsibility for an inferior solution."

Meanwhile, in the first days of August, the population of Warsaw rose against the Nazi armies. Churchill offered air supplies immediately, and wired Stalin to ask that he also help. Stalin replied: "I think that the information which has been communicated to you by the Poles is greatly exaggerated and does not inspire confidence." As the battle for Warsaw raged, Vyshinsky summoned the American Ambassador and read a statement clarifying the Soviet Union's position on the rising; it said: "The Soviet Government cannot of course object to English or American aircraft dropping arms in the region of Warsaw, since this is an American and British affair. But they decidedly object to American or British aircraft, after dropping arms in the region of Warsaw, landing on Soviet territory, since the Soviet Government do not wish to associate themselves directly or indirectly with the venture in Warsaw." Roosevelt and Churchill responded by drafting a joint appeal to Stalin, urging that the anti-Nazis in Warsaw not be abandoned. Stalin's answer was discouraging: it was all an adventure by a small group anxious to seize power. The only hope for Warsaw's liberation lay in the advancing Red Army. As Churchill gained new information on the Polish resistance, he passed this on to the President. Roosevelt, in replying, said that, given the Soviet position, he could not see that any further aid could be given the Warsaw combatants. Churchill urged another joint message, explicitly asking for permission to send American aircraft with the right to land on Russian territory. Roosevelt refused to go along with this proposal; he could not see that it would produce any good effect. The British Cabinet proceeded to make an appeal of its own to Stalin. Churchill, writing in 1953, could not find words to describe the shock he felt about Soviet brutality; on the American failure, he said nothing.

At Quebec, in September 1944, Churchill and Roosevelt reached agreement on important issues. Churchill was able to wire the War Cabinet: "The Conference has opened in a blaze of friendship. The Staffs are in almost complete agreement already." On a subject close to his heart, he informed the Cabinet: "The idea of our going to Vienna, if the war lasts long enough and if other people do not get there first, is fully accepted here." Henry Morgenthau accompanied Roosevelt to Quebec, and presented his scheme for making Germany an agricultural state. Churchill was not much impressed with it, but on the insistent urging of his Ally, "agreed to consider it." That Churchill had no great belief in the possibility of "pastoralizing" Germany, his account makes perfectly evident.

If relations were good in September, they did not long remain so. The greatest difficulty developed out of British policy in Greece. Although the country was cleared of Germans by early November, the Government in Athens did not enjoy an effective authority over the various political and guerilla movements which had come into existence during the war. Churchill understood that the E.A.M. and E.L.A.S. bands had to be controlled, and was prepared to urge the Greek and British forces to take even the most extreme steps to maintain order. By early December, the E.L.A.S. forces controlled the greater part of Athens. The British were pitted against these Greek forces in fighting in and around Athens. In the United States, the reaction was violent; Churchill was accused of every sort of reactionary design. In Great Britain, the censure was only slightly less severe; everyone demanded to know why the British should be involved in fighting "the friends of democracy in Greece." Churchill sought to clarify the Government's position in a speech delivered in the House of Commons on December 8. "Democracy," he said, "is not based on violence or terrorism, but on reason, on fair play, on freedom, on respecting the rights of other people." Noting the criticisms leveled at him, he said: "We are told that because we do not allow gangs of heavily armed guerillas to descend from the mountains and install themselves, with all the bloody terror and vigour of which they are capable, in power in great capitals, we are traitors to democracy." For the moment, the criticism waned, but by mid-December,

Harry Hopkins was warning Churchill that public opinion in the United States was deteriorating rapidly. In Athens, street fighting between British and Greek forces continued. Churchill decided to fly to Greece to see the situation for himself. Partly as a result of his intervention, a truce was effected, and a regency established. Churchill never doubted that the British action in Greece had saved the country from falling to the Communists.

In February 1945, Churchill, Roosevelt, and Stalin met at Yalta. The discussions centered on Germany and Poland. With respect to Germany, Stalin wished to know what plans the others proposed for its dismemberment. Churchill answered that such a matter was far too complicated to resolve in five or six days. "It would require," he said, "a very searching examination of the historical, ethnographical, and economic facts, and prolonged examination by a special committee, which would go into the different proposals and advise on them." Roosevelt suggested, according to Churchill, that the Foreign Secretaries "produce a plan for studying the question within twenty-four hours and a definite plan for dismemberment within a month." Churchill saw no need to comment on this. He did, however, emphasize the shock he experienced in hearing Roosevelt say that the United States had no intention of keeping a large army in Europe after the war, and that he hoped for an occupation which would be limited to two years. Churchill wrote: "Formidable questions rose in my mind. If the Americans left Europe Britain would have to occupy single-handed the entire western portion of Germany. Such a task would be far beyond our strength." For this reason, he pressed for the creation of a French zone of occupation. As he explained, "To give France a zone of occupation was by no means the end of the matter. Germany would surely rise again, and while the Americans could always go home the French had to live next door to her. A strong France was vital not only to Europe but to Great Britain. She alone could deny the rocket sites on her Channel coast and build up an army to contain the Germans."

The question of Poland occupied the Conference in seven

of its eight plenary sessions. Great Britain and the United States accepted Russia's proposals for Poland's frontiers, though not with any great enthusiasm. On the government to be established in Poland, the rift between the Western Allies and the Soviet Union seemed large. In what Stalin said about the "London Poles," he indicated that he intended they should play only a minor role, if any, in the new Polish state. Both Roosevelt and Churchill understood the implications of these remarks and resisted them. After prolonged conversations, Molotov produced a draft which gave assurance that the Lublin Government would be "reorganised on a wider democratic basis, with the inclusion of democratic leaders from Poland itself, and also from those living abroad." Churchill was still not happy, but as he recognized, the situation gave no other option; as he explained in his history, "what would have happened if we had quarrelled with Russia while the Germans still had three or four hundred divisions on the fighting front?"

The only sensible solution was to take Russia at its word. Churchill had hardly returned to London, however, when he had reason to regret the compromises reached. Russia was acting in total disregard of the Yalta accord. Molotov, while pretending to consult "non-Lublin" Poles, was doing so only to make a farce of the whole procedure. As Churchill explained, his intention was to make the new government the existing one "dressed up to look more respectable to the ignorant." Churchill felt that an immediate message to Stalin, emphasizing again the character of the Yalta agreement, was called for. He asked Roosevelt for his views. The President agreed with Churchill's objectives but had reservations about his tactics. Roosevelt recalled that Stalin had made a great point at Yalta about London Polish opposition to the Red Army and the Lublin Poles. If, he argued, Great Britain and the United States sought to pressure the Lublin Poles to cease persecuting their political opponents, Stalin would reject the plea, claiming that the persecution was as great on the other side. Also, Roosevelt feared that the British and the Americans would be "charged with trying to halt the land reforms." He preferred further approaches to Molotov, before any effort was made to bring Stalin into the picture. Churchill, knowing that he could make no progress in this if he lacked American support, reluctantly agreed to go along with the President. Churchill's unhappiness was registered in a personal telegram to Roosevelt, sent on March 13. He wired: "At Yalta also we agreed to take the Russian view of the frontier line. Poland has lost her frontier. Is she now to lose her freedom? That is the question which will undoubtedly have to be fought out in Parliament and in public here. I do not wish to reveal a divergence between the British and the United States Governments, but it would certainly be necessary for me to make it clear that we are in presence of a great failure and an utter breakdown of what was settled at Yalta, but that we British have not the necessary strength to carry the matter further and that the limits of our capacity to act have been reached. The moment that Molotov sees that he has beaten us away from the whole process of consultations among Poles to form a new Government, he will know that we will put up with anything. On the other hand, I believe that combined dogged pressure and persistence along the lines on which we have been working and of my proposed draft message to Stalin would very likely succeed." The reply which came, Churchill implied, sounded like the work of the State Department. It denied a divergence of views on Poland. Before the end of the month Roosevelt agreed that a personal appeal to Stalin was necessary. Both Roosevelt and Churchill sent letters to which Stalin replied. The fault, he claimed, lay with the British and American ambassadors in Moscow for getting "the Polish affair into a blind alley." The ambassadors, instead of seeking to reconstruct the Lublin Government, were trying to abolish it, and form a completely new one. This, he said, went counter to the Yalta accords. He then proceeded to offer some positive recommendations on how the negotiations might "escape from the blind alley."

In April 1945 Roosevelt died. Churchill wrote eloquently of the help the American President had given Great Britain. There was no need to emphasize the differences that had frequently arisen; they were explicitly and implicitly given in their appropriate place. In May the German armies collapsed and Britain cheered its victory. As Churchill moved among the admiring throngs, he felt considerable anxiety. He explained: "My prime thought was a meeting of the three great Powers and I hoped that President Truman would come through London on the way. As will be seen very different ideas were being pressed upon the new President from influential quarters in Washington. The sort of mood and outlook which had been noticed at Yalta had been strengthened. The United States, it was argued, must be careful not to let herself be drawn into any antagonism with Soviet Russia. This, it was thought, would stimulate British ambition and would make a new gulf in Europe. The right policy should, on the other hand, be for the United States to stand between Britain and Russia as a friendly mediator, or even arbiter, trying to reduce their differences about Poland or Austria and make things settle down into a quiet and happy peace, enabling American forces to be concentrated against Japan. These pressures must have been very strong upon Truman. His natural instinct, as his historic actions have shown, may well have been different. I could not of course measure the forces at work in the brain centre of our closest Ally, though I was soon conscious of them. I could only feel the vast manifestation of Soviet and Russian imperialism rolling forward over helpless lands."

When Churchill urged Truman to join in issuing an invitation to Stalin for a "tripartite meeting," Truman answered that he preferred that the initiative be taken by Stalin. Also, he suggested that he and Churchill go to any such meeting separately, so that they not give the impression of "ganging up." Churchill, in a long telegram to Truman, sought to impress the President with some notion of his own misgivings. The withdrawal of American troops and equipment from Europe gave Churchill real concern. "Anyone can see that in a very short space of time our armed forces on the Continent will have vanished, except for moderate forces to hold down Germany. Meanwhile what is to happen about Russia? . . . What will be the position in a year or two, when the British and American Armies have melted and the French has not yet been formed on any major scale, when we may have a handful of divisions, mostly French, and when Russia may choose to keep two or three hundred on active service? An iron curtain is drawing down upon their front. We do not know what is going on behind. . . . Surely it is vital now to come to an understanding with Russia, or see where we are with her, before we weaken our armies mortally or retire to the zones of occupation. This can only be done by a personal meeting. I should be most grateful for your opinion and advice. Of course we may take the view that Russia will behave impeccably, and no doubt that offers the most convenient solution. To sum up, this issue of a settlement with Russia before our strength has gone seems to me to dwarf all others."

Truman's response to this was to inform Churchill that he was sending Joseph E. Davies to London as his personal emissary, to discuss matters which he preferred not to handle by cable. Davies arrived with the proposal that Truman and Stalin meet in Europe before Churchill joined them. Churchill was astonished at the proposition. Annoyed by the earlier suggestion that Great Britain and the United States might be accused of "ganging up" against Stalin, the notion that the President should meet Stalin separately seemed to him an insult and a tactical mistake. "I would not agree in any circumstances to what seemed to be an affront, however unintentional, to our country after its faithful service in the cause of freedom from the first day of the war. I objected to the implicit idea that the new disputes now opening with the Soviets lay between Britain and Russia. The United States was as fully concerned and committed as ourselves." Churchill expressed his feelings strongly in a note which he handed Davies for the American President.

In late May, Stalin urged that "the Three" meet "in the very near future" in Berlin. Truman seemed agreeable to a meeting on July 15. Churchill pressed for a meeting earlier that month, believing that events were moving so swiftly as to require an almost immediate gathering, but Truman insisted on his date. Churchill's laconic comment: "I could not press the matter further." His desire for an earlier meeting rested on his belief that an Allied withdrawal to the zones prescribed in the occupation agreement was impending, and that this would deprive the British and Americans of their last chance to influence events in Poland. As Churchill wrote: "Now, while the British and American Armies and Air Forces were still a mighty armed power, and before they melted away under demobilisation and the heavy claims of the Japanese war — now, at the very latest, was the time for a general settlement." On June 4, he wired the President: "I am sure you understand the reason why I am anxious for an earlier date. . . . I view with profound misgivings the retreat of the American Army to our line of occupation in the central sector, thus bringing the Soviet power into the heart of Western Europe and the descent of an iron curtain between us and everything to the eastward. I hoped that this retreat, if it has to be made, would be accompanied by the settlement of many great things which would be the true foundation of world peace. Nothing really important has been settled yet, and you and I will have to bear great responsibility for the future. I still hope therefore that the date will be advanced."

Truman's answer suggested that these were all closed issues. The tripartite agreement about occupation zones had been approved after "long consideration and detailed discussion," and could not be reopened. He had been advised, he wrote, that the Russians would resent any postponement of Allied withdrawal till the meeting in July. He was preparing to order the American withdrawal on June 21. Churchill wrote: "This struck a knell in my breast. But I had no choice but to submit." Churchill called his chapter "A Fateful Decision"; it followed closely on one titled "The Chasm Opens." The moral of his history was evident; the Western Allies had gained a great military victory but had failed to secure the peace. A sense of propriety prevented him from criticizing more severely the mistakes made by the

United States, first under Roosevelt, and then under Truman, but his narrative gave evidence of the efforts he had made to persuade the United States to adopt other policies. Churchill failed in this endeavor. He could not extinguish a distrust which existed in high Washington circles, and which looked constantly for signs of British imperialist ambition. He saw Europe as an entity, and felt for Poland as he did for Greece. These feelings were misinterpreted, and thought to be proof of a surviving expansionist interest. Washington gave too much attention to propitiating the Russians, and too little to the complaints raised by London. Churchill, anti-Bolshevik for almost three decades, was thought to be baiting Russia, and American official sympathy was extended more readily to Stalin than to the British Prime Minister. Churchill's record as an anti-Bolshevik caused him great trouble at a moment when Americans in high places wished only to think well of their Soviet ally. Roosevelt could not appreciate Churchill's emotional response to the Nazi destruction of Warsaw; Truman failed to understand his views on the relation between military power in Europe and diplomacy. In both instances, Churchill's effort seemed to threaten so-called "good relations" with Russia, and this seemed sufficient reason for spurning it. Churchill, grateful for all that the Americans had done, refused to dwell on the rebuffs he suffered, but the record spoke eloquently of them.

In the 1945 General Election the British electorate chose to withdraw its confidence from the Conservative Party. For the next six years, Churchill took his place as Leader of the Opposition. He used these years to compose his history, but also, to give new warnings to his country and to the West about the unprecedented and unanticipated crises which overwhelmed them. From his seat in the Commons, and in numerous public places, he renewed his warnings about Soviet power and the necessity of Allied unity. His son, Randolph Churchill, collected the more important of these statements in four volumes. They provide an additional proof of extraordinary insight and of a remarkable capacity to anticipate and prophesy events. As early as November 1945, he was able to say: "I must tell the House, speaking with my own knowledge, that the world outlook is, in several respects, today less promising than it seemed after the German capitulation of 1918, or after the Treaty of Versailles in 1919." The only hope of peace lay in the United States maintaining its vast military power and joining with others in preventing new aggressions. "It would be a mistake," he said, "to suppose that increasingly close and friendly relations between Great Britain and the United States imply an adverse outlook towards any other Power. Our friendship may be special, but it is not exclusive."

It was on March 5, 1946, at Fulton, Missouri, that Churchill made his most important pronouncement on the world situation. Introduced by the President of the United States, Churchill said: "The President has told you that it is his wish, as I am sure it is yours, that I should have full liberty to give my true and faithful counsel in these anxious and baffling times. I shall certainly avail myself of this freedom, and feel the more right to do so because any private ambitions I may have cherished in my younger days have been satisfied beyond my wildest dreams." Churchill provided specific recommendations and then came to what he called "the crux of what I have travelled here to say." It was that "neither the sure prevention of war, nor the continuous rise of world organization will be gained without what I have called the fraternal association of the English-speaking peoples." This meant "a special relationship between the British Commonwealth and Empire and the United States." Churchill warned that time might be short, and that any delay was dangerous. He spoke of the nature of Communist rule in Eastern Europe: "this is certainly not the Liberated Europe we fought to build up. Nor is it one which contains the essentials of a permanent peace." The only hope was for "a grand pacification of Europe, within the structure of the United Nations and in accordance with its Charter." Churchill believed that the Soviet Union had no wish for war. "What they desire," he said, "is the fruits of war and the indefinite expansion of their power and doctrines." A settlement was immediately needed; "from what I have seen of our Russian friends and Allies during the war," he said, "I am convinced that there is nothing they admire so much as strength, and there is nothing for which they have less respect than for weakness, especially military weakness." He reminded his audience that he had warned constantly of the German menace, and that before 1935, it might have been met and defeated without the loss of a single life. "There never was," he said, "a war in all history easier to prevent by timely action than the one which has just desolated such great areas of the globe." The solution to present difficulties, Churchill said, would come through a "good understanding on all points with Russia under the general authority of the United Nations Organisation and by the maintenance of that good understanding through many peaceful years, by the world instrument, supported by the whole strength of the English-speaking world and all its connections."

Churchill, as Leader of the Opposition, enjoyed a limited power to influence events. His reputation assured him a platform, which he used to good advantage, but he never mistook his new position for the one which he had recently held. Divested of authority, he spoke with the freedom which age and international renown afforded him. As caustic as in his youth, but no more disillusioned, he took the Labour Government to task for mistakes committed and for opportunities neglected. For six years he busied himself with various political chores but also with his history. When he wrote the Preface to *The Gathering Storm* in March 1948, he thought it necessary to say: "It must not be supposed that I expect everybody to agree with what I say, still less that I only write what will be popular." Churchill felt a compulsion to recall the events of his lifetime, and to comment on them. He asked that his criticism of others be understood, and that "no one look down on those honourable, well-meaning men whose actions are chronicled in these pages, without searching his own heart, reviewing his own discharge of public duty, and applying the lessons of the past to his future conduct." Just as the interwar years carried their lesson, so did the war period. A sense of modesty and obligation impelled Churchill to soften his criticism of those who had been friends and faithful allies, but the demands of the future required that he not conceal the truth. The Anglo-American alliance, for all of its magnificent achievement, had not held together as he hoped it would. For reasons which Churchill never analyzed, Roosevelt, Truman, and a large number of those who made American policy, while admiring Britain for what she had done in 1940, distrusted her intentions and sought to thwart her ambition. This, for Churchill, was the tragedy of the war.

As an old man, Churchill began to publish the last of his histories — *A History of the English-Speaking Peoples*. This was a work which he had begun before the outbreak of war; a half million words had been produced before he went to the Admiralty in 1939. In the four volumes which emerged between 1956 and 1958, Churchill left a final testament. The simplicity of the work — with its heroes and villains, its conventional chronology and its uncomplicated theories of causation — reflected the calm self-assurance of its author. The Europe of his youth was now irretrievably lost; there was no advantage in mourning it. Great Britain and the whole English-speaking world needed to look to the future. "Another phase looms before us, in which alliance will once more be tested and in which its formidable virtues may be to preserve Peace and Freedom." Churchill, in the end, had no other message to give to his time.

The autobiography of Winston Churchill is contained in his histories. The image is of a restless adventurer, devoted to his country, faithful to his friends, and incapable of keeping that discreet silence which is said to be a virtue for the political man not entirely in accord with the opinions of his day. Churchill thought that he lived in a bronze age, only occasionally illumined by the light characteristic of more golden times. Instead of deploring his fate, he accepted and exploited it. Outspoken even as a youth, he clashed with authorities who called him bumptious and conceited; in later years, the charge changed to irresponsible and unstable. Excluded because of his opinions, at the moment when he most wished to influence events, he knew how to bide his time, while preparing for the day when he would again exercise power. At the moment of the nation's greatest peril, it turned to him, expiating its own error in his elevation. But the reputation remained, and it came to haunt him in yet another crisis. In the end, his American friends shared the suspicions which had led Bonar Law, Stanley Baldwin, Neville Chamberlain, and the British electorate to prefer men more hospitable to the ideas and practices of the twentieth century. Churchill — critic and Cassandra — paid a price for his independence, but thought it small for the victory achieved. A more discreet opinion would have saved him disappointment, but would have denied him glory. As a Marlborough, he sought the latter even at the price of the former.

BIBLIOGRAPHICAL
NOTE
❖
INDEX

ACKNOWLEDGMENTS

Grateful acknowledgment is made to the following publishers for permission to quote from the works of Winston S. Churchill:

Great Contemporaries by Winston S. Churchill. Copyright 1937 by Winston S. Churchill. Used by the permission of G. P. Putnam's Sons, publishers.

Great Contemporaries by Winston S. Churchill. 1937. London. Odhams Press, Ltd.

The Gathering Storm by Winston S. Churchill. 1948. Boston. Houghton Mifflin Co.

The Gathering Storm by Winston S. Churchill. 1948. London. Cassell & Co., Ltd.

The Grand Alliance by Winston S. Churchill. 1950. Boston. Houghton Mifflin Co.

The Grand Alliance by Winston S. Churchill. 1950. London. Cassell & Co., Ltd.

Closing the Ring by Winston S. Churchill. 1951. Boston. Houghton Mifflin Co.

Closing the Ring by Winston S. Churchill. 1952. London. Cassell & Co., Ltd.

Triumph and Tragedy by Winston S. Churchill. 1953. Boston. Houghton Mifflin Co.

Triumph and Tragedy by Winston S. Churchill. 1954. London. Cassell & Co., Ltd.

Marlborough: His Life and Times by Winston S. Churchill. 6 vols. 1933, 1933, 1935, 1935, 1937, 1938. New York. Charles Scribner's Sons.

Marlborough: His Life and Times by Winston S. Churchill. 4 vols. 1933, 1934, 1936, 1938. London. George G. Harrap & Co., Ltd.

A Roving Commission: My Early Life by Winston S. Churchill. 1930. New York. Charles Scribner's Sons.

My Early Life by Winston S. Churchill. 1947. London. Odhams Press, Ltd.

The World Crisis by Winston S. Churchill. 4 vols. 1923, 1927. New York. Charles Scribner's Sons.

The World Crisis by Winston S. Churchill. 4 vols. 1938. *The Aftermath*. London. Odhams Press, Ltd.

The Aftermath by Winston S. Churchill. 1929. New York. Charles Scribner's Sons.

BIBLIOGRAPHICAL NOTE

Testimony to the importance of Edmund Burke, Benjamin Disraeli, and Winston Churchill is afforded by many different sorts of evidence, not the least being the numerous books and articles devoted to their careers which issue from British and American presses. Because, in my own essays, only certain themes have been emphasized, to the neglect of others, an extensive bibliographical statement would be superfluous. In what follows, two criteria have been used: first, to list those writings of Burke, Disraeli, and Churchill on which my own interpretations are based; and, second, to cite the secondary works which influenced my judgments, positively or negatively.

EDMUND BURKE

Any study of Edmund Burke must begin with an examination of his *Works*. These appeared first in eight volumes, prepared by his literary executors, F. Laurence and W. King, and published between 1792 and 1827. Later editions, of which there are many, are all based on this original edition. I have used the 1846 new and improved edition, in nine volumes, published in London in 1846 as *The Works of the Right Honourable Edmund Burke*. Burke's correspondence, which appeared in a four-volume edition in 1844 as *The Correspondence of the Right Hon. Edmund Burke; between the Year 1744 and the Period of his Decease, in 1797*, was edited by Charles William, Earl Fitzwilliam, and Sir Richard Bourke. In the twentieth century, Arthur P. I. Samuels, in *The Early Life, Correspondence and Writings of the Right Hon. Edmund Burke* (Cambridge, 1923) made available important additional correspondence. A definitive edition of the whole of Burke's correspondence, under the editorship of Thomas W. Copeland, is now being prepared; the first volume, *The Correspondence of Edmund Burke, April 1744–June*

1768, was published in 1958 by the Chicago and Cambridge University Presses. The *Annual Register,* to which Burke contributed, needs to be consulted; I have used the volumes for 1759, 1760, 1761, 1762, 1764, 1767, 1770, 1771, and 1773.

Burke's French Revolutionary writings aroused immense controversy in his day and spurred the publication of numerous tracts and pamphlets, most of them hostile to Burke's ideas. This literature is described by Carl B. Cone in "Pamphlet Replies to Burke's Reflections," *Social Science Quarterly,* XXVI (June 1945). The most important early biography of Burke was written by James Prior, *Memoir of the Life and Character of the Rt. Hon. Edmund Burke* (London, 1824); this work went through many editions, the fifth appearing in 1854. The second edition (London, 1826), in two volumes, is perhaps the best. Thomas Macknight wrote a three-volume biography, *History of the Life and Times of Edmund Burke* (London, 1858), which, until the appearance of John Morley's *Edmund Burke: A Historical Study* (London, 1867), threatened to hold the field for Victorian readers. Morley wrote a further study for the English Men of Letters Series, *Burke* (London, 1879). This established his claim as the principal authority on Burke, a claim challenged only by Sir Leslie Stephen, whose *History of English Thought in the Eighteenth Century,* 2 vols. (London, 1876) contained a superb chapter on the eighteenth-century Whig. It is interesting to note, in this connection, that the major nineteenth-century studies were produced by men of Liberal sympathies and not by Conservatives, who ignored Burke until fairly recently.

In the last quarter of Victoria's reign, and during the Edwardian decade that followed, Burke received little attention from biographers or critics, Tory or Liberal. Lord Hugh Cecil, in *Conservatism* (London, 1912), repudiated the bias which a generation habituated to reading Morley or Stephen had been led to accept. John MacCunn, in *The Political Philosophy of Burke* (London, 1913), wrote the first major interpretative work in this century. After the 1914–1918 war, interest in Burke grew, and several important studies appeared. Mention should be made particularly of Alfred Cobban, *Edmund Burke and the Revolt Against the Eighteenth Century* (London, 1929), who set out to prove that Burke was in fundamental revolt against Locke's psychology and philosophy; Sir Ernest Barker, *Burke and Bristol, 1774–1780* (Bristol, 1931), who explored Burke's relations with the populous borough that he represented in Parliament; Mario Einaudi, "The British Background of Burke's

Political Philosophy," *Political Science Quarterly* (December 1934); Lucy S. Sutherland, "Edmund Burke and the First Rockingham Ministry," *English Historical Review*, 1932; Dixon Wector, "The Missing Years in Edmund Burke's Biography," *Proceedings of the Modern Language Association*, 1938; Donald Cross Bryant, *Edmund Burke and his Literary Friends* (St. Louis, 1939). As is suggested by the last titles, much of the effort in this period involved filling gaps in the story of Burke's life. Sir Philip Magnus, in *Edmund Burke: A Life* (London, 1939), demonstrated the advantages of gaining access to the Burke papers, still in the keeping of the Fitzwilliam family. Magnus, ignoring none of the personal and financial scandals about which Burke's Victorian biographers had been uninformed or reticent, produced a volume which touched subjects never previously examined.

The interest in Burke grew rapidly after the Second World War. A model of biographic research was Thomas Copeland's *Our Eminent Friend Edmund Burke* (New Haven, 1949). These six essays, monographic in style and content, showed what new scholarship in this field might produce. Ross J. S. Hoffman, in *Edmund Burke, New York Agent* (Philadelphia, 1956), made available important new correspondence. When the Fitzwilliam manuscripts were moved from Wentworth Woodhouse to the Central Public Library of Sheffield, new research opportunities opened. Carl B. Cone, having gained access to the papers, concluded that a major new biography was called for; the first of his two volumes appeared as *Burke and the Nature of Politics: The Age of the American Revolution* (Lexington, Ky., 1957). Thomas H. D. Mahoney, in *Edmund Burke and Ireland* (Cambridge, Mass., 1960), also made use of the Fitzwilliam manuscripts to explore an aspect of Burke's career on which there had been little previous work.

In the last decade, there have been several major new critical estimates of Burke as a political philosopher. Leo Strauss, in *Natural Right and History* (Chicago, 1953) argued that, though Burke used the language of modern natural rights, he incorporated his ideas into a classical or Thomistic background. This idea was further explored by the so-called "new Conservatives" who wrote in the United States in the 1950's. Russell Kirk's *The Conservative Mind* (Chicago, 1953), presented a portrait of Burke which neither John Morley nor Leslie Stephen would have recognized. Peter Stanlis, in his *Edmund Burke and the Natural Law* (Ann Arbor, 1958) argued that Burke's teachers were Aristotle, Cicero, and St. Thomas Aquinas, and that he intended his own philosophy to be a refutation of men like

Hobbes and Locke, who had betrayed the "true Natural Law tradition." Charles Parkin's *The Moral Basis of Burke's Political Thought* (Cambridge, 1956) asserted that Burke's writing could be understood only as an "expression of a coherent moral philosophy of man and community," and that any other approach missed the principal thrust of his argument. The most recent work which pursues these same themes is that of Francis P. Canavan, S.J., *The Political Reason of Edmund Burke* (Durham, NC., 1960). The image of Burke that emerges from these works is very different from that developed by Basil Willey even as recently as a decade ago in *The Eighteenth Century Background* (New York, 1950). It will be interesting to see how long it takes before the pendulum swings back, so that Burke's Whig bias and party spirit are again taken into account, and his Victorian commentators are restored to somewhat greater favor.

Benjamin Disraeli

Disraeli's novels are collected in several major editions. In 1870–71, a *Collected Edition of the Novels* was published with a Preface by Disraeli. In 1881, the year of his death, the *Novels and Tales* appeared in the Hughenden Edition; this is the edition that I have used. A collection of Disraeli's speeches, in two volumes, was edited by T. E. Kebbel, and published as the *Selected Speeches of the Late Right Honourable the Earl of Beaconsfield* (London, 1882). There is no definitive edition of Disraeli's correspondence. For the early years, Ralph Disraeli edited a collection, *Lord Beaconfield's Letters, 1830–1852* (London, 1887). This volume included the correspondence published previously as *Home Letters Written by the Late Earl of Beaconsfield in 1830 and 1831* (London, 1885) and *Lord Beaconsfield's Correspondence With His Sister, 1832–1852* (London, 1886). These volumes, also, were edited by Ralph Disraeli. In the twentieth century, the Marquis of Zetland edited correspondence which he published in two volumes, *Letters of Disraeli to Lady Bradford and Lady Chesterfield* (London, 1929); this was the correspondence of Disraeli's later life with two of his closest friends. *Letters to Frances Anne, Marchioness of Londonderry, 1837–1861* (London, 1938) told of the earlier period in Disraeli's life, when he was making his first moves to realizing his large ambitions. Disraeli's early polemical works are collected in *Whigs and Whiggism: Political Writings*, ed. W. Hutcheon (London, 1913). This is a particularly valuable source for the period before Disraeli found a place in the House of Commons.

Bibliographical Note

The standard biography of Disraeli is the monumental work of William F. Monypenny and George E. Buckle, *The Life of Benjamin Disraeli, Earl of Beaconsfield*, six volumes (London, 1910–1920). Monypenny wrote the first two volumes, Buckle, the remaining four, as well as the revised two-volume edition which appeared in 1929. It would not be an exaggeration to say that these volumes have deterred scholars from attempting new biographies. In their documentation, if not always in their interpretation, they cover the field so well as to seem almost definitive. Those who have published biographies since Monypenny and Buckle have generally chosen to write in a popular vein, appealing to a larger than scholarly audience. One thinks, in this connection, of André Maurois, *Disraeli* (New York, 1928); D. C. Somervell, *Disraeli and Gladstone; A Duo-Biographical Sketch* (New York, 1926); Hesketh Pearson, *Dizzy; The Life and Personality of Benjamin Disraeli, Earl of Beaconsfield* (New York, 1951). The best short biography of Disraeli is still probably that of James Anthony Froude, *Lord Beaconsfield* (London, 1890).

In The *Cambridge Bibliography of English Literature*, Disraeli is listed in the company of Thackeray, Dickens, Trollope, the Brontës, and Meredith, as a major novelist of the middle nineteenth century. This, however, has not led critics to give much heed to his work; in fact, no so-called "major" Victorian novelist has received less critical attention than Disraeli. The major study of Disraeli's work as a novelist is probably Morris E. Speare's *The Political Novel* (New York, 1924). Sir A. T. Quiller-Couch treats Disraeli in *Charles Dickens and Other Victorians* (Cambridge, 1925). In an earlier day, James Bryce considered him in *Studies in Contemporary Biography* (London, 1903), as did Sir Leslie Stephen in *Hours in a Library* (London, 1892), volume 2. Articles in periodicals have appeared from time to time, but few of these have contributed significantly to our understanding of Disraeli as an author. Muriel Masefield's *Peacocks and Primroses, A Survey of Disraeli's Novels* (London, 1953) is useful chiefly for its plot summaries.

Crane Brinton's *English Thought in the Nineteenth Century* (Cambridge, Mass., 1949) contains an important essay on Disraeli. The 1867 Reform Bill agitation, and Disraeli's role in it, is considered by Asa Briggs in his *Victorian People: A Reassessment of Persons and Themes, 1851–67* (Chicago, 1954). The most recent new biography is by B. R. Jerman, *The Young Disraeli* (Princeton, 1960); Jerman, in treating Disraeli's youthful escapades, makes perceptive comments on his early novels. Eighty years after Disraeli's death, the literature on his life and thought remains remarkably slight. It is to be hoped that new researches in the Disraeli papers at Hughenden and in the British Museum will lead to a revival of interest in his career. For the intellectual historian, particularly, there is ample room for new work.

WINSTON CHURCHILL

While every man cannot hope to be his own historian, there are many who aspire to that role. In the company of those who have succeeded, Winston Churchill must certainly be counted. His published works provide, in almost every instance, abundant materials for his biography. *The Story of the Malakand Field Force* (London, 1898) told of fighting along the Indian frontier in the sort of imperial wars which disappeared with the nineteenth century. *The River War* (London, 1899), in two volumes, described the British reconquest of the Sudan, an operation which Churchill witnessed. *London to Ladysmith via Pretoria* (London, 1900) and *Ian Hamilton's March* (London, 1900) were Churchill's Boer War histories. In *Lord Randolph Churchill* (London, 1906), two volumes, Churchill discharged an obligation to his father's memory; he sought to explain a meteoric career that ended in failure but which had its own peculiar dignity and authenticity. Churchill's conversion to Liberalism was attested to by many speeches; some were collected and published as *Liberalism and the Social Problem* (London, 1909); *The People's Rights* (London, 1910); and *Home Rule from the Treasury Bench* (London, 1912). The World War put an end to writing, but provided the experience on which Churchill constructed his history of that terrible conflict. *The World Crisis 1911–1914* and *The World Crisis 1915* appeared in 1923. The next two volumes, on 1916–1918, were published in 1927. *The Aftermath,* which dealt with the postwar world, emerged in 1929. A volume titled *The Eastern Front,* which Churchill wrote without the advantage of first-hand knowledge, appeared in 1931. Churchill published *My Early Life* (London, 1930) to tell a new generation what the Victorian age in which he had passed his youth had been like. He made another attempt at autobiography in *Thoughts and Adventures* (London, 1932). In *Marlborough: His Life and Times,* published between 1933 and 1938 in four volumes in London and in six volumes in New York, Churchill made his most conscientious effort to write about an historical epoch removed from his own. While writing principally of his distinguished ancestor, Churchill told also a great deal about his own intellectual and political preferences. In *Great Contemporaries* (London, 1937), a collection of essays, Churchill spared neither praise nor blame in writing of men, British and foreign, of his own day. War interrupted authorship a second time in 1939, but again provided the materials for a great new work. The Second World War histories appeared in six volumes; they were published in Great Britain and the United States as *The Gathering Storm* (1948), *Their Finest Hour* (1949), *The Grand Alliance* (1950), *The Hinge of Fate* (1951), *Closing the Ring* (1952), and *Triumph and Tragedy* (1954). In his four-volume *A History of the English-Speaking Peoples*, published between 1956 and 1958, Churchill wrote the last of his histories.

There are many collections of speeches by Churchill. Attention needs to be directed particularly toward his *India* (London, 1931), *Arms and the Covenant* (London, 1938), *Step by Step* (London, 1939), *Into Battle* (London, 1941), *The Unrelenting Struggle* (London, 1942), *The End of the Beginning* (London, 1943), *Onwards to Victory* (London, 1944), *The Dawn of Liberation* (London, 1945), *Victory* (London, 1946), *Secret Session Speeches* (London, 1946); also, *The Sinews of Peace* (London, 1948), *Europe Unite* (London, 1950), *In the Balance* (London, 1951), and *Stemming the Tide* (London, 1953).

Churchill's writings constitute his autobiography. If one wishes to know what others have thought of him, one may consult Lewis Broad, *Winston Churchill 1874–1952* (London, 1952); John Lockhart, *Winston Churchill* (London, 1951); Virginia Cowles, *Winston Churchill; the Era and the Man* (New York, 1953). Alfred L. Rowse, in *The Churchills, from the Death of Marlborough to the Present* (New York, 1958), treats Churchill's forbears, the famous and gifted, along with the less distinguished members of the family. Many years will pass before any biographer succeeds in rendering Churchill as faithfully as he has done in his own writings. When such a person does appear, he will have many of Churchill's talents, not the least, wit, courage, literary skill and the capacity to admire.

INDEX

Index

Index